Arthur Miller's New York

Related titles

A Student Handbook to the Plays of Arthur Miller: All My Sons, Death of a Salesman, The Crucible, A View from the Bridge, Broken Glass
Edited by Enoch Brater

All My Sons (Student Edition)
Arthur Miller
Edited by Claire Gleitman

Arthur Miller Plays 1: All My Sons; Death of a Salesman; The Crucible; A Memory of Two Mondays; A View from the Bridge
Arthur Miller

Death of a Salesman (Student Edition)
Arthur Miller
Edited by Claire Conceison

Modern American Drama: Playwriting in the 1940s: Voices, Documents, New Interpretations
Felicia Hardison Londré

The Crucible (Student Edition)
Arthur Miller
Edited by Soyica Diggs Colbert

Arthur Miller's New York

Visions of the City

Stephen Marino

methuen | drama
LONDON • NEW YORK • OXFORD • NEW DELHI • SYDNEY

METHUEN DRAMA
Bloomsbury Publishing Plc, 50 Bedford Square, London, WC1B 3DP, UK
Bloomsbury Publishing Inc, 1359 Broadway, New York, NY 10018, USA
Bloomsbury Publishing Ireland, 29 Earlsfort Terrace, Dublin 2, D02 AY28, Ireland

BLOOMSBURY, METHUEN DRAMA and the Methuen Drama logo are trademarks of Bloomsbury Publishing Plc

First published in Great Britain 2026

Copyright © Stephen Marino, 2026

Stephen Marino has asserted his right under the Copyright, Designs and Patents Act, 1988, to be identified as author of this work.

For legal purposes the Acknowledgements on p. xvi constitute an extension of this copyright page.

Cover design: Ben Anslow
Cover image © Arthur Miller working in New York City, November 18, 1945 (© Alamy); New York City Skyline (© CSA-Printstock / Alamy)

All rights reserved. No part of this publication may be: i) reproduced or transmitted in any form, electronic or mechanical, including photocopying, recording or by means of any information storage or retrieval system without prior permission in writing from the publishers; or ii) used or reproduced in any way for the training, development or operation of artificial intelligence (AI) technologies, including generative AI technologies. The rights holders expressly reserve this publication from the text and data mining exception as per Article 4(3) of the Digital Single Market Directive (EU) 2019/790.

Bloomsbury Publishing Plc does not have any control over, or responsibility for, any third-party websites referred to or in this book. All internet addresses given in this book were correct at the time of going to press. The author and publisher regret any inconvenience caused if addresses have changed or sites have ceased to exist, but can accept no responsibility for any such changes.

A catalogue record for this book is available from the British Library.

A catalog record for this book is available from the Library of Congress.

ISBN: HB: 978-1-3505-2476-7
PB: 978-1-3505-2475-0
ePDF: 978-1-3505-2478-1
eBook: 978-1-3505-2477-4

Typeset by Deanta Global Publishing Services, Chennai, India
Printed and bound in Great Britain.

For product safety related questions contact productsafety@bloomsbury.com.

To find out more about our authors and books visit www.bloomsbury.com and sign up for our newsletters.

To Katie:
"My Foundation and Support"

Contents

List of Figures	viii
Preface: A Pear Tree Bloomed in Brooklyn	xiii
Acknowledgments	xvi
Introduction: Arthur Miller and the New York Experience	1
1 The Brooklyn Plays: *The American Clock, Death of a Salesman, A View from the Bridge, Broken Glass*	37
2 The Manhattan Works: *A Memory of Two Mondays, After the Fall, The Price, The Ride Down Mt. Morgan, Mr. Peter's Connections, Homely Girl, A Life*	101
3 *Focus*: A Novel about Queens	131
4 Short Stories: The Presence of New York	163
Notes	195
References	203
Index	214

Figures

0.1	Miller's boyhood home at 45 West 110th Street, c. 1940	10
0.2	Miltext Coat and Suit Company factory, c. 1940	12
0.3	45 West 110th Street today. The Miller's occupied a sixth-floor apartment that overlooked Central Park	13
0.4	Skaters on Central Park lake, c. 1938	15
0.5	As a young boy, Miller saw vaudeville shows here that his father loved, c. 1940	16
0.6	The Regun theatre on West 116th Street, c. 1940	17
0.7	The Miller family home on East 3rd Street Brooklyn in 1940	21
0.8	Apartment house looms over small wood-frame house: "bricks and windows, windows and bricks," c. 2023	24
0.9	Miller's Brooklyn boyhood home as it looks today	25
0.10	The apartments in this building at 62 Montague Street, c. 2023 were called "French Flats." Miller and his wife Mary shared the apartment with her girlfriends	28
0.11	Miller's residence at 18 Schermerhorn, c. 2023 was a one family building in Brooklyn Heights converted into apartments	29
0.12	Miller and his wife lived in a duplex apartment in this building, c. 2023	31
0.13	Miller bought this home with the royalties from his success with *All My Sons*, c. 1940	32
0.14	Arthur Miller in Brooklyn Heights, c. 1954	33
0.15	Miller's fifth residence in Brooklyn Heights, c. 2023 is considered an architectual gem and served as a stop on the Underground Railroad	34
0.16	United States. New York City, 1961. View of the Brooklyn Bridge from the promenade	35
1.1	Coney Island boardwalk and the famous Parachute Jump, c. 1989. The Parachute Jump was originally constructed for use	

	at the 1939–40 New York World's Fair. It was moved to Coney Island in 1941	40
1.2	Depression encampments along the Hudson River, c. 1930	41
1.3	Construction of the Empire State Building, c. 1931	42
1.4	Manny Newman's home on East 4th Street, c. 1940	44
1.5	Pete Panto lay in an unmarked grave in St. Charles Cemetery for over eighty years. A tombstone was placed there on September 26, 2023	46
1.6	Red Hook home of Pete Panto, c. 1940	47
1.7	Contemporary picture, c. 2023, of 186 Remsen Street, location of Brooklyn Rank-and-File Committee in 1939	48
1.8	Gargiulio's Funeral Home in Red Hook, last known sighting of Pete Panto, c. 1940	49
1.9	ILA Headquarters, c.1940	50
1.10	Arthur Miller in front of the Brooklyn Bridge, c. 1954	54
1.11	Miller's Brooklyn boyhood today. To the rear left, the extension can be seen; note how close the neighboring house is on the right	62
1.12	Mielziner, Jo. Sketch of set design from *Death of a Salesman*. 1948–9. Note the apartment houses surrounding the Loman home	63
1.13	Narrow alley between houses on Miller's block; note the apartment house looming behind, c. 2023	64
1.14	Both Grand Central Station and the adjacent Commodore Hotel have storied histories in New York City, c. 1967	67
1.15	The AT Stewart Store, considered America's first department store, was located in what is known as the Sun Building, often called the "Marble Palace," c. 1978	71
1.16	The Standish Arms, the "Boston" Hotel where Biff discovers Willy with The Woman, is actually located in Brooklyn Heights, c. 1940	72
1.17	Ebbets Field, home of the Brooklyn Dodgers, c. 1950	73
1.18	Marilyn Monroe kicking a soccer ball at Ebbets Field, c. 1957	75
1.19	Hardware store on Sixth Avenue, c. 1940	76
1.20	New York once had a major trolley car system. Here is a trolley on the McDonald Avenue line under the El in Brooklyn, c. 1950	79
1.21	Union organizer speaks to longshoremen on Brooklyn docks, c. 1939	83

1.22	Moore-MacCormack Line Pier 3, c. 1940	84
1.23	Contemporary photo of the former Pier 41. Note the World Trade Center Tower in the background, c. 2023	85
1.24	Waterfront Barge in Red Hook, c. 2018	86
1.25	Bowling Association list shows the alleys located on Flatbush Avenue in the 1950s. *Brooklyn Eagle*, April 21, 1950, p. 21.	88
1.26	United States. New York City, 1961. Raf Vallone, Carol Lawrence, and Arthur Miller during the making of *View from the Bridge*.	90
1.27	United States. Brooklyn, New York. 1961. Arthur Miller signing autographs for longshoremen during the production of *A View from the Bridge*.	91
1.28	Former bridle path on Ocean Parkway, c. 2023	92
1.29	Landmarked buildings that housed the National Title Guarantee Building and the Brooklyn Trust Company, c. 2023	93
1.30	The famous Schrafft's restaurant in Downtown Brooklyn, c. 1940	95
1.31	The Rialto Theatre in Flatbush, c. 1940	96
1.32	Cable Bldg 611 Broadway, c. 1940	97
1.33	The famous Wanamaker's Bldg at Broadway and 8th Street, c. 1999	98
2.1	Cast on the set of *The Price* with Augusta Miller's dining room table on stage, c. 1968	104
2.2	Miller lived at the famous Chelsea Hotel after his divorce from Marilyn Monroe and during the early years of his marriage to Inge Morath, photo, c. 1973	107
2.3	Central Park benches line the west side of Fifth Avenue, c. 2024	108
2.4	First Lady Jacqueline Kennedy christening a ship at the Groton Shipyard, c. 1962	109
2.5	The exclusive Carlyle Hotel, c. 2024	111
2.6	Fruit and vegetable market on Ninth Avenue, c. 1940	112
2.7	Many buildings in the San Juan Hill neighborhood of Manhattan were razed to construct Lincoln Center. Among those was the Chadick-Delameter Auto Parts Warehouse. United States. New York City, 1963	115
2.8	Contemporary view of the Lincoln Center complex, c. 2024	116

2.9	B. Altman's flagship store on Fifth Avenue at 34th Street signified the best in luxury shopping, c. 1940	124
2.10	Crowd gathers in Times Square to get the news about the invasion of France, c. 1939	125
2.11	Janice and Herman wind up in an Irish bar on 84th Street and Broadway, c. 1940	126
2.12	The fictional Crosby Hotel is modeled after the many resident hotels on Manhattan's Upper West Side, c. 2024	128
3.1	Home at Newman's address in Woodside, c. 2025	139
3.2	Attached homes in Woodside in 1940 as described in the novel, c. 1940	140
3.3	Same attached homes in Woodside today, c. 2025	141
3.4	Still from the film version of *Focus*.	141
3.5	Miller may have modeled the Woodside National Bank as the location for the hate rally, c. 2025	142
3.6	The Fisk Theatre, c. 1940	143
3.7	Part of the Fisk Theatre structure survives as a tire shop, c. 2025	144
3.8	The Loew's Woodside Theatre, c. 1940	145
3.9	Today, the Woodside Theatre functions as St. Sebastian Roman Catholic Church, c. 2025	146
3.10	Bernard Perlin's *Orthodox Boys*, 1949	149
3.11	Trinity Church, c. 1940	153
3.12	Trinity Church graveyard	154
3.13	Radio City Music Hall, c. 1985	155
3.14	Entrance to Central Park facing the Plaza Hotel, c. 1969	156
3.15	Nazi rally at Madison Square Garden, c. 1939	159
4.1	Sid Luckman formerly Erasmus Field, c. 2023	166
4.2	18 Schermerhorn Street, c. 1940	167
4.3	One of the north entrances to Central Park across from Miller's 110th Street home, c. 2024.	168
4.4	The Miller family spent their summers in a bungalow in Far Rockaway, c. 1940	170
4.5	Rows of bungalows, c. 1940	171
4.6	Dry cleaning store in Harlem, c. 2024	177
4.7	Restaurant on Lenox Avenue, c. 1940	178

4.8	Site of former restaurant on Lenox Avenue, c. 2024	179
4.9	French battleship *Richelieu* passes Brooklyn Bridge, New York, with damaged turret for refitting at New York Navy Yard on January 30, 1943	181
4.10	Aerial photo shows the vastness of the Brooklyn Navy Yard, c. 1940	182
4.11	The *USS Missouri* under construction at the Navy Yard. The Japanese surrendered on the battleship at the end of the Second World War, c. 1942	183
4.12	The Five Sullivan brothers at the Navy Yard in 1942.	184
4.13	United States. New York City, 1961. View of the Brooklyn Bridge.	185
4.14	New York's landmarked Municipal building, c. 1966 which the shipfitters passed after crossing the Brooklyn Bridge on their way to the ship repair on the Hudson River	186
4.15	The East 3rd Street home of Moe Fishler, his wife Jean, and her mother is located across the street from the Miller family home, c. 1940	189
4.16	Athletic field and the adjacent Washington Cemetery where Moe Fishler is buried, c. 2023	191
4.17	In his final recorded visit to Brooklyn on April 23, 2004, Arthur Miller crosses Remsen Street to attend the Arthur Miller Conference at St. Francis College. Pictured with him are Stephen Marino (l) and Christopher Gibbons (r)	193

Preface

A Pear Tree Bloomed in Brooklyn

This book had a twenty-year gestation. In April 2004, I delivered a paper, "Arthur Miller's Yoknapatawpha," at the Ninth International Arthur Miller Conference held at my home institution, St. Francis College in Brooklyn Heights, the same neighborhood where Miller lived from 1940 to 1956. My paper examined the astonishing fact that many plays in Miller's canon are located in New York settings that are vital to the action. I had done previous work on the importance of Brooklyn as a setting in *Death of a Salesman*, *A View from the Bridge*, and *Broken Glass*, but in 2004 came to the realization that other New York boroughs, Manhattan and Queens, also are as important in Miller's plays as Faulkner's mythical Yoknapatawpha is in his fiction. I also served as chair at that conference and arranged an appearance by Mr. Miller where he was interviewed by his biographer and keynote speaker, Christopher Bigsby, and signed the books and programs of hundreds of students and conferees.

The next day, I drove Chris Bigsby and Miller Society member Jane Dominik to visit Miller's boyhood home on East 3rd Street, to where the family moved in 1928 when he was thirteen. The block where the Miller family lived was, and still is, a dead end street in what is technically the "Gravesend" section of Brooklyn, an appropriate name because of the cemetery that lies beyond a baseball field at its north end. One can still see and hear, like the young Arthur, the "El" train as it heads south toward Coney Island and north toward Manhattan. What is particularly striking is how the block evokes *Death of a Salesman*. The two-story wood-frame houses resemble Willy Loman's house with the "bricks and windows, windows and bricks" of apartment houses lurking over them.

Our visit took place on a Saturday that is the Sabbath for the largely Hasidic population that now lives in the neighborhood. As we drove down the block, we had to steer carefully through the young children playing on that warm spring day. Many male adults, all clothed in their distinctive white shirts and black pants, lingered on the sidewalks and stoops enjoying the afternoon weather. Because I had to double park on the crowded street, we immediately caught the attention of the kids and their parents, for we were obviously strangers. The three of us stopped, admittedly awe-struck at standing in front of the house that had served a pivotal role in the formation of Miller's artistic life. Chris went to the front door to speak with the residents while Jane started snapping pictures from every angle. I fended off the inquiries of some neighbors who wanted to know if the residents had "won something." I laughed at how Chris, Jane, and I must have looked to them—like the employees of Publisher's Clearing House bestowing some grand prize. When I explained that Arthur Miller had lived in that house, many recalled *Salesman* and a few, of course, knew about his marriage to Marilyn Monroe.

Chris conversed with the younger residents of the house who were initially reluctant to speak with us. However, an older woman, the grandmother, explained that they could not invite us into the home on their Sabbath, but we were welcome to walk around outside. The house looks much like it did when Miller lived in it with some modern alterations of brick face on the front porch, stucco on the first floor, and aluminum siding on the second floor where the bedrooms are located. The grandmother explained that the only major renovation to the house occurred in 2003 when the family added a two-story addition to the rear which created a larger kitchen and an additional bedroom. Chris was especially anxious to see the backyard because Miller had planted a pear tree there when the family moved to the house. And lo and behold, the tree was there just coming into bloom! The grandmother explained that their religion forbade them to destroy any living thing, thus the extension to the home ended right at the tree line. Oh, how the three of us recalled Willy's lament in *Salesman* at the builder having cut down the elm trees.

At the next Miller Conference in 2005, I delivered a paper, "*Homely Girl, A Life*: The Landscape of Manhattan," that expanded to Miller's fiction the importance of New York settings. I then began a book-length study of the subject in his canon. In the fall of 2012, I had completed 2/3 of the manuscript and was gathering photos of New York City locations that would complement the discussion. Superstorm Sandy hit New York on October 29, inundating many areas of the city, including my Queens neighborhood lying along Jamaica

Bay. The basement of my home—that I used as a study—completely flooded, destroying much of the manuscript—hard copies, notes, and computer files. I was able to retrieve some material, but largely abandoned thought of completing the project.

In 2015, I was heavily involved in many events celebrating the Miller Centennial. BBC Radio recorded a special program about Miller's life in New York, and I guided the *New York Times's* theater critic Ben Brantley on a tour of Arthur Miller's residences in Brooklyn Heights and the Red Hook docks where he researched *A View from the Bridge*, and our conversation was taped for broadcast. We traveled to Miller's East 3rd Street home. The same people owned the house, and curious residents on the block once again gathered round and asked questions. One asked if Marilyn Monroe had ever been there.

I was keen on showing Ben the pear tree in the backyard. To my surprise, the tree was gone with only a 3 foot jagged stump remaining. Three years earlier, the owner informed me, it blew down in the terrible winds of Superstorm Sandy. Struck by the amazing connection between my lost manuscript and the pear tree, I resolved to complete the project. I like to think that the pear tree that once bloomed in Brooklyn bears final fruit in this book.

Acknowledgments

I would like to thank the many people whose advice, encouragement, and support helped me complete this book. My stalwart colleagues in the Arthur Miller Society—Jane K. Dominik, Sue Abbotson, Josh Polster, David Palmer, Ramón Espejo Romero, Jan Balakian, and Chris Bigsby—always were invaluable sounding boards. I must also recognize Rebecca Miller and the Arthur Miller Trust for their sustained interest and single out Julia Bolus for her enthusiasm for this project.

The accompanying photos are a vital part of this book. I owe much to Katie Murray's keen eye and for allowing me to take her all over Brooklyn. I am also grateful for Jane Dominik's ability to snap fine pictures while dodging Manhattan traffic. I also must recognize the technical expertise of Addie Marino for superb and prompt photo editing, even at all hours of the night.

I appreciate the efforts of Sana Manzoor of the Inge Morath Estate in securing permission for Inge Morath's Magnum photos, the Elliott Erwitt Estate for granting permission for his photos, Michael Schreiber of the Estate of Bernard Perlin and Tate Images for allowing the use of *Orthdox Boys*, Krista Errickson for granting use of Jo Mielziner's sketch, and Ken Cobb of the New York City Municipal Archives for his extreme cooperation with the archival photos.

Finally, I am indebted to senior editor Mark Dudgeon of Methuen Drama for recognizing the value of this book and his editorial guidance. I must also mention assistant editor Ella Wilson for her fine work with the minutiae of my manuscript.

The author and publisher gratefully acknowledge the permission granted to reproduce the copyright material in this book

Every effort has been made to trace copyright holders and to obtain their permission for the use of copyright material. However, if any have been inadvertently overlooked, the publishers will be pleased, if notified of any omissions, to make the necessary arrangements at the first opportunity.

Introduction

Arthur Miller and the New York Experience

In the fall of 1915, a woman started her labor pains in an apartment on West 111th Street in Manhattan. It was the Sabbath, and her labor extended into the next day. And on Sunday, October 17, a screaming baby boy, named Arthur Asher Miller, was delivered to the world. As he sucked in his first breaths, the air of New York City filled the fiber of his being.

More than a century later, we hear the voice of that baby who grew into a man and became a celebrated American dramatist of the twentieth century and one of the greatest writers America has produced. Arthur Miller clearly ranks with the other truly major figures of United States playwrights—Eugene O'Neill, Tennessee Williams, and Edward Albee—and the pantheon of great world dramatists such as Chekhov, Strindberg, Shaw, and Beckett.

Miller earned this reputation during a more than seventy year career in which he achieved critical success in the 1940s and 1950s with the dramas *All My Sons*, *Death of a Salesman*, *The Crucible*, and *A View from the Bridge*, refused to "name names" at his appearance before the House Un-American Activities Committee (HUAC), had a celebrated marriage to the film actress Marilyn Monroe, served as president of the literary organization International P.E.N., produced an acclaimed autobiography, *Timebends*, in 1987, and premiered new plays, such as *Broken Glass* and *The Ride Down Mt. Morgan*, on Broadway and in London in the 1990s and the new millennium.

Arthur Miller was not only a literary giant, but also one of the more significant political, cultural, and social figures of his time. He was a man of conviction with rock-solid integrity who frequently took stands, popular and unpopular, on the ethical issues that engage societies throughout the world. At his death in 2005, the front-page headline of the *New York Times* called him the "moral voice of [the] American stage" (Berger 2005: 1). Miller's strong voice dominates his plays, his fiction, and his extensive commentary on the theatrical, political, moral, and social issues of his time. Throughout his seventy-year career, Miller asked questions about how we make our way in the world.

Arthur Miller also was a quintessential man of the twentieth century: his life and career immersed in the cataclysmic events that defined what often is called "America's Century." Miller's ninety years spanned almost the entire time period. Born in 1915 while the First World War raged, he died in 2005 in the Age of Terrorism. His worldview and moral principles were formed in the crucible of the political, economic, and social events of the era: the Roaring Twenties, the Great Depression, the Second World War, the Red Scare and Communist Witch Hunts, the cultural revolution of the 1960s and Vietnam, the Cold War, Reaganism, the Arab-Israeli conflicts, the fall of the Soviet Union, and the New World Order. In his professional and personal life, Arthur Miller boldly confronted the conflicts of his time. In his plays, fiction, and essays, he frequently took stands, popular and unpopular, on moral, social, and political problems—whether we liked hearing them or not. The great themes of his work and career—family and society, individual and social conscience, private and public responsibility, and guilt and betrayal—are what engaged societies throughout the world in his time and continue to do so in our own.[1]

Literary critics have long focused on how certain writers create geographical locations that function as central settings throughout many of the works in their canons. Of notable examples are Thomas Hardy's Wessex, James Joyce's Dublin, Saul Bellow's Chicago, and William Faulkner's American South. For these novelists, the cultural, political, social, and religious histories of the geographical regions in which they were born and/or lived became the raw material for their work: transforming real places into fictional landscapes.

In the same way, New York City was vital to Arthur Miller's experiences throughout his almost ninety years and thus figures prominently in his literary work. The influence of his native city on his life and career cannot be ignored. Just as Shakespeare remained a Warwickshire man his entire life, so did Arthur Miller remain a New Yorker.

In many interviews, articles, and his autobiography, *Timebends*, Miller detailed the importance of his defining experiences in Manhattan and Brooklyn as a boy growing up in the 1920s and 1930s and as a young playwright, husband, and father in the 1940s and early 1950s and how those experiences were formative for the writer that he would later become. Miller spent his first thirteen years living in Manhattan with his Jewish family in upper middle-class splendor at 45 East 110th Street in Harlem in an apartment overlooking Central Park. Miller's father, Isidore, owned a successful suit and coat factory and the family was quite well-off, but the hard times had come for them early, even before the Stock Market crash of 1929, when the coat and suit factory collapsed. Consequently, Isidore moved his family in 1928, when Arthur was thirteen, from Manhattan. The move to Brooklyn was clearly a step down, and the family relocated to the Midwood section of the borough to a little six-room house on East 3rd Street where Miller shared a bedroom with his maternal grandfather. Miller relished his teenage years growing up in Brooklyn until he left for the University of Michigan in 1934.

When Miller graduated in 1938, he lived briefly at the family's East 3rd Street home before his marriage in 1940 to Mary Slattery, whom he met in college. The couple moved to the Brooklyn Heights section of the borough and would live in five different residences until 1956 when Miller divorced Slattery and married Marilyn Monroe. Miller's fifteen years living in Brooklyn Heights were crucial to his artistic development: he moved into the neighborhood as an unknown aspiring writer, created his most famous plays while living there, and later moved out as one of America's most important playwrights married to the most famous woman in the world.

After his divorce from Monroe, Miller took up residence at Manhattan's famous Chelsea Hotel. When he married the photographer Inge Morath, the couple spent most of their lives on Miller's property in Roxbury, Connecticut. He also maintained an apartment in Manhattan for which Miller retained an innate feeling into his later years often shuffling back and forth from his country home. He wrote at the end of *Timebends*, "I have lived more than half my life in the Connecticut countryside, all the time expecting to get some play or book finished so I can spend more time in the city, where everything is happening" (Miller 1987: 599).

New York City became a crucial component of Miller's creative DNA. He transformed the experiences of his youth and early adulthood—formed on the streets and in the neighborhoods of the New York boroughs of Manhattan and Brooklyn—into art. This book examines how Miller placed a staggering number of his plays and fiction in New York, creating a dramatic landscape where his characters encounter the cultural, ethnic, religious, and economic issues indigenous to twentieth-century New York City. Nine of his major plays are set in New York: *Death of a Salesman* (1949), *A Memory of Two Mondays*

(1955), *A View from the Bridge* (1955, 1956), *After the Fall* (1964), *The Price* (1968), *The American Clock* (1982), *The Ride Down Mt. Morgan* (1991), *Broken Glass* (1994), and *Mr. Peter's Connections* (1998) all have settings in which the characters' interactions with the cityscape significantly mesh with the events of the plays. Much of the action of Miller's only novel, *Focus* (1945), occurs in the borough of Queens and boldly confronts, for the first time in American literature, the issue of anti-Semitism. In addition, most of Miller's short fiction depicts New York settings that are integral to the main characters' conflicts. In particular, his novella, *Homely Girl, A Life* (1992) creates a sweeping landscape of time and emotion in Manhattan.

From the start of his career, Miller had a strong inclination to use his life as the raw material for his drama and fiction. He clearly tapped into his impulse for autobiography for the plots, characterizations, and themes of New York plays such as *Death of a Salesman, A Memory of Two Mondays, After the Fall, The Price, and The American Clock*. In other works, he transferred his experience living in the city and his encounters with people and places in the metropolis onto his characters.

Miller's use of New York is distinguished by how the plays and stories are not only set in locations in the boroughs but also how characters mention scores of streets and avenues, department stores and shops, movie theaters, restaurants, famous New York landmarks, and subway routes, indicating just how much the city is an integral part of their lives. Miller's New Yorkers are immersed in the cultural, social, and economic life of the so-called Capital of the World and often possess a strong identification with neighborhoods of the diverse population of the city's boroughs. Stimulated to make art out of his life experience, Miller accurately depicted the vibrancy of life in the city that he knew so well.

Miller's use of New York settings in his canon is quite pervasive, so it is surprising how little scholarship has explored this aspect. Some critics, such as Barry Gross, Kay Stanton, and Linda Ben Zvi, have explored how the city in *Death of a Salesman* contrasts with the frontier, pastoral, or "Green World" for which Willy Loman longs. I have written about the importance of Brooklyn as a setting in *Death of a Salesman, A View from the Bridge*, and *Broken Glass*. Aysha Viswamohan produced an important essay, "Arthur Miller and the New York State of Being" that notes how extensively Miller portrayed the "ethos" of the city in his work, in which he "repeatedly presents a view of the city, encompassing its streets, its multi-ethnic character, its people, culture and, of course, its unique language" (Viswamohan 2014). However, Viswamohan acknowledges that the discussion does not cover the full extent of Miller's use of New York because of his prolific output. *The Cambridge Companion to Literature of New York* offers a wide range of writing by and about New Yorkers including Whitman, Melville, Wharton, O'Neill, and Ginsberg, but only offers two paragraphs on the Red Hook setting of Miller's *A View from the Bridge*. Similarly, in 2005, Randy Cohen of the *New York Times* proposed creating a literary map which would show the homes and haunts of the fictional characters who lived in New York City's most famous borough and invited *Times* readers for their suggestions. The result produced not one character, play, or work of fiction by Miller. Thus, *Arthur Miller's New York: Visions of the City* opens a new area of scrutiny for critics.

The book shows how America's great playwright saw America's great city during the country's great century. Those who are familiar with Miller's famous works, particularly *Death of a Salesman* and *A View from the Bridge*, will discover just how much New York City is an indelible part of his work. Those readers interested in the history of New York will learn how Miller's life was rooted in the political, cultural, economic, and social movements of his native city, and how he subsequently infused his characters with his experience. Through the vision of America's great playwright, the book highlights the diversity, vitality, and rich history of New York City.

There are two unique features of this book. The text offers analyses of Miller's plays and stories that focus on the centrality of the New York settings in influencing the characters' actions. In his 1945 review of Miller's only novel, *Focus*, Charles Poore observed that, "Mr. Miller knows New York well, and his pictures of it are truly drawn. He can give you a subway ride, or a tour through a suburban wasteland, or a picture of the city on a sweltering night that would make any New Yorker in exile homesick" (Poore 1945: 17). Therefore, I found it vital to include many archival and contemporary photographs of the New York settings in Miller's work. I also include pictures of the residences and neighborhood places where Miller lived in Manhattan and Brooklyn, which he mentions in his autobiography *Timebends*, and that he later used in his work. These photos are not only vivid complements to the discussion of his drama and fiction but also have detailed captions that provide intriguing information about past and present locations and landmarks in New York that Miller mentions in his work.

A few examples: Miller modeled the Brooklyn home of Willy Loman in *Death of a Salesman* after his family's home at 1350 East 3rd Street in the same borough. The book contains a vintage photo of the house (real estate tax photos taken by New York City in 1940) and contemporary photos that show the building and its surroundings in their current state. Moreover, photos of large apartment buildings astride wood-framed homes show the physical change of Brooklyn in the era between the world wars, during the borough's quick and dramatic transition to the wholly urban environment of today, a physical change that had a great effect on Miller and his most famous character, Willy Loman. The discussion of *A View from the Bridge* is accompanied by past and present photos of the docks and piers in the Brooklyn Heights and Red Hook neighborhoods where Miller conducted his research for his tragedy about the Italian immigrant society whose homes he visited. The discussion of *Broken Glass* is accompanied by a photo of Ocean Parkway; in 1938—the year of the play—there was a bridle trail that extended to the Atlantic Ocean at Coney Island which the character Dr. Hyman uses daily for his horseback riding. Also, the famous department store Wanamaker's in Manhattan plays a significant role in the play's action, and the book contains an image of the store as it existed on the corner of Broadway and 8th Street which in recent years has been occupied by Meta, Yahoo, and Wegman's. Miller's short story, "I Don't Need You Anymore" (1967), is based on an autobiographical event in Miller's boyhood at his family's summer beach bungalow in Far Rockaway, Queens. The accompanying photos and text provide intriguing information about the history of the ethnic enclaves that populated the length of Rockaway Peninsula during the twentieth century.

I have organized the book to show the vital importance of New York in Miller's life and his entire oeuvre, including his plays and fiction.

Chapter 1: "The Brooklyn Plays" reveals how Miller was so influenced by his experiences in Brooklyn that the borough became the prime setting for three of his major plays: *Death of a Salesman*, *A View from the Bridge*, and *Broken Glass*, as well as *The American Clock*. Thus, all three major plays use physical geography as a metaphor for emotional dislocation. The chapter includes photos with explanatory captions about the specific neighborhoods where Miller set the plays and the actual locations that the characters mention.

Chapter 2: "The Manhattan Works" focuses on the action of five plays and a novella set in Manhattan. *A Memory of Two Mondays, After the Fall, The Price, The Ride Down Mt. Morgan, Mr. Peter's Connections,* and *Homely Girl* show the borough as an economic, social, and cultural force in the lives of the characters. The action is rooted in vital physical locations in Manhattan that provide a measure of reality for the reveries of the characters. The accompanying photos not only vivify the plays but illustrate just how accurately Miller depicted life in the city.

Chapter 3 concentrates on Miller's only novel *Focus* and its significant action in the borough of Queens. Published in 1945, *Focus* is one of the first novels that boldly confronted the issue of American anti-Semitism. The novel extensively portrays the biases pervasive in every aspect of New York City society. The New York settings, with the associated photos, reinforce the prejudices at the heart of the novel. Thus, *Focus* provides a sweeping panorama of the city and its inherent ethnic, racial, religious, and class divisions.

Chapter 4 considers the prodigious number of short stories Miller produced throughout his long career. Many of Miller's short stories are set in New York locations that are germane to the situations of the texts.

Life in Manhattan

Arthur Miller's life experiences in New York occurred when it emerged as the preeminent city in the United States. During the nineteenth and early twentieth centuries, New York City earned a reputation as the quintessential melting pot of the United States as waves of mostly European immigrants settled in the city. However, the growing metropolis as a melting pot where people shed identification with their native lands to live side by side in democratic harmony was a romanticized version. In reality, immigrants tended to settle—by choice or not—in their own communities with their own kind who shared similar cultures, languages, and religions, living together without wholly assimilating into a heterogenous America. Thus was born the many famous and infamous Manhattan neighborhoods identified by their origins in the Old World: Germantown or Little Germany, Dutchtown, Irish Five Points, Little Italy, Chinatown, Spanish Harlem, and the Jewish Lower East Side. In fact, many people could live the bulk of their lives rarely leaving the boundaries of their communities—having most of their needs satisfied in shops, markets, schools, churches, synagogues, and temples. In *Timebends*, Arthur Miller acknowledged this reality: "The miracle of New York was the separation of one group from the experiences of others. The city is like a jungle cut through by a tangle of separate paths used by different species, each toward its own nests and breeding grounds" (62). This phenomenon continues in the twenty-first century, particularly in the outer boroughs: for example, Asian immigrants have settled in Flushing, Queens, and Sunset Park, Brooklyn; Hasidic communities thrive in Williamsburg; Guyanese and Indians prosper in Richmond Hill and South Ozone Park, Queens.

Arthur Miller was born and raised in predominantly Jewish neighborhoods in Manhattan and Brooklyn, and his unique experiences in those insular communities contributed mightily to his moral and religious belief systems, cultural attitudes, and his later artistic vision.

In the 1880s, Miller's immigrant grandparents settled in the famous Jewish enclave on the Lower East Side of Manhattan: the Millers on Stanton Street and the Barnetts on Broome Street, where his mother Augusta ("Gussie" appears on her birth certificate) was born on March 18, 1891. Both his maternal grandfather, Louis Barnett, and paternal grandfather, Samuel Miller, were from the same village, Radomizel, in current day Poland[2] and were likely related. Like many immigrants, they escaped the poverty of their village and the pogroms against Jews to achieve the American Dream which became a dominant theme in Arthur Miller's work. Miller's father Isidore and his six siblings were born in that village.

Louis Barnett and Samuel Miller thrived in New York's Jewish-dominated garment industry, both owning manufacturing companies that eventually made both families so well-off that they were able to move from the squalid tenements of the Lower East Side: the Millers to a large house in the Flatbush section of Brooklyn, the Barnetts to the then more respectable Jewish area of Harlem, which by 1910 had a hundred thousand Jews, the second largest concentration of immigrant East European Jews in America (Bigsby 2008: 21). Despite Harlem's reputation as a primarily Black community, Harlem in the late nineteenth and early twentieth centuries was comprised of many different ethnic and racial groups and given monikers such as Spanish Harlem and Irish Harlem. In fact, Little Italy in Harlem developed much before the famous Little

Italy on the Lower East Side, and Miller had decidedly negative encounters with Italian boys from East Harlem.

Louis and Samuel retained their Radomizel roots in the new world through their garment industry connections and "arranged" a marriage between Isidore and Augusta (see Miller 1987: 17–18; Bigsby 2008: 18–19, 26–9). Isidore at that time worked for his father's company, S. Miller and Sons, which he would spin off after the First World War into his own business, the Miltex Company, which would become the second largest coat and manufacturing company in the United States (Bigsby 2008: 12, 13, 16). Both Miller in *Timebends* and Bigsby offer accounts of Augusta's attitude toward a marriage that stifled the gifted and intelligent woman who had planned to attend college. Her comment that she was "sold like a cow" (Miller 1987: 18) sums up her resentment toward Isidore, especially when she discovered barely two weeks into the marriage that her new husband was illiterate (Miller 1987: 19). Miller offers various fictionalized accounts of this in *After the Fall* and *The American Clock*.

The family lived in an apartment at 127 West 111th Street where Miller's older brother Kermit was born in 1912 and where Arthur also was born.[3] After Miller's birth, the family moved to 45 West 110th Street between Lenox and Fifth Avenues, and this residence became the center of Miller's boyhood life experience in Manhattan (Figure 0.1).[4]

Miller realized just how crucial a role growing up in New York played in his development. In *Timebends*, he relates how he would have had an entirely different life if his father had given a loan to the soon-to-be famous Hollywood producer, William Fox, who in 1915 was beginning the company that would grow into the movie empire, Twentieth Century Fox, and was raising funds from New York garment industry owners. Despite the temptation, Isidore turned down the investment opportunity and Miller concluded that had his father taken the risk, he would have been raised in Los Angeles and never learned what he did on the streets of Harlem and Brooklyn, been spared the Depression, and "arrived no doubt at a different personality" (Miller 1987: 20). The literary world benefited from Isidore's decision not to make that fateful move, for the artistic personality that formed in Arthur was nurtured by the young boy's unique experiences in Harlem.

The family lived in a sixth-floor apartment overlooking New York's Central Park. At the time, many residences were grand living spaces—the Millers

Figure 0.1 Miller's boyhood home at 45 West 110th Street, c. 1940. Courtesy Municipal Archives City of New York.

occupied eleven rooms—very often with space for support help such as a maid, like Sadie who assisted Augusta in running the household. Interestingly, Miller's sister, the actress Joan Copeland, bought an apartment in 1972 at 88 Central Park West. She explained in an interview that when her brother Kermit saw her apartment, he said that it reminded him of their West 110th Street apartment.[5]

Stephen Marino: So what kind of memories do you have of living here in New York? You were only six years old when you moved to Brooklyn.

Joan Copeland: Well, it's interesting. This apartment that we're in at this moment. When my brother Kermit saw it after I just bought it, he said, "You know, you won't remember this, but this is what our apartment at 45 West 110th Street was like." He said, "Not exactly like this, but it was open and airy and sunny and large rooms." And he remembered that very well, since he was older when they moved to Brooklyn. (Copeland 2008: 43–4)

Copeland inherited her mother's Baby Grand Knabe piano, one of three identical instruments that Augusta and her two sisters owned, although as Miller relates, she was the only one who could play. The piano bench was filled with sheet music of the New York plays and shows that Augusta frequented. The piano plays a significant role in the Millers' semi-autobiographical play *The American Clock* (see Chapter 2), and Copeland intended to will the piano to Rebecca Miller, Miller's daughter from his third wife, Inge Morath.

Miller's lively recollections of his thirteen years living in Manhattan clearly reflect the upper middle-class splendor that the family enjoyed in their Harlem neighborhood. The family had a Polish-speaking maid, had owned a chauffeur-driven seven-passenger "National" automobile, and rented a summer bungalow on the beach in Far Rockaway. Miller recalls being driven with his mother downtown to visit the Miltext Coat and Suit Company factory at 22–26 West 32nd Street (Figure 0.2) in the Seventh Avenue garment district and his privilege at understanding that he and Kermit were the boss's sons. Miller would use his experience at the factory in the first play he wrote at the University of Michigan, *No Villain* (1935) (see Chapter 1) and fictionalize the family's summers in Rockaway in his short story, "I Don't Need You Anymore." (See Chapter 4.)

The young Miller also had a fascination with cars as symbols of wealth and power. In *Timebends*, he details how he and his boyhood chum Sid Franks, who lived in the same building in the apartment next door, would watch a line of chauffeur-driven cars from their apartments. "We could hang out our sixth-floor window, Sid and I, and call out the names of every car passing on 110th, recognizing them from above, so distinctive were they" (Figure 0.3) (Miller 1987: 45). Miller would take his fascination with cars into his adulthood and would later use them as significant objects in many of his plays and fiction[6] as

Figure 0.2 Miltext Coat and Suit Company factory, c. 1940. Courtesy Municipal Archives City of New York.

later chapters in this book discuss. His boyhood chum Sid and his father were models for characters in *The Price*.

Miller's mother Augusta reveled in the cultural and social life of the city, and Miller recalls her and Isidore's evening attire as they went to the theater: "High heels with rhinestone buckles, a black beaded knee-length dress, and silver and black cloche hat (Miller 1987: 4), diamond and a silver fox"—recollections

Figure 0.3 45 West 110th Street today. The Miller's occupied a sixth-floor apartment that overlooked Central Park. Photo by Jane K. Domink.

he would also fictionalize in plays such as *After the Fall*, *The Price*, and *The American Clock*.

Miller attended PS 24 on 111th Street, and he vividly captures the atmosphere of public education in New York in the 1920s: the discipline of the Palmer Method of handwriting, the emphasis on good conduct as an equal part of the graded curriculum, the morning inspection of hands and fingernails and shined shoes, the spinster Irish teachers cracking the backs of the students who talked during lessons, students carting all their belongings—pen, pen wiper, blotter, notebook, galoshes, sweater—up to the blackboard for fear of them being stolen by their classmates (22).

His mother Augusta had attended the same school and had been an excellent student, as was his older brother Kermit—unlike the young Arthur who clearly was never a serious student in grammar school, something which would continue in his high school years. Miss Fisher was the principal when Augusta attended (Miller used her as an offstage character in *After the Fall*), still held that position (Miller 1987: 28) and Miller admits that his roguish ways frequently got him into so much trouble that his mother was called to the principal's office to account for his "unruliness."

Although Miller describes Harlem as an "ambiguous place," he proclaims that community was packed nevertheless with "the living and much hope" (Miller 1987: 55), and in *Timebends* he describes his memories of the neighborhood as "deceptively warm" (1987: 55). He became quite sensitive to the rhythmical repetitions of life during the Roaring Twenties: Daily activities included horses on the streets pulling the milkman's wagons, the iceman delivering blocks of ice (Miller 1987: 23) to the homes, buying a live chicken at the butcher's market, selecting pickles from the open barrel, building a wagon out of a soap box (Miller 1987: 65), the mothers cleaning linens, boiling laundry, and carrying rugs to the roof to beat the dust (Miller 1987: 64), images he used in plays such as *The American Clock*, *The Price*, and *Broken Glass*. Miller vividly described children's street games such as ring-a-levio and stoop ball, and the cycle of games that could only be played, for some reason no one understood, only in their proper season, such as shooting checkers in the spring and immies in the fall (Miller 1987: 44). In the winter, he and Sid at their sixth-floor windows watched the flagpole at the Central Park boathouse, waiting for the red ball flag to fly, indicating the hardening of the ice on the North lake (Miller 1987: 56) (Figure 0.4).

When he was five years old, Miller saw his first movie at a makeshift theater on the roof of his apartment house one summer night, with a sheet as a screen. He was mesmerized and haunted by the appearance of the people on the sheet, and when the image disappeared as the film ended, the boy asked his father where the people were. Miller recalled how this experience "deepened my misunderstanding of the real" (Miller 1987: 57). Over the next years, Miller

Figure 0.4 Skaters on Central Park lake, c. 1938. Underwood Archives, Inc/Alamy Stock Photo.

would learn the crucial differences among the reality of life depicted on the screen, in the theater, and the streets of Harlem.

Harlem during the 1920s was filled with restaurants, clubs, and theaters on Seventh and Lenox Avenues and 125th Street. The famous Cotton Club was located in predominantly Black Harlem but had a largely white clientele. Legitimate theater organizations played road productions of Broadway shows. Miller regularly attended vaudeville shows that Isidore particularly loved at venues such as the Lenox Theatre on 111th Street (Figure 0.5). (60).These shows included opening acts such as Chinese flying acrobats, songs delivered by busty sopranos, and famous comics and singers such as Al Jolson, Eddie Cantor, George Burns, George Jessel, and Bill "Bojangles" Robinson. Miller relates how Augusta loved to attend play matinees, and Miller recalled that when he was eight, she took the boy who would become one of America's greatest playwrights to see his first play at what he identifies as the Shubert Theatre. (However, the Shubert organization did not operate theaters in Harlem. Miller is quite clear that the theater he attended is on Lenox Avenue and 115th Street [Miller 1987: 58] [Figure 0.6]. The theater was likely the Regun or the Loew's, both located off Lenox Avenue with structures extending from 116th Street

Figure 0.5 As a young boy, Miller saw vaudeville shows here that his father loved, c. 1940. Courtesy Municipal Archives City of New York.

to 115th Street.) The melodrama vividly impressed him. The young Miller understood the suspension of reality of the movies that he had been attending every Saturday afternoon, but the lad was alarmed by seeing a deck of a ship on the theater stage moving up and down and witnessing people moving in and out of stage doors. And the nascent playwright discovered that the reality of the stage could seem more real (Miller 1987: 58) than life outside on 115th

Figure 0.6 The Regun theatre on West 116th Street, c. 1940. Courtesy Municipal Archives City of New York.

Street. He was enthralled by the suspense enacted on the stage—a bomb about to go off—and he clawed at his mother's arm in real fear but kept looking at the theater's walls to make sure the action on the stage was not actually real. At this first impression, certainly Miller learned the power of manipulating reality for an audience—for years later he would enthrall millions of theatergoers into believing the reality of the stage action in his own plays.

Miller maintains that by the time he was six and entered school, he had never heard an anti-Semitic remark. "Indeed, if I had thought about it at all, I would have imagined the whole world was Jewish, except for Lefty the Cop and Mikush the janitor"—such was life in the ethnic New York enclaves. "Except for our teachers and Mikush, our family knew almost no gentiles, and our prosperity helped seal us inside our magical apartness" (Miller 1987: 82) However, Miller ultimately became aware of the differences and similarities among the racial, religious, and ethnic communities that constituted Harlem in the 1920s. When he was seven or eight, Italian kids in the park mugged him for his roller skates (Miller 1987: 22) an incident he would fictionalize in his first short story, "Ditchy" (1944) (see Chapter 4).

As an adult, Arthur Miller rejected the practice of his Judaism, declaring himself a "Jewish atheist." Miller's biographer Christopher Bigsby has judged that despite this, being Jewish was his "default setting"(Bigsby 2005a: 477). And how could it not be? Miller developed a unique and complicated view of his Jewish culture and Judaism from his observant Yiddish-speaking grandparents and parents. Even though Miller claims that he was shielded from anti-Semitism as a young boy, he admits that nevertheless, his skin absorbed the Jews' part in two thousand years of European history and "I had become a part, a character floating on the surface of the mythic American melting pot" (Miller 1987: 24).

Miller eventually learned how Mikush, the Polish janitor, hated the Jews in the building just as much as other gentiles did, but the man could be kind to the boy, as when he straightened his badly bent bicycle (Miller 1987: 26, 27), so that Miller had less than total fear of him. Miller absorbed the Jewish apprehension for Catholics from his grandfather Louis Barnett, who once instructed the young Arthur never to walk under a large cross overhanging the sidewalk outside a church on Lenox Avenue. If he did so by accident, the grandfather insisted, he must spit when he realized it in order to cleanse himself. But the man never explained the theology behind this, leaving it to the realm of superstition for the boy. Miller included his and Kermit's Bar Mitzvah instruction among the Jewish inclination not to explain things rationally.

However, Miller explains that his "more overtly Jewish memories, in fact, are suffused far less with fear and flight than with power and reassurance" (36). Miller had a particularly moving recollection when he was four or five years old of sitting in his great-grandfather Barnett's lap in the 114th Street

Synagogue where Kermit would have his Bar Mitzvah: his great-grandfather pointing out the letters in the prayer book; the "movingly male" assemblage of his father, grandfather, and his brother sitting in a row as the women, consigned to the balcony, looked down, with Augusta weeping with the pride of it (Miller 1987: 37); the young boy told "Shh!" by the questions he asked; the Torah scrolls moving out their ark. Miller learned that the "transaction called believing comes down to the confrontation with overwhelming power" (Miller 1987: 37).

Miller relates that the climax of his childhood fascination with religion came one day when he was alone with his great-grandfather sitting at shul. The old man instructed the boy to close his eyes and warned him not to look. Miller recalls that the man removed his own shoes and in only his white socks, put his prayer shawl over his head and joined a large group of men at the altar. The obedient boy kept his eyes closed and covered with his hands, fearful of seeing something forbidden, when he heard the men singing, not in unison but in individual voices, in different melodies. The boy was unable to contain himself, peeked, and saw the most astonishing thing—about fifteen old men, bent over and covered completely by their prayer shawls, all of them in white socks—dancing! The boy gasped in fright, thinking he was seeing something forbidden but could not figure out what. But he knew that he had never heard music "so wild and crazy, and each man dancing without any relation to another but only toward the outer darkness that enveloped the spaces beyond family and men, the spaces you might say listened to prayers" (Miller 1987: 39).

Why was this event with his grandfather, which Miller later learned was the annual celebration of Simchat Torah, so significant in the young boy's life? Miller concluded that "in some osmotic way it was he that I would strive to imitate as a writer though he died before I even started to go to school" (Miller 1987: 39). What was it about his grandfather that he would imitate as a writer? Is not a writer a religious man singing and dancing his words in the outer darkness? Is not writing a religious experience? Can we conclude that Miller's writing is rooted in Judaic prayer and ritual? This was clearly an epiphanic moment in Miller's life that remained so fixed in his memory that he saw his great-grandfather as the source of his art. (Marino 2024: 23–4). And Miller would transform his experiences with Jewish religion and culture in his so-called "Holocaust" plays, *After the Fall, Incident at Vichy, Playing for Time*, *and Broken Glass*. His short story, "I Don't Need You Anymore" occurs on the holy day of Yom Kippur, whose rituals are essential to the tale (See chapter 4).

A Boy Grows in Brooklyn[7]

Miller's glorious boyhood changed when hard times came for the Millers, even before the Stock Market crash of 1929. Because of the collapse of his coat and suit factory (Gussie blamed Izzy for hiring too many of their relatives from his own father's dissolved business as the cause (Miller 1987: 12)), Miller's father moved his family in 1928, when Arthur was thirteen, from Manhattan to Brooklyn. The move was clearly a step down, and the family relocated to the Midwood/Gravesend neighborhood of the borough. The Millers bought for $5,000 a six-room house at 1350 East 3rd Street, off Avenue M in the Parkville section, a few blocks from Gussie's family (Figure 0.7).[8] Miller shared a bedroom with his maternal grandfather, Louis Barnett, whose wife had recently passed.

In his final interview with Christopher Bigsby in 2004, Miller explained the family's financial descent and his transition to life in Brooklyn.

> AM: Well, it, the first, you know the big crash of '29 occurred in pulses. It didn't occur in one day for a lot of people. We went downhill in bumps. You didn't really, you were not convinced the end had come for three or four years. So that the move to Brooklyn from Central Park North, which was 110th Street, was not so much a catastrophic thing as a recognition that you had to tighten your belt a little bit, and we lived in a perfectly lovely house on a nice street on Ocean Parkway and I loved it there. It was terrific. And then gradually we had to move to a smaller house because things got tighter and pretty soon you couldn't pay the mortgage on the small house and pretty soon the possibility was there that you might be evicted like a lot of other people and then God knows where on the street. But this took from I'd say '29 to '32.
>
> CB: You were a teenager. A sense that I get is that in some way Brooklyn is a kind of liberation for you.
>
> AM: Oh, I loved it! It was like going to the country. We were out in Midwood. There were empty lots where we could play football and wonderful weeds and trees and just a couple of years earlier I had an aunt who could watch her children go to school 6, 7, 8, 10 blocks with no houses. It was all open. That's Willy Loman country and it gradually got built up,

Figure 0.7 The Miller family home on East 3rd Street Brooklyn in 1940. Courtesy Municipal Archives City of New York.

of course, very crowded. But in those days, Flatbush was never beautiful. It was flat and kind of ugly. But I thought it was great. (Miller 2006: 61–2)

Miller often described Brooklyn as if it were a rural, frontier outpost, and it certainly must have seemed so to the boy who had lived his thirteen years in Manhattan and to his family whose financial and cultural lives had embraced the city. Miller captured their attitude toward Brooklyn in *The American Clock*, a play which partly chronicles his family's downfall during the Depression in the guise of the Baum family. The sisters Rose and Fanny, (characters based on Miller's mother and aunt), argue over their father's objections to moving to Brooklyn. Fanny says: "And what is he going to do with himself in Brooklyn? He never liked the country" (Miller 1989: 110). This description of Brooklyn as "the country" typifies an attitude toward the borough in the 1920s and 1930s—a point of view which impressed Miller so much he would later use it in *Death of a Salesman*. For despite the borough's size and population (when Brooklyn joined New York in 1898, it had been the fourth largest city in the country with a population of 1.1 million), surprisingly many areas remained relatively rural even though the infrastructure of the city—streets, trolleys, buses, subways, and elevated train lines—were being built. And life in an "outer" borough like Brooklyn greatly contrasted with life in Manhattan, what people then (and now) called "the city." As Grandpa says in *The American Clock*: "Brooklyn is full of tomatoes" (Miller 1989: 111).

Miller's recollections of life during his Brooklyn youth are remarkably consistent in emphasizing the rural and pastoral. In a piece he wrote in 1955 for *Holiday* magazine, "A Boy Grew in Brooklyn," he described the Midwood section thirty years before:

> As a flat forest of great elms through which ran the elevated Culver Line to Coney Island, two and a half miles distant . . . Children going to school in those days could be watched from the back porch and kept in view for nearly a mile. There were streets, of course, but the few houses had well-trodden trails running out their back doors which connected with each other and must have looked from the air like a cross section of a mole run; these trails were much more used than streets, which were as unpaved as any in the Wild West and just as muddy. (Miller 1955a: 54)

In both the *Holiday* piece and *Timebends*, Miller recounts the life of his two pioneer uncles, Manny Newman and Lee Balsam, (who were married to Augusta's sisters and lived two blocks away) both salesmen, who had moved their families to Brooklyn after the First World War, almost ten years earlier than his own family. Miller describes the Midwood area as "so empty they could watch their kids walking all the dozen blocks to the school across the scrubby flatlands" (Miller 1987: 121). He used descriptions of this in *The American Clock, After the Fall*, and *Broken Glass*. In *Holiday*, Miller also tells how the families kept rabbits and chickens and hunted squirrels and other small game. Miller was aware of how greatly his relatives' lifestyle contrasted with his own:

> In the twenties, when the Millers came out from Manhattan in their limousine to visit, the Newman-Balsam connected houses were flanked by only four other pairs, a line of little wooden homes with flat roofs and three-step stoops. . . . With no stores closer than a couple of miles, they bought potatoes by the hundred-pound sack and canned the tomatoes they grew, and their basements smelled hauntingly of earth, unlike Manhattan basements with their taint of cat and rat and urine. (Miller 1987: 121)

Miller was concerned particularly with the physical change of Brooklyn in the era between the world wars, when he witnessed the borough's quick and dramatic change to the wholly urban environment of today. Miller recalls how the nation and Brooklyn were mired in the Great Depression: "Inevitable changes had helped to destroy so much that was human and lovely in my neighborhood... The woods were gone now and there were houses everywhere and even the last lot left to play football on was turned into a fenced-in junk yard" (Miller 1987: 122–4).

Today, Miller's boyhood home still looks much as it did in 1928. East 3rd Street is a few blocks from the wide boulevard known as Ocean Parkway. This famous Brooklyn thoroughfare traverses directly through the borough with its terminus, as the name indicates, at the Atlantic Ocean. In *Timebends*, Miller recollects how, as a young boy, he worked for a bakery, a block and a half from his home, and one cold winter morning, his bicycle toppled over on the icy road, spilling bagels, rolls, and bread over this six-lane parkway (Miller 1987: 107, 8). In *Broken Glass*, Dr. Harry Hyman rode his horse on the bridle paths—now pedestrian walkways—which formerly lined this boulevard. (See Chapter 1.)

Driving down Ocean Parkway through the Midwood section clearly gives a real sense of how much Miller used Brooklyn in his work, especially *Death of a Salesman*. The elevated line still runs parallel to the wide parkway where many grand brick houses of the wealthier Brooklyn residents stand. Many of these single-family homes are shadowed by the larger apartment buildings that were constructed during the rapid growth of Brooklyn in the era between the world wars, when Miller witnessed the borough's quick and dramatic change to the wholly urban environment of today. The side streets off Ocean Parkway are occupied by many of the same small wood-frame houses which dominated

Figure 0.8 Apartment house looms over small wood-frame house: "bricks and windows, windows and bricks," c. 2023. Photo by S. Marino.

the neighborhood when Miller lived here, interspersed with the more recently built brick apartment buildings (Figure 0.8).

The block of East 3rd Street also is the same as when the young Miller played football and baseball there—a dead-end street with a baseball field at its north end. Miller's house, number 1350, sits two-thirds down the dead end on the left side, and one can see how it served a pivotal role in Miller's life as a writer, especially how it evokes Loman house in *Death of a Salesman*. Across from Miller's boyhood home (Figure 0.9) is the house where his cousin Jean and her husband Moe lived with his mother and which Miller used as the setting for

Figure 0.9 Miller's Brooklyn boyhood home as it looks today. Photo by Katie Murray.

his most autobiographical short story, "The 1928 Buick" (see Chapter 4). The front of the house looks much like it did when Miller lived in it.

Miller had an admittedly undistinguished academic career at Abraham Lincoln High School.[9] In the 2004 interview with Christopher Bigsby, Miller's final public interview, Bigsby asked about his high school education. Although Miller was not a stellar student, in the library at Abraham Lincoln he discovered his passion for reading, a significant intellectual experience for him:

CB: When you went to school, you weren't exactly a serious scholar, were you?
AM: No.

CB: I'm interested in the moment you ceased being the high school student who wanted to be a second baseman who suddenly wanted to go to University.

AM: I went through high school invisibly. I was the invisible man. On my last week or so I ran into somebody who had a camera. I was sort of interested in cameras, and he was in school and he had the camera. And I said "What do you do with that?" And he said, "Well, I'm in the camera club." Well, I had been in that school four years and I didn't know there was a camera club. Years later the man named Mason, who was the principal of the school, everybody loved him, and he retired. This was already probably in 1955, something like that. They invited me to attend the dinner. I sat next to a teacher who said that they had all been looking through their records because these teachers were of an age, many of them, who would have been my teachers. Some of them were 70; they were all retired. None of them could find a trace. I left no footsteps behind, and it was a little embarrassing.

CB: Does that mean that there was never a teacher who ignited your interest in literature?

AM: They ignited my interest in leaving the school. (*Laughter*) It was a total loss. The only thing I got out of it was at some point in that four-year period at Abraham Lincoln High School, it was a perfectly good school, a lot of people loved it and I didn't mind it either because they left me alone. I had to write a book report and I knew nothing about anything, so I went into the library and found my eye came upon a book called *The Brothers Karamazov*. Well, I was a brother. My older brother and I were at sore points a lot of times and I thought well, maybe I could read that. And I read it and I was completely swept away. That's where my life began with Dostoevsky. In fact, I thought *Crime and Punishment* was a detective story. I had absolutely no background whatsoever about Dostoevsky. It meant nothing to me. He could have been Joe Smith, and I read all his works because he was—something in it meant something in me, and then I began to read some, a lot of Russian literature Tolstoy, Turgenev, Chekhov they were the great teachers for my education first. (Miller 2006: 62–3)

In 1932, Miller graduated from Lincoln during the depths of the Depression. His poor grades and his family's finances kept him out of college. Miller worked in a succession of odd jobs.[10] For two years, he toiled as a stock clerk in the Delamater-Chadwick auto parts supply warehouse, an experience he would turn into his 1955 one-act play, *A Memory of Two Mondays* (see Chapter 2). Miller finally entered the University of Michigan at Ann Arbor in 1934. Miller's playwriting career began during his college years when he won three

Avery Hopwood Awards for plays that are clearly autobiographical and are set in Brooklyn.

A Writer in Brooklyn Heights

After Miller graduated from the University of Michigan in 1938, he returned home to live with his parents. In 1940, Miller married Mary Slattery, a student and a Catholic, whom he had met at the University of Michigan. The couple lived from 1940 to 1956 in various apartments and homes in Brooklyn Heights, which Miller describes in *Timebends* as "a quiet, leafy village" (1987: 70). Miller's time living in Brooklyn Heights is crucial to his artistic development, for his dramatic vision congealed there. He moved into the neighborhood as an unknown, aspiring writer and left as one of the most famous literary, political, and social figures in America. Miller's dramatic reputation rests upon the four tragedies he produced between 1947 and 1956: *All My Sons*, *Death of a Salesman*, *The Crucible*, and *A View from the Bridge*. His residence and experiences in the neighborhood obviously influenced the conditions under which he produced those masterpieces and other significant works in his canon.

Brooklyn Heights is a national historic district that had the reputation in the early nineteenth century as New York's first suburb. But Brooklyn Heights in the 1930s, 1940s, and 1950s had a downtrodden reputation, and consequently was a haven for artists and writers such as Miller, Norman Rosten, Thomas Wolfe, Henry Miller, Richard Wright, W. H. Auden, Norman Mailer, Truman Capote, and Carson McCullers. As Miller said, "There were a lot of boarded up houses, especially along Columbia Heights" (Miller 2006: 61) and, as a result, Miller proclaimed: "Brooklyn Heights in the 40s was the cheapest place you could live in New York City" (Miller 2006: 65).

Today, the Downtown Brooklyn Civic Center has exploded with condos and towering office buildings. When Miller attended the Arthur Miller Conference at St. Francis College in 2004, he was asked how he felt returning home to Brooklyn. Miller quipped, "I don't recognize it. It looks like Philadelphia ((Miller 2006: 61). . . . I would get lost here and I used to walk these streets all the time. It got much richer, it seems to me. I wasn't there today, but I can't imagine anything is boarded up now" (Miller 2006: 65). Despite Miller's reaction to the many physical changes in his Brooklyn Heights neighborhood, all of the residences where he lived in the 1940s and 1950s survive. Miller would recognize the houses of his Brooklyn neighborhood.

Miller and Mary Slattery lived in five residences between 1940 and 1956, and it is intriguing to trace his dramatic development during those years as the couple frequently moved from place to place. Miller's first Brooklyn Heights residence was at 62 Montague Street. During the couple's time living at 62 Montague Street (Figure 0.10), Miller started writing radio plays and the novel version of *The Man Who Had All the Luck* (1944).

Figure 0.10 The apartments in this building at 62 Montague Street, c. 2023 were called "French Flats." Miller and his wife Mary shared the apartment with her girlfriends. A plaque recognizing his residence there was dedicated in 2016. Photo by Katie Murray.

In 1941, the Millers moved from Montague Street to 18 Schermerhorn Street[11]—a street where he placed his late short story "Bulldog" (2001). Norman Rosten, a friend of Miller's from the University of Michigan, also lived in the building (Figure 0.11). Miller explained:

> My first apartment was on Schermerhorn Street after I got married and that was a newly remodeled brownstone building. Nobody had ever lived in this apartment before and it was a living room, and a kitchen and a bedroom— beautiful. It went right through the building. And that cost $35 a month. Now even then, elsewhere you'd have to pay double that, and a lot of writers and artists moved to Brooklyn Heights because of that, because it was cheap. But it was also beautiful. (Miller 2006: 65)

Figure 0.11 Miller's residence at 18 Schermerhorn, c. 2023 was a one famly building in Brooklyn Heights converted into apartments. Photo by Katie Murray.

Miller's apartment window looked out on the backyard of a mosque. "I used to sit and watch the Moslems holding services," Miller wrote. "They had a real Moorish garden symmetrically planted with curving lines of white stones laid out in the earth, and they would sit in white robes— twenty or thirty of them, eating at a long table, and served by their women who wore the flowing purple and rose togas of the East." (Miller 1955a: 54.)

During this time, Miller worked as a fitter in the Brooklyn Navy Yard and he wrote half-hour radio plays for DuPont's "Cavalcade of America," the Columbia Workshop, and US Steel. In early 1943, Miller left the Navy Yard to conduct background research for the screenplay of *The Story of G.I. Joe* (1943) that he adapted from columns by American war reporter Ernie Pyle. Miller's script was too raw and realistic for the studio executives and the producer replaced Miller who did not receive a film credit (Abbotson 2007: 322). However, Miller used his research to publish *Situation Normal* (1944). While living on Schermerhorn Street, he also wrote his first Broadway play, *The Man Who Had All the Luck* that he had written as a novel but was rejected by publishers, so he transformed it into a play. [12]

In 1944, the Millers moved again, to a duplex apartment at 102 Pierrepont Street (Figure 0.12). As Miller remembered it: "The rooms were very dark— wood-paneled. It had been a very elaborate home. We never could see anything. Norman Mailer lived upstairs, but much of the time he was away at war" ("He Was No Misfit . . . "). In *Timebends*, Miller paints an unflattering account of Mailer. One afternoon, Miller intervened in an argument between Mailer and a woman occurring in the hallway. Mailer later approached Miller on the street, introduced himself, and having apparently seen *All My Sons*, Mailer proclaimed, "I could write a play like that." Miller laughed at his bravado (1987: 139). After suffering the disappointment of the Broadway flop of *The Man Who Had All the Luck*, Miller wrote in that Pierrepont residence his only novel, *Focus*, and his first Broadway hit, *All My Sons*.

With the success of *All My Sons*, Miller realized how "the word *royalty* took on a more exact meaning" (Miller 1987: 141). The play and film rights that Miller sold gave him financial and artistic freedom. He reasoned that it made little sense for his family to stay in the small apartment on Pierrepont Street. In 1947, Miller purchased his first home, 31 Grace Court, near the steep hill that at that time led down to the East River.[13] With his royalties, Miller

Figure 0.12 Miller and his wife lived in a duplex apartment in this building, c. 2023. His daughter Jane was born in 1944 during their residency. Photo by Katie Murray.

also purchased a country home on some 44 acres of property in Roxbury, Connecticut (Figure 0.13).

While Miller lived on Grace Court, he conceived and completed his masterpiece, *Death of a Salesman*, although he actually wrote the first draft of the play in the studio he built on his country property in Connecticut (*Timebends* 182–4) (see Chapter 1). Miller also wrote his version of Henrik Ibsen's *An Enemy of the People* (1950) on Grace Court, and the long gestation

Figure 0.13 Miller bought this home with the royalties from his success with *All My Sons*, c. 1940. Courtesy Municipal Archives City of New York.

of *A View from the Bridge* (See chapter 1) began while Miller resided there. After the success of *Salesman*, Miller wrote the screenplay, *The Hook*, (1951) about his experience researching the Mafia hiring practices on the Brooklyn docks. During this time, Miller also took a trip to Hollywood with the director Elia Kazan to promote *The Hook*. While there, Kazan introduced Miller to Marilyn Monroe, which marked the start of their relationship. In 1951, Miller sold the home on Grace Court that was purchased anonymously through an

Figure 0.14 Arthur Miller in Brooklyn Heights, c. 1954. Photo courtesy of the Estate of Elliot Erwitt.

agent for the historian W. E. B. DuBois. As a vocal member of the Communist Party, Du Bois was hounded so much by the FBI that he could not find a home to rent. Finally, he was able to purchase Miller's Grace Court home (Figure 0.14).

Miller's 151 Willow Street home[14] is located one block from the famous Brooklyn Promenade (which Miller called the "Esplanade") that sits atop a hill

Figure 0.15 Miller's fifth residence in Brooklyn Heights, c. 2023 is considered an architectual gem and served as a stop on the Underground Railroad. Photo by Katie Murray.

on which two levels of the Brooklyn-Queens Expressway are built (Figures 0.15, 0.16). During Miller's residence there, the highway had not been constructed, and a steep hill inclined to the East River, where the Brooklyn docks were located. Miller remembered:

> Before the esplanade was built, the promenade there, and you looked down on the docks where ships were still being loaded and unloaded, and there were longshoremen bars down there. It was a whole life going on at the edge of the river. Later it dried up because of the container ships that didn't require so many longshoremen, but it was an interesting place to live. Out of that came *A View from the Bridge* because I got to know some of the people down there. (Miller 2006: 65)

Figure 0.16 United States. New York City, 1961. View of the Brooklyn Bridge from the promenade. © Inge Morath/Magnum Photos.

While Miller lived on Willow Street, he wrote *The Crucible* (1953) after researching the trial transcripts in Salem. Miller also wrote the one-act version of *A View from the Bridge* at this time, and no play illustrates better the effect of Miller's years in Brooklyn Heights. *A View from the Bridge* was born on the streets of this Brooklyn neighborhood (see Chapter 1). The title refers to the famous Brooklyn Bridge that spans the East River between Manhattan and Brooklyn at the foot of Brooklyn Heights. By the time he was writing the one-act version of *A View from the Bridge*, Miller had embarked on his affair with Marilyn Monroe, was about to divorce his wife, and was becoming a target of HUAC, as his friends and colleagues had. After the divorce filing, Miller had his celebrated hearing before HUAC. He and Monroe married in late June 1956; then the famous couple flew to England where Monroe was to star with Laurence Olivier in a film, *The Prince and the Showgirl*, and where Miller revised *A View from the Bridge* into a two-act play for a London production.

After 1956, Miller would never live in Brooklyn again. The fledgling writer who moved to the Heights left the neighborhood a celebrated playwright and controversial figure married to the most famous woman in the world.

Return to Manhattan, The Chelsea, a Connecticut Yankee

Miller and Marilyn Monroe planned to center their lives in a second home that Miller bought at 232 Tophet Road in Roxbury. They had even enlisted America's most illustrious architect, Frank Lloyd Wright, to renovate the farmhouse. However, the famous couple also spent much time in Manhattan in Monroe's subleased apartment high up in the Waldorf Tower, eventually renting a Sutton Place apartment at 444 East 57th Street, right off the East River (398). There was ample newspaper coverage of the couple's appearances in New York and their visits to Brooklyn to visit Miller's parents. The couple also rented a house on the south shore of Long Island—where after an incident on the beach with Monroe, Miller wrote the story, "Please Don't Kill Anything" (1960). In 2021 and 2022, the sales of the Sutton Place apartment and the Hamptons rental house attracted media attention.

After his divorce from Monroe, Miller's New York residence was at the famous Chelsea Hotel at 222 W 23rd Street where, he reported in his lively essay, "The Chelsea Effect," that he wrote the bulk of *After the Fall*. In the 1970s, Miller purchase a coop apartment at 315 East 68th Street that he and Inge Morath—established in Roxbury—used as their New York base for their many appearances in the metropolis for play rehearsals, premieres, and public appearances. Also, Miller spent his final days in New York City at his sister Joan Copeland's apartment on 88 Central Park West before traveling to his Roxbury home where he passed on February 10, 2005.

1

The Brooklyn Plays

The American Clock, Death of a Salesman, A View from the Bridge, Broken Glass

Arthur Miller used his experiences living in Brooklyn in four plays where, in Faulkner's own words, he transformed the "postage stamp of native soil" (Faulkner 2007: 57). He once proclaimed that "Brooklyn is the world" (Miller 1955a: 54) and was so influenced by his life there that the borough became the prime setting for *The American Clock, Death of a Salesman, A View from the Bridge,* and *Broken Glass*. As a writer, he adhered to the age-old axiom: "Write what you know"—and Miller clearly knew Brooklyn. The autobiographical impulse in him was strong, and his Brooklyn plays are rooted in encounters with people and places that stimulated his instinct to make art out of life.

From the start of his career, Miller had a strong inclination to use biographical events as the raw material for his drama. In fact, he based the very first play that he wrote, *No Villain*, on his family's experiences in Brooklyn during the Depression. *No Villain* holds an important place in Miller's canon as the first of the three plays he wrote at the University of Michigan. During spring break 1935, he decided to try his hand at playwriting in order to win the annual Avery Hopwood Award that came with a $250 cash prize, money that he desperately needed. Miller's natural bent for drama was born: the clearly autobiographical play won first prize when Miller submitted it for the 1936 contest in his sophomore year. The next year he penned *Honors at Dawn* (1937) which won him his second Hopwood Award; a third play, *The Great Disobedience*, (1938) won him second place in his senior year. Miller also revised *No Villain* with the titles *They Too Arise* (1937) and *The Grass Still Grows* (1939).

In *No Villain*, Miller for the first time drew from his family's experiences. The plot is his thinly disguised dramatization of crucial events in the Miller Brooklyn household during the spring of 1935 when Arthur returned home from his freshman year at the University of Michigan filled with the liberal, radical ideology that pervaded the Ann Arbor campus. In New York, his father Isidore (named Abe) and his brother Kermit (named Ben) were contending with union organizers at their factory in the garment district in Manhattan.

The plot revolves around the Simon family anxiously awaiting the arrival home of Arnold—Miller's name for himself—who is hitchhiking home during a school break. The Simon teenage daughter Maxine is modeled on Miller's sister Joan (Maxine was her middle name) and displays her spoiled precociousness; the Simon grandfather depicts the sensitivity and vulnerability of Augusta's father, Louis Barnett. The character Esther typifies the love, anxiety, and strength of a Jewish mother modeled on Miller's mother Gussie. Her role is responsible for establishing the serio-comic tone of the play, but Esther also voices shock and wonder at how new political ideas threaten the fabric of Esther's family. She is particularly fearful—as was Augusta about Arthur—that Arnold has become a Communist. Arnold clearly portrays the commitment to social change that Miller embraced at Michigan, but also shows understanding for the plight of his elder brother, who left college to help with the family business. Miller balances the action in the family home with Abe and his son Ben in their factory contending with the effects of union organization. The political and moral issues that Miller brought with him from Michigan are at odds with the business and economic interests of his family.

As Miller's first play, *No Villain* can be variously classified as a seminal play for his later works, an ur-text for his subsequent revisions, or even a dramatic bildungsroman given that the play emphasizes the transformation of Arnold's (and Arthur's) political, economic, and social beliefs in his time at college. The conflicts among the self, family, and society—so evident in Miller's masterpieces—also are present in *No Villain*. In addition, the complicated clashes between fathers and sons, crucial in *All My Sons*, *Death of a Salesman*, and *The Price*, are dramatized in the interactions among Abe, Ben, and Arnold. Arnold's politics and the workers' strike are existential threats to Ben's business—and also to the Simon family. As such, *No Villain* deftly balances between being a social play and a family drama—a balance that Miller would use in many plays over his seventy-year career.[1]

Winning the Hopwood Award entitled Miller to study with Kenneth T. Rowe at the University of Michigan, under whom Miller acknowledges he honed his craft: "His chief contribution to my development was his interest in the dynamics of play construction" (Miller 1987: 227). Thus, when Miller began his professional playwriting career, he knew that dramatizing personal experience was not enough. In his important 1956 essay, "The Family in Modern Drama," he explained how he recognized in writing *Death of a Salesman* the need for the play to "extend itself out of the family circle and into society . . . and lift it out of the merely particular toward the fate of the generality of men" (Miller 1978: 74).

Miller's 1980 play *The American Clock* is a splendid example of how Miller used his personal family experiences as a counterpoint to the experience of society, giving truth to his declaration that "Brooklyn is the world" (Miller 1955a: 54). Of the plays set in Brooklyn, *The American Clock* is the least well-known, but is the most autobiographical—although the entire play is not about Miller's family. Based on Studs Terkel's *Hard Times*, *The American Clock* offers a kaleidoscope of individual stories of economic loss, political turmoil, and social upheaval of Americans caused by the Great Depression against thinly disguised episodes from Miller's family experiences during those turbulent times of the 1920s and 1930s. Using the pseudonym of the Baum family, he combines their episodes with the traumatic events of actual Americans whom Miller had read about in Studs Terkel's *Hard Times*. The play shows how the individual stories are an integral part of the landscape of the entire American society—and Miller's family story is part of that landscape. The overall effect is to show Americans' steely determination, innate sense of hope for recovery, and the promise of prosperity in the future.[2]

Many of the scenes of the Baum family are thinly disguised dramatizations of the effects of the Depression on Miller's family. Events that are blatantly autobiographical include: Isidore's chauffeured limousine; his dabbling in the stock market; Gussie going to the theater; the family moving from Manhattan to Brooklyn; his maternal, elderly grandfather shuffled among his daughters and sharing a bedroom with Arthur; Miller's college decision-making and applying for relief aid with his father; his father borrowing train fare from him; and Gussie hosting illegal card parties, playing the piano, hiding from a bank collector, and hating her mother-in-law. The character Lee Baum is also the narrator of the play, and he is clearly a stand-in for the young Miller.

Moreover, the play blatantly mentions specific locations, streets, and neighborhoods in Brooklyn and Manhattan that Miller and his family knew so well—a technique that he used in every play set in New York City—such as Coney Island, the Brooklyn Bridge, and Gramercy Park (Figure 1.1). Union Square is referred to as a place of political gatherings for Communists

Figure 1.1 Coney Island boardwalk and the famous Parachute Jump, c. 1989. The Parachute Jump was originally constructed for use at the 1939–40 New York World's Fair. It was moved to Coney Island in 1941. Courtesy of the New York City Landmarks Preservation Commission.

and Fascists (Miller 1982: 178). Because the events of the play occur during the Great Depression, Miller also depicts historical events in New York. For example, the character Robertson looks out from his Riverside Drive apartment and describes the "Hoovervilles" he can see from his window: "It's Calcutta on the Hudson thousands of people living in cardboard boxes right next to that beautiful drive. It like an army encampment down the length of Manhattan Island. At night you can see the campfires flickering ... the flames reflecting off the river through the night" (Miller 1982: 154). Robertson also describes other Depression-era scenes in New York (Figures 1.2 and 1.3):

> Along the West Side of Manhattan you had or ten of the world's greatest ocean liners tied up—I recall the SS *Manhattan*, the *Berengaria*, the *United States*—most of them would never sail again. But at the same time they were putting up the Empire State Building, highest in the world. But with whole streets and avenues of empty stores who would ever rent space in it? (Miller 1982: 174)

Figure 1.2 Depression encampments along the Hudson River, c. 1930. Everett Collection/Alamy Stock Photo.

Figure 1.3 Construction of the Empire State Building, c. 1931. American Photo Archive/Alamy Stock Photo.

Birth of the Famous Brooklyn Plays

Arthur Miller's famous Brooklyn plays, *Death of a Salesman*, *A View from the Bridge*, and *Broken Glass*, are not entirely autobiographical plays; he did not directly base their exact plots on his family life; rather, they are rooted in encounters with people and places in Brooklyn that stimulated his writer's instinct to turn life into art.

Both *Death of a Salesman* and *A View from the Bridge* had long creative gestation periods that intertwined starting in 1946 and were crucially influenced by Miller's life in Brooklyn. Brenda Murphy's volume, *Death of a Salesman*, is a critical history of the play from its creation to its premiere, and to the significant American and world productions that have spawned in the ensuing years. Murphy devotes more than a third of her book to an exhaustive study of the collaborative strands of writing, producing, directing, and performing that contributed to the acclaimed original Broadway production.

In Murphy's section on the writing of the play, she details how the direct impetus for Miller starting the play was his chance meeting with his Uncle Manny Newman in the lobby of the Colonial Theatre in Boston in late 1946 during the pre-Broadway tryout of *All My Sons*. As the introduction explained, Manny Newman was one of Miller's two "pioneering" uncles, married to Miller's mother, Augusta's sisters (Lee Balsam married Esther; Manny married Annie) who had moved to Brooklyn at the end of the First World War, some ten years before the Millers. They lived a few blocks from the East 3rd Street home of the Millers. In *Timebends*, Miller recalls how Manny had raised his two sons, Buddy and Abby, to be competitive alter egos of Miller and his older brother Kermit. Miller had not seen Manny in years and his uncle's greeting to him in the lobby theatre was "Buddy is doing very well" (Miller 1987: 131). Miller was struck that after all those years, Manny remained a "competitor, at all times, and all things, and at every moment" (Miller 1987: 122). This encounter with him remained in Miller's mind. When he found out a short time later that Manny, a traveling salesman, had committed suicide, he decided to dramatize Manny's story and his strong connection to his sons. The character who would become Willy Loman was actually a composite of other salesmen Miller had known through his father's coat and manufacturing business in New York's garment district (126).[3]

However, to Miller, Manny clearly remained the model for Willy. In a 1999 *New Yorker* interview that Miller gave to John Lahr during the play's fiftieth anniversary Broadway run, he recalled that fateful meeting with Manny. Miller explained that Manny's proclamation about his son doing well made him realize that, "Manny was living in two places at the same time. And I thought, Wouldn't it be marvelous to be able to do a play where somebody is in two or three different places concurrently. That's when the penny dropped."(Miller 1999: n.p.). He described Manny as the "ultimate climber up the ladder who was constantly being stepped on . . . by those climbing past him. My empathy for him was immense." Miller wanted to contrast Manny's "failure in the face of surrounding success" (Miller 1999: n.p.). When he learned of his uncle's suicide, it confirmed his feeling that "this man was always half in darkness" (Miller 1999: n.p.). Miller's view that the "play was basically looking from the edge of the grave at life" (Miller 1999: n.p.) resonates strongly in how he used the circumstances of Manny's suicide in the play. Manny's death certificate states his cause of death as "illuminating gas poisoning" in his home on East 4th Street in Brooklyn (Figure 1.4) and the means of injury as "inhaled

Figure 1.4 Manny Newman's home on East 4th Street, c. 1940. Courtesy Municipal Archives City of New York.

illuminating gas poisoning—1 jet & tub" ("Historical Vital Records"). Miller wove this into *Salesman* in Willy crafting the rubber tube for the hot water heater. Biff's discovery of it leads to his dramatic confrontation with Willy at the end of act 2, an action that pushes Willy, like Manny, to the edge of the grave.

Miller's plans to write the salesman play were interrupted by his sudden interest in a topic that would turn into *A View from the Bridge*. In *Timebends* (Miller 1987: 144), Miller relates how, after his success with *All My Sons* in 1947, he had been looking for a subject for another play and had gone on long walks in his Brooklyn Heights neighborhood and over the Brooklyn Bridge into Manhattan. He had noticed graffiti dotting the walls and sidewalks around the piers located at the foot of the neighborhood. The graffiti read: "Dovè Pete Panto?" which in Italian translates to: "Where is Pete Panto?" (Miller 1987: 146). The message also appeared in subway stations and on office buildings at the Court Street Civic Center in Downtown Brooklyn. Miller writes that he learned from newspaper coverage that Pete Panto was a young longshoreman who had challenged the powerful Mafia leadership of the seamen's union (Figure 1.5). In "Chi è Pete Panto?" Joey Skee explains:

> Working conditions on the Brooklyn docks were horrid, with endemic problems such as the "shape-up" hiring system (where men waited daily to be chosen to work), mandatory salary kickbacks, extortion, and high rates of work-related injuries. Enforcing the status quo of this corrupt fiefdom, was gangster Albert Anastasia, head of the crime syndicate "Murder, Inc." and his brother Anthony "Tough Tony." (Skee 2009: 2)

An Italian immigrant who worked the Brooklyn docks, Panto had lived at 128 Sackett Street (Figure 1.6) and worked out of the Brooklyn Rank-and-File Committee at 186 Remsen Street (Figure 1.7), where he was trying to organize the dockworkers against the hiring practices. After Panto sponsored a union rally in June of 1939, he mysteriously disappeared.

> After work on July 14, 1939, having warned his fiancée, Alice Maffia, aged twenty, and her brother, Michael Maffia, that he was off to meet two people he "didn't trust," twenty-eight year-old Pietro Panto, a hiring boss for the Moore McCormack lines on Montague Street's Pier 3, left the Maffia household on 11 North Elliott Place in Ft. Greene, across the street from the Navy Yard, and arrived at Gargiulo's Funeral Home on 56 President Street. in

Figure 1.5 Pete Panto lay in an unmarked grave in St. Charles Cemetery for over eighty years. A tombstone was placed there on September 26, 2023. Photograph by Joseph Sciorra. Available under a CC BY-SA 4.0 licence.

Red Hook at 7 PM, across the street from ILA headquarters at 33 President Street. (Hylton 2014; see Figures 1.8 and 1.9)

Panto's disappearance effectively ended the threat to the union's corruption. His body was discovered in 1941 in New Jersey.

The circumstances of Pete Panto's disappearance and murder are well-documented. News coverage was widespread in New York, and in the ensuing years, historians and journalists have unearthed more information. Panto's

Figure 1.6 Red Hook home of Pete Panto, c. 1940. Courtesy Municipal Archives City of New York.

tragic ending has been the focus of films and books such as Benjamin Appel's pulp novel *The Raw Edge* (1958), Elia Kazan's *On the Waterfront* (1955), a 1941 play written by two former crime reporters, *Brooklyn USA*, and *Waterfront* by Fergus Findley. Interest continues even today, with the *New York Times* publishing a front-page story on Panto in July 2022 after it was discovered that he lay in an unmarked grave at St. Charles Cemetery (Stapinski 2022: 1)

Figure 1.7 Contemporary picture, c. 2023, of 186 Remsen Street, location of Brooklyn Rank-and-File Committee in 1939. Photo by Katie Murray.

in Suffolk County on Long Island. Through the efforts of the Calandra Italian American Institute at Queens College of the City University of New York, a tombstone was placed on Panto's grave on September 26, 2023 (Barron 2023: n.p.).

Miller was fascinated by the idea of writing about the tragic ending of this heroic man and became intrigued with learning about the Italian immigrant society of the Brooklyn docks. He began researching the criminal underworld by visiting the piers to find out the truth behind Panto's fate. From his research, Miller likely knew all the addresses associated with Pete Panto because he included references to many of these locations in *A View from the Bridge*. Miller claims he was stymied by the intimidated silence of the longshoremen who

Figure 1.8 Gargiulio's Funeral Home in Red Hook, last known sighting of Pete Panto, c. 1940. Courtesy Municipal Archives City of New York.

feared speaking out against their bosses and the hiring traditions transported from their native Sicily. Nearly deciding to give up his project, Miller details that he "unexpectedly" received a phone call from Mitch Berenson, a union organizer, and Vinny Longhi, a lawyer, who were attempting to continue Pete Panto's resistance to the longshoremen union's power structure. After

Figure 1.9 ILA Headquarters, c.1940. Courtesy Municipal Archives City of New York.

Miller offered to write about their plight, they gave him the opportunity to enter the mysterious underbelly of this corrupt world. He learned about the lives and culture of the longshoremen, many of whom he befriended, often visiting their homes in their Red Hook neighborhood, south of Brooklyn Heights. In 1947, Miller even accompanied Longhi on a trip to Sicily where Longhi hoped to solicit support among the natives (Miller 1987: 155) for his cause in an upcoming union election. In Italy, Miller absorbed the roots of the

Sicilian society and came to understand the cultural connection between the American immigrants and their native land. Ironically, in Sicily, Miller had a chance encounter with Salvatore Giuliano who was known as the Sicilian Bandit. The irony of Miller investigating Italian corruption on the New York piers and meeting the infamous mobster was not lost on the playwright.

Stephen Schwartz in "True Life Tales 'On the Waterfront'" has noted many inaccuracies in Miller's account of learning about Pete Panto and Miller's relationship with Vinny Longhi. Panto disappeared in 1939, before Miller's residence in the Brooklyn Heights neighborhood, and it is questionable that the graffiti that Miller mentions would still dot the Brooklyn cityscape in 1947. Schwartz details that by 1947 newspaper coverage had stopped and that the longshoremen's silence was likely a result of Panto being considered old news by the time. Schwartz also details the interest in Panto's story by Communist and political organizations in Brooklyn and that Miller's relationship with Longhi may have occurred before Miller implies in *Timebends*. Schwartz details Longhi's political ambitions, including his run for Congress in 1946 supported by the Communist Party of America. In fact, a recently published book, *Bernie's Brooklyn*, details a rally held in Flatbush in 1946 headed by the musician and political activist Woody Guthrie, at which Miller was a featured speaker because he had received fame as a novelist after *Focus* was published in 1945. Longhi apparently was enthralled by the novel as he was about Pete Panto's story, which he later turned into his own play, *Two Fingers of Pride* (Ward 2019). Schwartz details that Longhi and Miller developed a close relationship before he implies, and Longhi's phone call in 1947 was not so unexpected. Schwartz's information may lead to the conclusion that in *Timebends*, Miller perhaps wanted to gloss over his association with Longhi's leftist politics that had caused him so much trouble during the Red Scare of the 1950s.

Despite the inconsistencies in how and when Miller learned about Pete Panto and why Miller fudged the truth, what is important is that during this time, Longhi told him the story of another longshoreman who had informed on two brothers who were related to him and living illegally in his house. In order to break up the relationship between his niece and one of the cousins, the longshoreman informed the immigration authorities, an action which made him a pariah in his neighborhood. Local gossip had him killed by one of the brothers. Miller was awed by the destiny of the immigrants and their informer that seemed almost the work of fate. Miller fiddled with a screenplay about the story but eventually became consumed with writing *Death of a Salesman* in 1948 and with the production of that masterpiece in 1949.

In *Timebends,* Miller relates that after his return from Italy (Miller 1987: 177–9), he reviewed his notes on the salesman character. He was in Manhattan on business and decided to go see a Fritz Lang film, *The Testament of Dr. Mabuse,* at a 42 Street movie house. Miller had not seen the film in five years (in his 1999 interview with Lahr, Miller relates this a bit differently), and he was struck by a final scene in an insane asylum where a man is screaming into a nonexistent phone: "Lohmann, Lohman, Get me, Lohman." The name suddenly meant to him "a terror-stricken man calling into the void for help that will never come" (Miller 1987: 179). Thus Willy Loman was born.

When Miller decided to write the salesman play in the spring of 1948, he felt compelled to create it "in a single sitting, in a night or a day " (Miller 1987: 182) He did not write the play in his Brooklyn home on Grace Court. He decided to drive up to the Roxbury, Connecticut home he had bought with his royalties from *All My Sons,* and with his own hands, he built a ten by twelve studio cabin that is still on the property to this day. On the day he sat down, Miller recalls that, "All I had was the first two lines and a death" (Miller 1987: 183), although Murphy reports that Miller had worked out an original three-act plot in his notes (Murphy 1995: 4). He worked through most of the day and into the night, completing the first act. Miller recalls in *Timebends* that "When I lay down to sleep I realized I had been weeping—my eyes still burned and my throat was sore from talking it all out and shouting and laughing. I would be stiff when I woke, aching as if I had played four hours of football or tennis and now had to face the start of another game" (Miller 1987: 184) He completed act 2 during the next six weeks.

Miller sent the completed play to Elia Kazan, who immediately recognized *Salesman*'s merit and together with Miller began the casting of what is now widely considered to be one of the greatest American plays of the twentieth century. Lee J. Cobb played the original Willy Loman, while Mildred Dunnock portrayed Linda. Kazan also enlisted the services of Jo Mielziner, who had designed the set for *A Streetcar Named Desire.* Miller, Kazan, and Mielziner collaborated to produce innovative staging and a revolutionary set that would become legendary in the American theater.

During the long run of *Salesman* in 1949, Miller wrote a screenplay, *The Hook*, about his experience on the Brooklyn docks, focusing on Pete Panto's doomed attempt to overthrow the Mafia gangsters who ruled the New York waterfront. After he read the script, Elia Kazan thought the film was a viable project for him to direct. Consequently, in early 1950, Miller and Kazan took a trip to Hollywood to get backing from a major studio. The negotiations for the film broke down when the Hollywood producers were reluctant to make a film critical of unions and demanded unrealistic changes, such as making the union crooks into communists, which Miller patently refused to do. The studios additionally performed background checks of Miller and Kazan—an indication of the coming Communist hysteria just beginning. In Hollywood, Miller also met the starlet Marilyn Monroe for the first time.

After his trip, disappointed by the unsuccessful Broadway production of his re-write of Henrik Ibsen's *An Enemy of the People*, Miller returned to the tale of the Italian longshoreman who had snitched on his relatives, working on the play for several months under the title, *An Italian Tragedy*, before abandoning it again in 1952 to research and write *The Crucible*, his controversial Salem Witch Trials play.

After his frustration with the critical reception of *The Crucible*, in 1954 Miller received a phone call from the actor Martin Ritt, who asked him to write a one-act play for a group of actors who had a theater available for use on Sunday evenings (Miller 1987: 352–3) and who wanted to act in a play without any commercial restraints. Miller agreed and wrote his one-act play *A Memory of Two Mondays* for these dedicated professionals (See Chapter 2). *A Memory of Two Mondays* is based on a biographical time in Miller's life—the dramatized recollection of the two years he spent working as a clerk in an auto parts factory in Manhattan before he attended the University of Michigan. Ritt loved the play and asked Miller if he had another one-act play to begin the evening, a so-called "curtain raiser." Thus, Miller returned to *An Italian Tragedy* which suddenly "seemed to fall into place as a one-act with a single rising line of intensity leading inevitably to an explosive climax" (Miller 1987: 353). Miller realized that his difficulty in dramatizing the story of the longshoreman who had informed on his relatives was that he had worried too much about making it a full-length play for the Broadway theater. Miller transformed *An Italian Tragedy* into the drama of Eddie Carbone and his niece, Catherine, writing the one-act version of what he now called *A View from the Bridge* in ten days. The title refers to the famous Brooklyn Bridge which spans the East River between Manhattan and Brooklyn Heights (Figure 1.10). However, when the original

Figure 1.10 Arthur Miller in front of the Brooklyn Bridge, c. 1954. Courtesy of the Estate of Elliott Erwitt.

theater for Sunday performances became unavailable, Kermit Bloomgarden, the producer of *Death of a Salesman*, became enthusiastic about the two one-act plays being played by the same actors, and he offered a full-fledged Broadway production.

Miller explained in "On Social Plays" that he originally wanted to dramatize the story of the informer without embellishment, exactly in "its exposed skeleton" because he did not want to interfere with the "myth-like march of the tale" (Miller 1978b: 67) toward its tragic ending. At this stage in his career, Miller was quite interested in writing modern American tragedies. For example, a few weeks after the production of *Death of a Salesman* opened, Miller wrote an op-ed piece for the *New York Times* entitled "Tragedy and the Common Man" where he made the case for Willy Loman as a modern tragic hero. Miller maintained that modern literature did not require characters to be royalty or leaders like in the tragedies of other eras and therefore, fall from some great height to their demise. Rather, Miller insisted:

> I think that the tragic feeling is evoked when we are in the presence of a character who is ready to lay down his life, if need be, to secure one thing—his sense of personal dignity. From Orestes, to Hamlet, Medea to Macbeth,

the underlying struggle is that of the individual attempting to gain his 'rightful' position in his society. (Miller 1978e: 4)

Thus, Miller argued that a lowly man like Willy could be considered a tragic hero. Miller clearly set his dramatic sights on achieving this in *A View from the Bridge*. Of course, the original attraction to Miller about Pete Panto's story was that he seemed a modern hero whose demise was a tragedy. Miller had also explored this notion just two years before in *The Crucible* with his hero John Proctor, and he aimed at similarly depicting Eddie Carbone and also further illustrating the themes of betrayal, informing, and adultery. For by the time he was writing the one-act version of *A View from the Bridge*, Miller had embarked on his relationship with Marilyn Monroe and was becoming a target of the HUAC, as his friends and colleagues had.

Miller wrote the play to keep to the tale Vinny Longhi had told him, trying not to change its original shape—although Miller did add the crucial depiction of Eddie's desire for Catherine. He wanted the audience to feel as he felt when he heard it for the first time—not with sympathy but with wonder. Miller admits that the meaning of Eddie's fate remained a mystery to him during and after writing the one-act play, and he was dissatisfied with the final result. The reviews were mixed, and the production consequently had a disappointing run, closing after 149 performances, though Miller won his third Drama Critics Circle Award. In *Timebends*, Miller also acknowledged that personal and professional distractions in his life caused him to not fully focus on writing the play as the Broadway hit that Bloomgarden wanted (Miller 1987: 354).

Miller was deeply involved in his relationship with Marilyn Monroe at this time and was contemplating the painful divorce from his wife and two children. Moreover, he continued to be distracted by personal attacks on him brought on by his political views. In 1954, the American government refused to grant Miller a passport and visa for the European premiere of *The Crucible* and his break with Kazan over his HUAC testimony received much press coverage. In addition, while casting and rehearsing the one-act *A View from the Bridge*, Miller had been researching and writing a screenplay for the New York Youth Board documentary about juvenile delinquents in Bay Ridge, Brooklyn. Sue Abbotson reports that Miller spent two months virtually living with various gangs, witnessing episodes of violence and secret mediation sessions" (Abbotson 2007: 82) clearly immersing himself in the Brooklyn community as he did a few years earlier in Red Hook for *A View from the Bridge*. An investigator from HUAC warned the city administration about being associated with Miller for his political opinions. In turn, the American Legion and the Catholic War Veterans applied pressure to stop the film because of Miller's "Communist ties." The City Council halted the project. Three years later, Miller published an essay in *Esquire*, "Bridge to the Savage World," in which he conveys the brutal realism of the youths' lives. His essay offers a grim picture of violence in New York in the 1950s, yet he is hopeful that social services offer prospects for better lives (Abbotson 2007: 82).

Miller had the opportunity to revise *A View from the Bridge* in 1956, which was a tumultuous year for him. Committed to Monroe, he spent six weeks in April in Nevada to establish residency for a "quickie" divorce. After the divorce filing, Miller had his celebrated hearing before HUAC, after which he and Monroe married in late June; then the famous couple flew to England, where Monroe was to star with Laurence Olivier in a film, *The Prince and the Showgirl*, and where Miller revised the play into a two act for a London production which was directed by Peter Brooks.

Broken Glass

Miller's late-career play, *Broken Glass*, was his first new full-length play on Broadway since *The American Clock* in 1980. In *Broken Glass,* Miller explores the subject of the Holocaust—a topic which he first dramatized in *After the Fall* and *Incident at Vichy*, plays he premiered in 1964 for the newly formed Lincoln Center Repertory Company. In 1980, he also wrote a television screenplay for *Playing for Time,* based on the memoirs of the French chanteuse Fania Fenelon, who led a female band at the Auschwitz concentration camp; he later turned the screenplay into a full-scale stage production.

Broken Glass takes place in Brooklyn in 1938, and its central concern is the cause of Sylvia Gellburg's paralysis: her hysteria about the persecution of Jews in Germany after Kristallnacht. Miller stated that her paralysis also signified the world's political paralysis at stopping the Holocaust. But writing *Broken Glass* in the early 1990s, Miller also wrote it as a response to contemporary events, particularly the Western world's paralysis at intervening in the war in Bosnia, at that time the most significant European war since the end of the Second World War.

Even late in his career, Miller went back to the well of personal experience for this play. He set the action in the very Brooklyn neighborhoods where he had lived. The time of the play, 1938, was a significant year for him as he had graduated from the University of Michigan and returned to the family home on East 3rd Street. He remembered that during that time he knew a woman in his neighborhood who inexplicably became paralyzed from the waist down. He recalled that the husband always dressed in black. The prototypes of Sylvia and Phillip Gellburg were born in Miller's creative mind for the play he initially called *The Man in Black* and then *Gellburg*. He only decided on the title *Broken Glass* at the suggestion of the English director, David Thacker (Rosenthal 2010: n.p.; Bigsby 2011: 418).

Literal and Figurative Brooklyn: Location and Dislocation

Death of a Salesman, *A View from the Bridge* and *Broken Glass* are plays rooted firmly in Brooklyn soil—but in their action, Brooklyn becomes a microcosm of the world. The personal struggles of the characters are the same struggles with which audiences and readers identify. For example, Miller's most famous character, Willy Loman, is, as Marius Bewley said, the American Dream personified. Willy's desire for economic success, personal satisfaction, a home, a family are what audiences in the United States and throughout the world identify with—Willy's struggle to achieve it is our struggle too.

It is striking how in these plays Miller uses the literal settings in Brooklyn as a contrast to other places—both geographic and symbolic. The main characters live in a Brooklyn which is the focal point of a reality with which they are in conflict. In *Death of a Salesman*, Willy Loman's idyllic memory of Brooklyn as an unspoiled wilderness contrasts with the reality of a post-Second World War technological culture which has boxed in his wood-framed house with "bricks and windows, windows and bricks," and a business culture in which he is no longer relevant. In *A View from the Bridge*, the Sicilian-American society living in the Red Hook section of the borough is consistently connected to its roots in the "Old World" of ancient Italian civilizations. Eddie Carbone succumbs to the same mythic fate as his ancestors. In *Broken Glass*, Sylvia Gellburg, an American Jew living in Brooklyn in 1938, suffers hysterical paralysis because of her concern for the persecution of German Jews during the Holocaust. The play details Sylvia's persecution on this side of the Atlantic by the figurative Nazi in her life: her husband Phillip. Thus, all three plays use physical geography as a metaphor for emotional dislocation.

Brian Robinson has pointed out that one of the main characteristics of modern literature is its use of juxtapositions which rely less on experience in a defined environment and more on fragmentation of experience in settings that may be difficult to define. In many modern texts, the city becomes the geographical locus where the tension between reality and fragmentation of experience is heightened. Despite his reputation as a social realist, Arthur Miller created characters for whom fragmentation of experience results in an emotional dislocation from the reality of the very places in which they live—the Brooklyn depicted in *Death of a Salesman*, *A View from the Bridge*, and *Broken Glass*.

In both *A View from the Bridge* and *Broken Glass*, Eddie Carbone and Sylvia Gellburg physically live in Brooklyn but are connected to other physical geographic locations. For example, *A View from the Bridge* takes place in the Red Hook section of Brooklyn in the mid-1950s, and Miller sought to place Eddie Carbone squarely in relation to his Sicilian-American immigrant society. However, when Miller first heard in his Brooklyn neighborhood the true tale of Eddie Carbone's desire for his niece and his informing on immigration authorities, he thought he had heard it before as "some re-enactment of a Greek myth" (Miller 1978: 67). In the writing and production of both the one-act and two-act versions, Miller created a character, the lawyer Alfieri, whose speeches to the audience directly connect Eddie to what Miller sees as the mythic level of the play: Eddie's destiny to enact tragic action. Therefore, many of Alfieri's speeches connect Eddie with his mythic fate, not in Brooklyn but across the sea in Italy. Alfieri uses the images of the tide, the sea, and blood to connect the Brooklyn immigrant society of the play to its savage roots in Sicily.

Similarly, in *Broken Glass*, Miller uses Brooklyn as a literal setting from which the characters connect emotionally to another physical place. The play focuses on the cause of Sylvia Gellburg's paralysis: her hysteria about the persecution of Jews in Germany in 1938. However, paralysis works on literal and figurative levels in the play: Sylvia's literal paralysis is symptomatic of an emotional and sexual paralysis between her and her husband, Phillip. Phillip and Sylvia Gellburg's emotional paralysis is connected consistently to the crucial "broken glass" image, and the image forces us to jump back and forth from the literal setting in Brooklyn to events occurring across the sea. Of course, Sylvia's anxiety ostensibly refers to "Kristallnacht"—the night of glass—the literal smashing of the stores and synagogues in Germany in 1938 which began the Nazi pogrom against the Jews. However, the play clearly parallels Sylvia's paralysis over the persecution of Jews with the paralysis in her marriage. Sylvia and Phillip's marriage is clearly as shattered as glass, and the play ultimately depicts Phillip as the cause of Sylvia's paralysis and the destruction of their marriage. For he is capable of Nazi-like violence as the play often depicts, and he actually is the figurative German she fears. Sylvia ultimately recognizes the connection between her anxiety over the affairs in Germany and her anxiety over her marriage. In fact, she blatantly connects the torture of German Jews with her own torment in Brooklyn.

Death of Salesman uses emotional dislocation from Brooklyn quite differently. For although Willy Loman physically lives in Brooklyn, he does not, like Eddie Carbone and Sylvia Gellburg, connect to a physical geographic location far from Brooklyn. Even though he is a traveling salesman, the center of his physical world is Brooklyn, but more importantly, the center of his fragile emotional existence is Brooklyn, too—the Brooklyn of the present and the Brooklyn of the past. Thus, for Willy, Brooklyn becomes the place of conflict between reality and fragmentation of experience.

Certainly, the dramatic tension at the heart of *Death of a Salesman* is Willy Loman's inability to differentiate between reality and illusion. The play depicts the last day in the life of Loman, who for thirty-six years as a traveling salesman has fought to achieve the material success and personal satisfaction which the American Dream promises, and the play captures the dramatic moments when Willy confronts his failure to achieve them and his failure to reconcile with his son Biff. Willy increasingly escapes the reality of his failures in reveries of the past, so that he often cannot differentiate between reality and illusion. In fact, from early in the play, Willy's lament for the Brooklyn of the past is inextricably tied to his conflict between reality and illusion. In the very first scene, Willy complains about the physical changes in Brooklyn over the years:

The street is lined with cars. There's not a breath of fresh air in the neighborhood. The grass don't grow any more, you can't raise a carrot in the back yard. They should've had a law against apartment houses. Remember those two beautiful elms trees out there? When Biff and I hung the swing between them? (Miller 1949: 17)

These elm trees exist in the Brooklyn of Willy's past, a Brooklyn which does not exist anymore. More importantly, they exist in the "imaginings" of Willy's mind, the place where the more important dramatic action of the play takes place. Miller's working title for *Death of a Salesman* was *The Inside of His Head*, and certainly Willy's internal longing for the Brooklyn of the past illustrates how dreaming and illusion work in his mind. Willy longs for an idyllic past, a world when his sons Biff and Hap were young, when Willy thought himself a hot-shot salesman, when Brooklyn seemed an unspoiled wilderness. However, the beautiful elms have been cut down and replaced by apartment houses which signify the reality from which Willy escapes in his imaginings. Willy's wistful longing for the Brooklyn trees includes his complaint about how the "bricks and windows, windows and bricks" (Miller 1949: 17) have boxed in his house. These buildings represent a modern post-Second World War technological culture which encroaches not only on Willy's house, but the very fabric of his existence. Willy longs for a place which does not exist in post-Second World War Brooklyn, but only in the memory inside his head.

Thus, in *Death of a Salesman*, Miller transformed his own perception of the physical changes he experienced into Willy's perception: the Brooklyn in Willy's mind—the pastoral, romantic, unspoiled wilderness; and the Brooklyn of the present time of the play—the place where the apartment buildings of the city loom over the smaller wood-frame houses. This contrast between Brooklyn as city and country touches upon many of the conflicts among Willy, Biff, and Hap.

Ultimately, the tension between the city and country is never resolved in the play. Even "Requiem" provides no definite insight. After Willy's burial, Biff is presumably returning to the West and even asks Hap to come with him. However, Hap declares his intention of "staying right in this city," where he is "gonna beat this racket!" (Miller 1949: 138). Perhaps Miller purposely left this tension. For after seventy-five years, we still wonder what legacy Willy has passed on to his sons and how his pursuit of the American Dream applies to us eking out our existence and creating our own dreams and illusions in whatever Brooklyn, or city, or suburb, or country we live in.[4]

Fictionalizing Brooklyn: Geography, Historical Events, Locations

In act 1 of *Salesman*, Willy's imagined character, his brother Ben, explains that he left South Dakota to find their father in Alaska, but, "At that age, I had a faulty view of geography, William. I discovered after a few days that I was heading due south, so instead of Alaska, I ended up in Africa." (Miller 1949: 48). As an artist, Miller certainly did not have the faulty view of geography that he gave to his creation.

A striking aspect of the Brooklyn plays is the geographical and historical accuracy that Miller used in the settings. Each play replicates the neighborhood that Miller lived in so that he deftly meshes fact with fiction. Characters in *Death of a Salesman*, *A View from the Bridge*, and *Broken Glass* not only specifically mention places and streets in Brooklyn, but also are immersed in the social and cultural activities that typify the ethnicity and economic class of the particular communities during the time period of each play. Moreover, Miller often intersperses historical references to actual world, city, and local news events that impact the lives of his fictional characters.

Death of a Salesman

Arthur Miller's most famous play, *Death of a Salesman*, is set in the same Gravesend/Midwood Brooklyn neighborhood where he grew up (Figure 1.11), and he modeled his conception for the little two-story wood-frame Loman home after his family's house on East 3rd Street. Most importantly, the play replicates the structural changes in Miller's and Willy Loman's neighborhood at the time that the play takes place in the late 1940s (Figure 1.12). In the very first scene of the play, Willy complains about the stink from the apartment houses built around the Loman home, trees torn down, and the builder having "massacred the neighborhood" (Miller 1949: 17). This is the exact phenomenon that Miller laments in "A Boy Grew in Brooklyn" (see Introduction) and that actually occurred on East 3rd Street. In fact, Joe Mielziner's set for the original Broadway production suggests this, and subsequent productions have emphasized it, most notably the 1985 Hallmark Hall of Fame TV broadcast that reprised the Broadway production of the previous year. The set for that TV production is striking for the apartment houses looming over the Loman

Figure 1.11 Miller's Brooklyn boyhood today. To the rear left, the extension can be seen; note how close the neighboring house is on the right. Photo by Katie Murray.

home and looks remarkably similar to the streets in Miller's neighborhood. In addition, the play accurately depicts the many single-family homes in Brooklyn that are closely built to each other on narrow plots of land (Figure 1.13). This explains the neighbor Charley's remark in act 1, that ""Can't we do something about the walls? You sneeze in here, and in my house, hats blow off" (Miller 1949: 42).

Miller had planted a pear tree in 1930 in the backyard of the East 3rd Street home, a tree that survived until Superstorm Sandy ravaged New York in October 2012 (see Preface). There were trees all over the neighborhood,

Figure 1.12 Mielziner, Jo. Sketch of set design from *Death of a Salesman*, 1948–9. Note the apartment houses surrounding the Loman home. Credit: Estate of Jo Mielziner, Billy Rose Theatre Division, The New York Public Library for the Performing Arts.

especially in the backyards of the homes. In *Timebends* and "A Boy Grew in Brooklyn," Miller recalls riding the Culver Line El train "over a forest of elms" (Miller 1955a: 54). But as zoning regulations changed, the builders of larger apartment houses used most of the land on a plot and removed many trees. These, of course, resulted in Willy's lament about the loss of trees.

The first scene of the play establishes a geographic sweep—ranging from North to New England, South to Florida, and out to the Western United States, but with the action always returning to Brooklyn. Of course, Willy is a traveling salesman, so the far-flung destinations of his "territory" as the vital New England man are referred to frequently in the play: Bangor, Boston, Hartford, Providence. Other geographic references relate to Willy's family history. He frequently laments that he stayed in Brooklyn and did not, like Ben or his father, light out for far-off places such as Alaska, the Gold Coast, Africa, the Yukon, and Ketchikan. Ben tells Willy how their pioneering father traveled with the family out west in a wagon through the western states. However, the geographic focal point of the play's action always returns to New York City, the Manhattan headquarters of the Wagner company and, most importantly,

Figure 1.13 Narrow alley between houses on Miller's block; note the apartment house looming behind, c. 2023. Photo by Katie Murray.

Willy's Brooklyn home. Biff, too, has been to far-flung places, but he returns home to Brooklyn from living out west in Texas, where he works as a farmhand after previous stints in the Dakotas, Arizona, and Nebraska, where he herded cattle. His wandering is a source of years-old conflict between father and son. Even Howard's son reciting the capitals of the states on the tape recorder enforces the geographical sweep of the play (But the seemingly precocious boy names an incorrect capital for Ohio).

Miller also uses geography for important implications about the characters. For example, Willy unexpectedly returns home to Brooklyn in the middle of the night "tired to the death" (Miller 1949: 13) and explains to Linda that "I got as far as a little above Yonkers" (Miller 1949: 13) and insists that it took nearly four hours to get home. Yonkers is the city directly north of the New York City borough of the Bronx and is approximately 30 miles from the presumed location of the Loman home in Brooklyn. So for Willy to judge that he drove a little above Yonkers would place him further north in Westchester County, perhaps in the towns of Dobbs Ferry, Hastings on the Hudson, or Tarrytown, about forty miles from his Brooklyn home, making the four-hour trip at ten miles an hour. But taking four hours to get to Brooklyn from Yonkers seems quite a long time, even considering the road conditions and highways of that era. Moreover, the action implies that Willy left the previous day, after Biff arrived home in Brooklyn. Miller's use of geography shows from the very start of the play that Willy's perceptions are inaccurate, which indicates the depth of his emotional conflict and dislocation. Linda says that his mind is not rested even though he just returned from Florida, the first mention in the play of a far-flung geographic location from New York. Later in act 1, his cry to his sons: "I couldn't get past Yonkers today! Where are you guys? The woods are burning! I can't drive a car!" (Miller 1949: 41) shows how his fragile emotions dictate his geographic limits.

Linda emphasizes the importance of Willy asking Howard to work in New York, but Willy resists that suggestion, claiming he is the New England man and he wants to send a wire to the Brown and Morrison company in Portland (presumably Maine) because he is supposed to show the line of merchandise the next day. But Linda insists that he must work in New York, and Willy proclaims that he would have been "in charge" of New York (Miller 1949: 14) if old man Wagner, the founder of the firm, were still alive. This too indicates Willy's dislocation from the reality of time and space. If Willy were supposed to be in Portland, Maine, the next morning, he would have driven 350 miles from Brooklyn the previous day, quite a trip with the road conditions and highway network (or lack of interstate system as today) that existed in the late 1940s. Linda's remark to Biff and Hap that Willy drives 700 miles seems geographically inaccurate, but she is probably referring to the round-trip total mileage.

Many of the locations that the play mentions that are not in Manhattan or Brooklyn represent places that are not only pastoral, but also offer economic opportunity from what Biff describes as "this nuthouse of a city" (Miller

1949: 61) Of course, the far-flung places that Ben mentions represent the achievement of economic success: Africa, the Gold Coast, and Alaska are all places where Ben has struck it rich—in contrast to Willy who stayed in Brooklyn. Florida is mentioned a number of times in the play, twice where Hap sent Willy for a rest. However, Hap also sees it as a place where he and Biff can achieve financial success. Hap tries to convince Biff to join him in a cockamamie scheme to form basketball teams to sell a Loman line of sporting goods in all the Florida hotels. This is part of the unrealistic dreams that are in the fabric of the Loman men.

Death of a Salesman, as well as *A View from the Bridge* and *Broken Glass*, shows the importance of Manhattan as the center of culture and business success as compared to Brooklyn. Its importance as a financial capital is perhaps best expressed in Willy's line to Ben that the "whole wealth of Alaska passes over the lunch table at the Commodore Hotel" (Miller 1949: 86), one of the more important New York hotels of the early twentieth century. (Located next to Grand Central Station, the hotel featured an ornate lobby, one of the largest ballrooms in the country, and was a gathering place for political, social, and business figures (Figure 1.14). In 1978, real estate magnate Donald Trump transformed the hotel into the Grand Hyatt New York, complete with a glass facade, and that hotel is planned to be replaced with a luxury tower called 175 Park Avenue ("Hotel Commodore: Past, Present, and Future" 2021: n.p.)). Of course, Willy wants a New York job, not only because he is tired of being "a road man," but he mistakenly believes that he can be successful by earning a decent salary to "set my table" at the company's headquarters. An amusing example of a New Yorker's superior attitude is evident in the act 2 restaurant scene in Frank's Chop House, located in the heart of Midtown Manhattan on Sixth Avenue and 48th Street in the Theatre District, which, of course, Miller knew quite well having lived with Sid Franks and his father on that block. When the waiter Stanley sets up the table for Hap in a back room, he says, "Y'know, there's a lotta people they don't like it private, because when they go out they like to see lotta action around them because they're sick and tired to stay in the house by theirself. But I know you, you ain't from Hackensack" (Miller 1949: 99). Stanley is conveying the attitude that he knows that Hap is not some country rube; a place like Hackensack, which is just across the Hudson River in New Jersey, was considered unsophisticated, similar to the way that today many Manhattanites look at the "outer" boroughs.

Figure 1.14 Both Grand Central Station and the adjacent Commodore Hotel have storied histories in New York City, c. 1967. Courtesy of the New York City Landmarks Preservation Commission.

Miller consistently uses the vivid idiomatic language that is the hallmark of New Yorkers and often needs some explaining to non-New Yorkers because there are rather subtle distinctions and implications in the dialect. The vernacular that characters speak to refer to New York places shows just how much Miller recreated regular life in the city that most New Yorkers/Brooklynites would recognize today. For example, when Hap tells Biff that he "drove into the city" with Willy, every New Yorker knows that "the city" means Manhattan, as opposed to the outer boroughs. But when Biff refers to this "nuthouse of a city" and declares, "I hate this city" ((Miller 1949: 58), he means all of New York, not just Manhattan. He would have used the definite article "the," that is, "the city" if he only meant Manhattan. He includes Brooklyn in his disdain because he hates returning to the Loman home in Brooklyn, which is the center of his unresolved conflict with Willy. Ironically, despite his love for the pastoral life out west, Biff still intuits that economic success is possible only in New York. He comes home because it is where, "I oughta be makin' my future" (Miller 1949: 22).

A number of times in the play, characters refer to "the train" or "the subway." For example, Linda chastises Willy about arguing with Biff "after he just got off the train" (Miller 1949: 15). Biff complains about the "measly manner of existence" (Miller 1949: 22) working in New York: "To get on that subway on the hot mornings in summer" (Miller 1949: 22). In act 2, Charley tells Bernard that he is "going to miss that train" (Miller 1949: 95). For New Yorkers, taking the train usually means traveling on one of the routes of New York's extensive subway system, usually heading toward Manhattan a.k.a. "the city" to which almost every line heads.[5] All of the system's trains do not run underground, for there are many elevated lines, mostly in the outer boroughs, although before the underground subway system, Manhattan had "elevated" train lines on the North/South street grid, such as the Third Avenue El and Sixth Avenue El. Although some New Yorkers may have said that they were "taking the el," in reality, most New Yorkers still say that they are taking the train or subway, even if they are taking an elevated line. In fact, this is exactly what Biff means in the play when he expresses his disgust at getting on the subway in the hot summer. Miller's home on East 3rd Street is a two-block walk from an elevated subway—still named the Culver Line today—that Miller describes taking in *Timebends*. This explains Linda's warning to Willy to: "Be careful on the subway stairs" (Miller 1949: 75). Today the "F" train runs on that line with its southern terminus at Coney Island only two miles or so from Miller's home.[6]

However, "the train" also refers to other instances of rail travel. New Yorkers also know that when Charley tells Bernard that he is "going to miss that train," he is not referring to subway travel, but rather travel out of New York City. Bernard is heading to argue a case in front of the Supreme Court, and he had to catch his train from New York's Pennsylvania Station (Today Penn Station) to Washington, DC. At the time of the play, the station was the magnificent building on Eighth Avenue between 31st and 32nd Streets that was demolished in 1963 to make way for Madison Square Garden, although the station still operates below ground but has expanded to the famous Post Office across Eighth Avenue (This was the same train that Miller famously took when he went to Washington, DC for his HUAC appearance in 1956.). Linda may very well be referring to this train station when she says to Willy that he should not have criticized Biff when he just got off the train. Biff has arrived in New York from Texas, so his train trip would have ended at Penn Station. The language implies that he may have been picked up at Penn Station—by either Willy or

Hap (Willy left for his road trip the previous day when Biff arrived and when they argued)—both of whom had cars. Perhaps the argument occurred in the car when Biff was picked up at the station. Similarly, when Ben says "I'll be late for my train" (Miller 1949: 52), he presumably means Penn Station if he is going to Ketchikan, Alaska. In addition, in the restaurant scene in act 2 Willy hears voices of the past echoing Biff's departure for Boston to find Willy. Bernard relates that Biff went to "Grand Central" (Miller 1949: 110). This, of course, is New York's famous Grand Central Station, which is the New York terminus of commuter trains and trains from the North. Biff would have taken the "New York, New Haven, and Hartford, going into Boston" (Miller 1949: 81), the same line to which Willy refers in the Dave Singleman speech.

Miller's obvious extensive familiarity with the subway system also is evident in other plays, such as in the later discussions of *A View from the Bridge*, *A Memory of Two Mondays*, his novel, *Focus*, and short stories such as "Bulldog."

Another example of particularly unique New York colloquial reference is when Willy demands that Bernard give Biff the answers on an exam. Bernard says: "I do, but I can't on a Regents. That's a state exam. They're liable to arrest me" (Miller 1949: 40). The importance of end-of-the-academic year New York State Regents Examinations is ingrained in every high school student in New York. The Regents exams have undergone tremendous changes in the past twenty-five years, so much so that in our times, passing Regents exams to show competency is required for graduation (although new changes eliminate the requirement in 2027). However, up until 2001, Regents exams were not required, but rather were considered upper-level final exams of a course designed for advanced students. Passing the exams and earning a Regents diploma had considerable cachet. Students were, and are, required to sign a "Declaration of Honesty" at the exam's conclusion to affirm that they had not cheated. A sort of urban legend was transmitted to students by New York teachers that cheating on a Regents exam had many consequences including never being able to get a civil service or state job—or even being arrested. This explains, of course, the strait-laced Bernard's fear. Bernard's answer, "I do," (Miller 1949: 40) to Willy's demand that he give Biff the answers does indicate he has cheated on other exams, but to him the Regents is an entirely different situation. Moreover, the fact that Biff is in a Regents course may indicate his high level of intelligence or capability, meaning that his academic failure is due to laziness. Also, was the University of Virginia admitting unprepared students—including student athletes—on the scholarship practices in 1932, the presumed time that Biff was a senior in high school?

Willy is a traveling salesman, and the play strongly suggests that the merchandise he sells is connected to New York's garment industry, where the Wagner firm is located, because Willy had to take the subway there. As Hap says to Biff, Willy "has the finest eye for color in the business" (Miller 1949: 20)—although exactly what he peddles is never identified—even though many have made the argument that it is stockings because he gives "The Woman" a box of "size nine sheers" in the imagining of the hotel scene in Boston. Stockings were widely available in colors and shades in the 1940s.

As a traveling salesman for the Wagner firm, Willy refers to many department stores in the play; most are outside of New York, with some notable exceptions. Some store names are real; some are fictional composites: F. H. Stewarts is in Baltimore, Filene's and Slattery in Boston, Brown and Morrison is located in Portland, but there is a branch in North Carolina, a state where Miller did some research in 1941 (Bigsby 188–194). In the hotel scene in act 2, Willy explains to Biff that The Woman is a buyer for J. H. Simmons. Hap criticizes Biff for whistling in the elevator when he was working for Harrison's, but it is unclear what kind of business this is. The play does not specifically mention New York stores, except for Stewarts. A. T. Stewarts was located in a famous landmarked building at 280 Broadway and is significant for housing America's first department store (Figure 1.15) ("Off the Grid"). Also, when Willy tells the boys to go to The Hub, he may be referring to a shopping area in the Bronx, where many department stores were located.

The play strongly implies that Hap works in a department store. He says about one of the buyers: "When he comes into the store, the waves part in front of him. That's fifty-two thousand dollars a year coming through the revolving door." (Miller 1949: 24) However, the store is not identified. Hap says the merchandise manager builds an estate on Long Island (23), nor is it clear what particular kind of merchandise. Because Hap and Stanley the waiter obviously know each other, Hap may very well work in a department store on Herald Square, such as Macy's, Gimbels, or on New York's Fifth Avenue, where famous department stores lined the Avenue from 59th Street to 34th Street. These were easily accessible for Hap, just a short subway ride or walk to Frank's Chop House.

Figure 1.15 The AT Stewart Store, considered America's first department store, was located in what is known as the Sun Building, often called the "Marble Palace," c. 1978. Courtesy of the New York City Landmarks Preservation Commission.

As a traveling salesman, Willy obviously stayed in many, many hotels, but only two are mentioned: the Parker House and The Standish Arms, sites of significant action in the play. The famous Parker House in Boston is where Willy tells Howard that he met the legendary salesman Dave Singleman, who inspired him to remain devoted to the profession. From that speech comes the title of the play. The Standish Arms is important in the play for its location as the penultimate scene in act 2 when Biff discovers Willy's infidelity with The Woman. Interestingly enough, the Standish Arms is not a Boston hotel; it is actually in Brooklyn at 171 Columbia Heights, one block from Miller's Willow Street home. The building has a significant history as a hotel in Brooklyn Heights, as housing for the Jehovah's Witnesses, and as recently converted high-end apartments. The actor Matt Damon bought a 6,000-square-foot luxury penthouse in the building for an eye-popping $ 16.745 million. The sale of this penthouse to Damon was the most expensive real estate sale in that area at that date. In the same building reside actor John Krasinski with his wife, the actress Emily Blunt. Miller's fictional use of the building was not the first. Comic book fans recognize the Standish Arms as the home of Clark Kent in Metropolis (Figure 1.16) (Laterman 2016: 2; Streeteasy 2023: n.p.).

Figure 1.16 The Standish Arms, the "Boston" Hotel where Biff discovers Willy with The Woman, is actually located in Brooklyn Heights, c. 1940. Courtesy Municipal Archives City of New York.

Death of a Salesman mentions other specific locations in Manhattan and Brooklyn; some are real, others are likely fictional, but all are stimulated by actual experiences that Miller had. Perhaps one of the most famous Brooklyn locations mentioned in the play is Ebbets Field, the legendary baseball park that was the home of the Brooklyn Dodgers, located in Flatbush in the heart of the borough. Most residents of Brooklyn were proud, even rabid, fans of their team. Their only World Series championship occurred in 1955, defeating the rival New York Yankees. It was the apex of professional sports in Brooklyn. Three years later, the team owner, Walter O'Malley, moved the team to Los Angeles, crushing the spirit of the borough's citizens. In 1962, New York was granted a National League franchise to replace the departed Dodgers and the New York Giants, who also had abandoned the city and relocated to San Francisco. The New York Mets built their ball field, named Shea Stadium, not in Brooklyn, but in Flushing Meadows Park in Queens. However, in a nod to the team's National League roots, when the franchise built a new stadium, Citi Field, in 2008, the ballpark was purposely built to resemble the facade of the demolished Ebbets Field (Figure 1.17).

As a boy, Miller was an avid sportsman, but he clearly preferred football; he played on the second team squad of the Abraham Lincoln High School team. In *Salesman*, Miller uses Ebbets Field as the location of Biff's championship football game. In its history, Ebbets Field actually was the site for many college, high school, and amateur football games at the end of the fall season which explains Charley's mocking line: "Baseball in this weather?" (Miller 1949: 89)—although

Figure 1.17 Ebbets Field, home of the Brooklyn Dodgers, c. 1950. Photo Researchers/Alamy Stock Photo.

high school and college baseball games were played there as well. Miller based Biff's football game—that Willy calls the "All Scholastic Championship Team of the City of New York"—on this. One of the first recorded games at Ebbets Field was a High School All-Star Game between the NYC Scholastic 1st team and the NYC Scholastic 2nd team on December 5, 1914 ("Football Games at Ebbets Field"). Ebbets Field also hosted soccer games. In an interesting coincidence, Marilyn Monroe appeared at Ebbets Field at a charity soccer event on May 12, 1957, during her marriage to Miller, and there was extensive newspaper coverage of the match between the Hapoel Tel Aviv Israeli club and a team of American All-Stars (Figure 1.18) ("When Marilyn 'Kicked Off' at Ebbets Field" 2021; Sokolovskyi 2025: n.p.). According to renowned scientist Ben Zinn, who was a star soccer player on the team, Miller attended the match ("Ben Zinn Remembers Marilyn at Ebbets Field" 2022).

Willy meets Biff and Hap at Frank's Chop House 48th near Sixth Avenue, and the establishment appears fictional. Miller knew the neighborhood well, not only because it is in the theatre district, but he located the restaurant one block from the apartment of his boyhood friend Sid Franks and his father, who lived on 47th Street and Sixth Avenue, the address that Miller used to falsify his claim for eligibility for the Federal Theatre Project. When Willy revives from his imagining in the Boston Hotel, in real time, he is actually in the bathroom at Frank's Chop House after Biff and Hap abandoned him to party with women. He asks Stanley about buying some seeds to plant, and Stanley tells him there are some hardware stores on Sixth Avenue, present-day Avenue of the Americas. Miller gets this exactly correct, as the photo shows (Figure 1.19).

In act 1, Hap recalls that he had his first sexual experience with a "Big Betsy something on Bushwick Avenue" (Miller 1949: 89). The Brooklyn neighborhood for which the avenue is named is quite far from the Midwood and Flatbush areas; Bushwick Avenue extends from the border of East New York to Williamsburg/Greenpoint. Miller may have known this northern Brooklyn area because many cemeteries are close by and extend into the Queens neighborhoods of Ridgewood and Glendale. In Miller's novel, *Focus*, Finklestein travels to a Brooklyn cemetery, taking a trolley along Bushwick Avenue. Miller's family burial plot is located at the Union Field Cemetery in Ridgewood, so his familiarity with traveling through the Bushwick neighborhood is likely and explains why he used it in *Salesman* and *Focus*.

Figure 1.18 Marilyn Monroe kicking a soccer ball at Ebbets Field, c. 1957. ARCHIVIO GBB/Alamy Stock Photo.

Even though Miller based the characters on Jewish salesmen he had known in the garment industry, used Jewish colloquialisms in the language, and set the play in Brooklyn, *Death of a Salesman* is not an obvious ethnic play, set in a specific neighborhood dominated by one ethnic group. In fact, Miller subsumes the identity of the Lomans. In early productions, they were played as mainstream Americans without an easily identifiable ethnicity or religion; for example, the neighborhood is not identified as such. Charley and Bernard's ethnicity is undetermined. The names of the boys in the cellar—George, Sam, Frank—are American names. Angelo, the mechanic, is perhaps the only

Figure 1.19 Hardware store on Sixth Avenue, c. 1940. Courtesy Municipal Archives City of New York.

identifiably ethnic one. Many of the actors cast in early productions, such as Lee J. Cobb, Mildred Dunnock, Frederic March, and George C. Scott, were purposely "Middle American." With the play's focus on the American Dream as a major theme, Miller perhaps wanted to universalize the play. Interestingly, in the 1975 New York revival, George C. Scott persuaded Miller, after much coaxing, to cast Charley and Bernard with Black actors. In the 1984 Broadway production, Dustin Hoffman tilted the characterization toward an ethnic portrayal. In fact, Miller observed that Hoffman was more like his original conception of Willy based on his Uncle Manny. Early criticism of the play did not assign a defined ethnicity to the Lomans, even though, interestingly enough, a Yiddish version of the play was performed in Brooklyn in 1950 and revived off-Broadway during the Miller centennial year in 2015.

In contrast, *A View from the Bridge* and *Broken Glass* proclaim their ethnic identities, and the Brooklyn neighborhoods in which they are set are ethnic enclaves and are vital in understanding the conflicts and the characters. The Carbones and the Gellburgs speak the language of their groups. Miller, who retained his strong Brooklyn accent his entire life, once said that he could not write dialogue unless he heard it. He told John Lahr in 1999 that when he wrote *Salesman*, "I was the stenographer. I could hear the characters. I could hear them literally. I've always said since then that playwriting is an aural art. You write it, but you are really hearing it" (Miller 1999: 10). He soundly re-created the language that he heard on the streets, in the stores, and in the homes in Brooklyn.

A View from the Bridge

The previous discussion of *Salesman* explains how, despite the geographic sweep to other places, the focal point of Willy's existence always returns to Brooklyn. In *A View from the Bridge*, Miller used a similar technique. Sicily is the far-flung place that is consistently evoked in Alfieri's monologues and Marco and Rodolpho's narratives about the post-Second World War conditions in Europe and their lives in the old world. However, Brooklyn's Red Hook neighborhood is the powerful center of the physical world for the Carbones and their fellow Sicilian-Americans who rarely stray from their community. In fact, the entire play (except for the jail detention scene) is set in the neighborhood—in scenes in the Carbone apartment, the lawyer Alfieri's office, and nearby streets. As explained in the introduction, this was quite typical of ethnic neighborhoods in New York where many people could live the bulk of their lives rarely leaving the boundaries of their communities—having most of their needs satisfied in shops, markets, schools, churches, synagogues, and temples. Certain women, such as housewives, were largely kept at home and never worked, and the assumption was that they knew little about the outside world. Eddie says to Beatrice: "You lived in a house all your life, what do you know about it? You never worked in your life." (Miller 1977: 15).

In *A View from the Bridge*, the insularity of Red Hook is so strong that straying out of the neighborhood often represents danger. The play indicates that Red Hook is not the safest neighborhood: Beatrice says, "Listen, if nothing happened to her in this neighborhood, it ain't gonna happen no place else" (Miller 1977: 13) Nevertheless, Eddie aims to keep Catherine within the confines of the community. For example, Eddie does not want her to take a secretarial job in a neighborhood near the Brooklyn Navy Yard: "I don't like that neighborhood over there" (Miller 1977: 12). His protective instinct is reinforced by his anger when Catherine and Rodolpho are late coming home from the movies. When Eddie asks if she went to the Paramount, Catherine explains that they went to the Brooklyn Paramount. At the time of the play, there were two Paramount Theaters in New York City: the Brooklyn Paramount, in Downtown Brooklyn on Dekalb and Flatbush Avenues, and the more famous New York Paramount located on Broadway and 43rd Street in Times Square, which held many famous concerts throughout its history. Of course, if Rodolpho and Catherine had gone to the New York Paramount, this would indicate considerable straying and danger to Eddie. The Brooklyn Paramount is geographically closer to Red Hook, accessible by public transportation, trolley, or even walking, whereas the New York Paramount required a long subway ride to Manhattan. To Rodolpho, the city is a magical place and he is especially enthralled by the bright lights of Broadway that he desperately wants to experience. However, Times Square represents danger to Eddie: "It's full of tramps there." (Miller 1977: 35), particularly sexual danger for Catherine. However, as in *Salesman*, Manhattan—the city—to Eddie also represents a better economic possibility for Catherine: as he says, "I want you to be in a nice office. Maybe a lawyer's office someplace in New York in one of them nice buildings" (Figure 1.20) (Miller 1977: 13).

Figure 1.20 New York once had a major trolley car system. Here is a trolley on the McDonald Avenue line under the El in Brooklyn, c. 1950. Photo by Max Hubacher © Milstein Division, The New York Public Library.

The lawyer Alfieri's opening monologue accurately describes the geography of the Red Hook neighborhood, its boundaries and streets, its culture, and historical events that characterize it. Alfieri draws us to the focal point of the action in Brooklyn, saying, "But this is Red Hook, not Sicily. The is the slum that faces the seaward side of Brooklyn Bridge" (Miller 1977: 4). Alfieri's office clearly is located in the neighborhood because he describes how "the flat air in my office suddenly washed in with the green scent of the sea" (Miller 1977: 5). He gives further insight into its location when he refers to specific historical events related to Mafia rubouts that occurred in Red Hook near his office. He says, "Al Capone was learning his trade on these pavements, and Frankie Yale himself was cut precisely in half by a machine gun on the corner of Union Street, two blocks away" (Miller 1977: 4). He also accurately describes the location of the entire stretch of docks that existed at the time of the play when he describes Eddie as "a longshoreman working the docks from the Brooklyn Bridge to the breakwater where the open sea begins" (Miller 1977: 5). The 1950s was the Golden Age of the New York Harbor and the piers stretched from the Brooklyn Bridge in Brooklyn Heights, down to Red Hook all along to the Brooklyn shoreline toward Bay Ridge to the Narrows between Brooklyn and Staten Island where the Verrazzano Bridge is now located.

Because of his research and knowledge of the intimate lives of the longshoremen and their families, Miller's familiarity with the neighborhood was extensive, which is quite evident in the play. Columbia Street is the major road which runs parallel to the lower East River west of the neighborhood and also extends into Brooklyn Heights before the Brooklyn-Queens Expressway and its famous cantilevered structure was built. Many longshoremen's homes were only a few blocks from the docks where they plied their trade. So when Beatrice says she could smell coffee all day, it was literally because a ship loaded with coffee had docked near their home. On their first night in America, Rodolpho and Marco actually walk from their docked ship to the Carbone home. After Rodolpho and Catherine return from the movies, he tells her that he is going to walk along the river before he goes to sleep. Miller even transmits his knowledge of similar dock areas in the New York metro area when Eddie recalls looking for work beyond Brooklyn: "When there was empty piers in Brooklyn, I went to Hoboken, Staten Island, the West Side, Jersey, all over" (Miller 1977: 46).

The most striking aspect of *A View from the Bridge* is the accuracy with which Miller blends historical figures and events, places, and streets into the narrative and dialogue. In its history as an Italian neighborhood, Red Hook had strong ties to the gangland world of the Mafia who dominated not only the docks and piers but also were involved in bootlegging, prostitution, illegal gambling, loan sharking, and forced protection payments. Alfieri accurately proclaims that Al Capone learned his trade on its pavements. Capone was one of the most famous gangsters in American history. Although "Scarface" is mostly associated with Chicago, he began his infamous career on the streets of Brooklyn and was allegedly involved in some of the most notorious crimes of the 1920s. In fact, Capone at one time worked for the famous gangster Frankie Yale in his Harvard Inn bar in Coney Island:

> He also was content to meet people that attended his bar, one of these was to be another great connection for Yale, Al Capone, whom Yale had employed to work at the bar as a bouncer. Capone earned the infamous nickname "Scarface" whilst working at Harvard Inn. He had gotten into an altercation

with a patron of the bar, after Capone had insulted his sister and as a result the Patron sliced him across the face. Capone eventually left the bar to join up with Yale's other mentor Torrio back in Chicago.

(Who was Frankie Yale..." 2014)

The evocation of Capone and Frankie Yale is important because of the underworld corruption and illegal activities that thread through much of the action of the play. In previous work on the play, I have noted that Miller accurately depicts how the law operates on many different levels in the Red Hook community: "In his role as a lawyer, Alfieri represents American civil law, but he is crucial in showing how civil law and its justice conflicts with the morals and tribal laws that operate in the Sicilian-American society" (Marino 2010: lix).

Frankie Yale's importance must be explained because little is known about him today. In his time, he was one of the more notorious gangsters in New York, especially in his home turf in Brooklyn. His rubout on a street in South Brooklyn on July 1, 1928, was particularly dramatic and marked a turning point in the wars among New York's Mafia families that continue up to our own time. For example, his shooting marked the first time that machine guns were used to kill a mobster. His funeral was lavish, and there was extensive New York media coverage. He is buried in Holy Cross Cemetery in Flatbush. (Bell 2017)

In the play, Alfieri gives the location of Frankie Yale's shooting as occurring on the corner of Union Street in Red Hook. His execution actually occurred on 44th Street, at that time called the Homewood section of Brooklyn. However, there was a shooting a few weeks later off Union Street in Red Hook when "a car was on its way to spew a rain of bullets at some unsuspecting Puerto Rican youth on the corner of Sackett Street at the end of Van Brunt" ("Site of 1928" 2013: n.p.). The shooting apparently was a case of mistaken identity of retaliatory killings for the murder of Frankie Yale. Miller may have confused this shooting with Yale's or purposely used this shooting in order to place Yale's murder in Red Hook to emphasize the mob violence in the neighborhood. Coincidentally, Pete Panto lived on Sackett Street before his disappearance in 1939.

In *A View from the Bridge,* Miller also gives vivid insights into how life for longshoremen was intimately tied to the hiring practices of the mob who dominated the piers. Marco and Rodolpho, referred to as "submarines," are indebted to the mob for "sponsoring" their illegal immigration.

Beatrice: "I just hope they get work here, that's all I hope.
Eddie: Oh, the syndicate'll fix jobs for them; till they pay 'em off they'll get work every day. It's after the pay-off, then they'll have to scramble like the rest of us."

(Miller 1977: 18–19)

Forest Hylton explains the hiring practices that Eddie describes:

> If you were a southern Italian man between the ages of 20 and 60, like two thirds of the men who worked on the Brooklyn waterfront in 1912—and half of those who worked on the entire New York waterfront in 1914—and if you lived in Red Hook, you probably woke up and walked to the corner of Columbia between Union and Carroll to "shape up" at 7:55 AM. In a "ritual enactment of the local social order" grounded in patterns of authority, hierarchy, and deference, you stood in a semi-circle with hundreds of others, ten to fifteen deep, to see who would be called for work and who would need to wait until the next shape-up at 12:55 PM, unless you were one of those fortunate enough to belong to a regular gang, which accounted for less than half of the city's 40,000–60,000 longshoremen between 1914 and 1938, and were concentrated mainly on the piers of the foreign lines on the North River, far from Brooklyn. (Hylton 2014; see Figure 1.21)

In "The Tragic Violent History of the Mob," Nathan Ward further explains that

> The five-mile stretch of Brooklyn shore that ran from Brooklyn Bridge to Twentieth Street was overwhelmingly staffed by lower-paid Italians who worked the less desirable cargoes and piers. Some four thousand dockers labored in "Camarda locals" like Panto's. Mob-held piers resembled company towns. On the Camardas' waterfront, wrote Brooklyn Assistant District Attorney Burton Turkus, everyone "from candy store proprietor to ship line operator" had "to pay tribute to the Mob." (Ward 2019)

These are exactly the conditions that Pete Panto was fighting against.

A View from the Bridge is filled with exact references to streets and geographic locations in Red Hook and the neighboring environs that show Miller's remarkable application of what he researched. For example, Eddie tells Beatrice that her cousins have arrived and their ship is in the "North River" (Miller 1977: 8), which generally refers to the Hudson River, but can

Figure 1.21 Union organizer speaks to longshoremen on Brooklyn docks, c. 1939. RBM Vintage Images/Alamy Stock Photo.

refer to various lengths of that river from the southern tip of Manhattan at the Battery to way North. It has particular meaning to the shipping industry of New York and New Jersey as the portion of the river from the western shore of Manhattan to the eastern shore of New Jersey where many of the docks were located, which is exactly how Eddie uses it. (In fact, the North River is a crucial scene in Miller's story 'Fitter' Night"; see Chapter 4.)

The Brooklyn docks and piers play a vital role in the action. Miller accurately places the names of "lines"—that is, shipping companies that were assigned to the Brooklyn piers—in their exact locations. For example, Mike observes that he saw Marco lifting coffee bags like a "regular bull" over by the "Matson Line" (33), which was located on Pier 11. Mike also refers to Marco and Rodolpho working on the Moore-MacCormack line (34) (Figure 1.22), which at the time was off Pier 3 at Montague Street. This dock also figured prominently in a union rally held by Pete Panto in 1939. In his opening monologue in act 2, Alfieri refers to (57) a case of Scotch whiskey falling off a boat at Pier 41 (Figure 1.23). This pier is located at 175 Van Dyke Street. Coincidentally, Pier 41 is located next to the Waterfront Barge Museum that in 2018 was the site of

Figure 1.22 Moore-MacCormack line Pier 3, c. 1940. Courtesy Municipal Archives City of New York.

performances of *A View from the Bridge* and in 2019 the United States premiere of *The Hook* which was never produced as a film (Figure 1.24). The Brave New World Repertory Theatre offered a site-specific production on a restored barge docked in New York's harbor off the shore of Red Hook.[7] Traveling to the barge takes you through the same streets where Miller did his research and that are mentioned in *A View from the Bridge*. The barge's location in New York Harbor connects much to the geography of the play. From the barge's loading dock, you can see the Narrows between Brooklyn and Staten Island that is

Figure 1.23 Contemporary photo of the former Pier 41. Note the World Trade Center Tower in the background, c. 2023. Photo by Katie Murray

the entrance to the harbor, where millions of immigrants sailed toward Ellis Island passing the Statue of Liberty, which stands directly opposite Red Hook. One can imagine the two "submarines"—Marco and Rodolpho—hiding in the hull of their ship and being dropped off at the piers just a few blocks away and walking to Beatrice and Eddie's ground floor apartment.

Miller uses the geography of Brooklyn streets and neighborhoods as part of the action of the play and to make significant implications about the characters, as he did for Willy in *Salesman*. The previous discussion of *Salesman* details the language that New Yorkers use to refer to the train and/or subway. In many of his other works, Miller also reveals an exactness about how his characters use the subway system. For example, in *A View from the Bridge*, Beatrice and Catherine tell Eddie that the big plumbing company which has offered her a job is located over on Nostrand Avenue near the Brooklyn Navy Yard. As detailed earlier, Eddie is reluctant for her to travel to what he perceives is a dangerous neighborhood. However, Beatrice and Catherine try to assuage his doubts by telling him that the office is located only a "block and half from the subway. She'll get out the subway and be in the office in two minutes" (Miller 1977: 13).

Figure 1.24 Waterfront Barge in Red Hook, c. 2018. Photo by S. Marino

It is interesting to scrutinize the validity of their assertion based on geography and the New York transit system as it existed at that time. From the Carbone home at 441 Saxon Street in Red Hook (a bit on this below) to get to the Brooklyn Navy Yard, Catherine presumably would walk to the nearest subway station to either the Carroll Street or Bergen Street stations on the "R" train, to 9th Street, transfer to the "GG" (now the "G") northbound, and get off at Flushing Avenue, which is exactly one block from Nostrand Avenue, and a few blocks from the Navy Yard, which reveals that Bea and Catherine are telling Eddie the truth. Of course, they would dare not lie to Eddie, as a powerful male figure in the play. Miller likely would have known an exact plumbing company in the area because he worked in the Brooklyn Navy Yard for two years at the beginning of the Second World War. He doubtless knew the four subway stops around the yard and may have walked past an actual plumbing firm in the neighborhood on his way to work.

The names of famous locations and streets give a sense of how significant these places in Brooklyn are to the residents of Red Hook. For example, Mike says to Eddie, "If you wanna come bowlin' later, we're goin' Flatbush Avenue"

(Miller 1977: 34). At the time of the play, Flatbush Avenue was, and still is, one of the most important thoroughfares in Brooklyn. Starting from the Atlantic Ocean and Jamaica Bay in the Rockaways to its terminus at the Manhattan Bridge, the avenue traverses some of Brooklyn's well-known neighborhoods from Marine Park, Flatlands, Flatbush, Prospect Park, into Downtown Brooklyn. In many ways, it was the spine of Brooklyn as shops, stores, movie theaters, entertainment establishments, and of course, bowling alleys lined the avenue (Figure 1.25). From Red Hook, Mike and Louis could have gone to a number of lanes that existed at the time. And of course, Beatrice evokes one of the world's most famous beaches and amusement areas when she asks why Marco and Rodolpho in Italy can't fish from the beach like, "You see them down in Coney Island" (Miller 1977: 48).

Miller's folding of actual Red Hook places and streets into the narrative and dialogue reveals much about how he used his research. In fact, we can pinpoint the exact locations and streets of fictional events, even where characters live. One of the most striking examples occurs in act 1 when Beatrice and Eddie tell Catherine the story of the teenager Vinny Bolzano, who snitched to Immigration. There are substantial differences between the original one-act play and the revised two-act version of this story. In the one-act version, Beatrice explains to Catherine:

> You were a baby then. But there was a kid, Vinny, about sixteen. Lived over on Sackett Street. And he snitched on somebody to the Immigration. He had five brothers, and an old man. And they grabbed him in the kitchen, and they pulled him down three flights, his head was bouncin' like a coconut—we lived in the next house. And they spit on him in the street, his own father and his brothers it was so terrible. (Miller 1955a: 517)

With this speech, Beatrice zones in on the exact blocks in Red Hook where the action of *A View from the Bridge* takes place. Sackett Street is a parallel street to Union Street, which Alfieri mentions in his opening monologue, and intersects Columbia Street, the main road in the waterfront neighborhood. Most importantly, she reveals that not only did the Bolzanos live on Sackett Street, but also apparently she and Eddie lived next door to them when Catherine was a baby. Her language implies that they now live in a different apartment on a different street. It is quite significant that Miller knew that Pete Panto lived on Sackett Street.

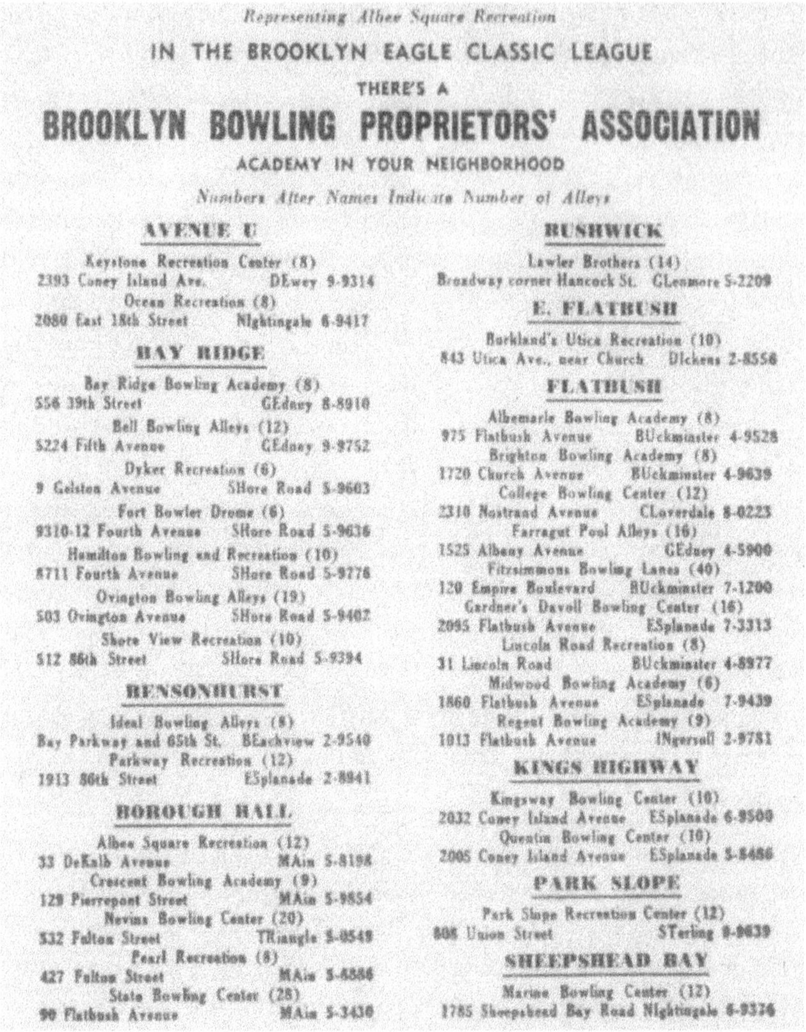

Representing Albee Square Recreation

IN THE BROOKLYN EAGLE CLASSIC LEAGUE

THERE'S A

BROOKLYN BOWLING PROPRIETORS' ASSOCIATION

ACADEMY IN YOUR NEIGHBORHOOD

Numbers After Names Indicate Number of Alleys

AVENUE U

Keystone Recreation Center (8)
2393 Coney Island Ave. DEwey 9-9314
Ocean Recreation (8)
2080 East 18th Street NIghtingale 6-9417

BAY RIDGE

Bay Ridge Bowling Academy (8)
556 39th Street GEdney 8-8910
Bell Bowling Alleys (12)
5224 Fifth Avenue GEdney 9-9752
Dyker Recreation (6)
9 Gelston Avenue SHore Road 5-9603
Fort Bowler Drome (6)
9310-12 Fourth Avenue SHore Road 5-9636
Hamilton Bowling and Recreation (10)
8711 Fourth Avenue SHore Road 5-9776
Ovington Bowling Alleys (19)
503 Ovington Avenue SHore Road 5-9402
Shore View Recreation (10)
512 86th Street SHore Road 5-9394

BENSONHURST

Ideal Bowling Alleys (8)
Bay Parkway and 65th St. BEachview 2-9540
Parkway Recreation (12)
1913 86th Street ESplanade 2-8941

BOROUGH HALL

Albee Square Recreation (12)
33 DeKalb Avenue MAin 5-8198
Crescent Bowling Academy (9)
129 Pierrepont Street MAin 5-9854
Nevins Bowling Center (20)
532 Fulton Street TRiangle 5-0549
Pearl Recreation (8)
427 Fulton Street MAin 5-4886
State Bowling Center (28)
90 Flatbush Avenue MAin 5-3430

BUSHWICK

Lawler Brothers (14)
Broadway corner Hancock St. GLenmore 5-2209

E. FLATBUSH

Burkland's Utica Recreation (10)
843 Utica Ave., near Church DIckens 2-8556

FLATBUSH

Albemarle Bowling Academy (8)
975 Flatbush Avenue BUckminster 4-9528
Brighton Bowling Academy (8)
1720 Church Avenue BUckminster 4-9639
College Bowling Center (12)
2310 Nostrand Avenue CLoverdale 8-0223
Farragut Pool Alleys (16)
1525 Albany Avenue GEdney 4-5900
Fitzsimmons Bowling Lanes (40)
120 Empire Boulevard BUckminster 7-1200
Gardner's Davoll Bowling Center (16)
2095 Flatbush Avenue ESplanade 7-3313
Lincoln Road Recreation (8)
31 Lincoln Road BUckminster 4-8977
Midwood Bowling Academy (6)
1860 Flatbush Avenue ESplanade 7-9439
Regent Bowling Academy (9)
1013 Flatbush Avenue INgersoll 2-9781

KINGS HIGHWAY

Kingsway Bowling Center (10)
2032 Coney Island Avenue ESplanade 6-9500
Quentin Bowling Center (10)
2005 Coney Island Avenue ESplanade 5-8486

PARK SLOPE

Park Slope Recreation Center (12)
808 Union Street STerling 8-9639

SHEEPSHEAD BAY

Marine Bowling Center (12)
1785 Sheepshead Bay Road NIghtingale 6-9376

Figure 1.25 Bowling Association list shows the alleys located on Flatbush Avenue in the 1950s. *Brooklyn Eagle*, April 21, 1950, p. 21.

In the two-act revised version, Miller somewhat alters this:

Eddie: Tell her about Vinny . . . . *To Beatrice*: Go Ahead, tell her. *To Catherine:* You was a baby then. There was a family lived next door to her mother, he was about sixteen.

Beatrice: No, he was no more than fourteen, cause I was to his confirmation in Saint Agnes. But the family had an uncle that they were hidin,' in the house, and he snitched to immigration.

Catherine: The kid snitched?

Eddie: On his own uncle!
Catherine: What, was he crazy? (Miller 1977: 18–19)

Miller made four substantial changes to the original play. The boy snitched on an uncle, whereas in the one-act version, the victim is not named. Perhaps Miller did this to make more evident the horror of informing on a family member, as he does to Marco and Rodolpho. He also deleted the Sackett Street location as the home of the Bolzanos; Beatrice's mother, instead of the Carbones, lives next door on the unnamed street. He also definitively gives Vinny's age as fourteen because Beatrice remembers going to his Confirmation ceremony. She remembers the location of the sacramental ceremony as Saint Agnes, which is an actual Red Hook church located at 433 Sackett Street, a few blocks from the waterfront. Why Miller deleted the exact street is unclear, but it is evident that the residences still are in the same vicinity. The church in which Marco is praying before his assault on Eddie may very well be St. Agnes.

An interesting footnote: Miller is quite clear that his research occurred all along the Columbia Street waterfront, including bars and eateries. One of the most famous saloons frequented by longshoremen at the time is Sunny's Bar at 253 Conover Street, which was there when Miller did his research—and is still operating today. The founders and owners of Sunny's Bar are the Bolzano family. It is intriguing to speculate that he may have named Vinny after the Bolzano family.

Finally, despite the accuracy with which Miller uses locations in the play, there is one significant location that is fictional: Eddie gives as his address 441 Saxon Street when he makes the fatal call to the Immigration Bureau. It seems that Saxon Street is entirely fictitious; no such street exists in Brooklyn—although there is a Saxon Street in Ann Arbor and Saxon Avenue in the Bronx, Staten Island, and Suffolk County. However, it is evident that Miller still intended the Carbone House on the fictional Saxon Street to be located in the same vicinity. The arresting immigration cop says he was born four blocks away from Saxon Street at 111 Union Street which is at the corner and around the block from the fictitious Saxon Street. So Miller clearly intended the play to take place here. Perhaps he wanted to keep Eddie's story in the realm of myth by not giving an exact address.

A film version of *A View from the Bridge*, titled *Vu du pont*, directed by Sidney Lumet, was released in 1962. The film featured a notable cast: Raf Vallone, who had starred in a Paris production, as Eddie; Maureen Stapleton,

Figure 1.26 United States. New York City, 1961. Raf Vallone, Carol Lawrence, and Arthur Miller during the making of *View from the Bridge*. © Inge Morath/ Magnum Photos

the renowned stage and screen actress, as Beatrice; and Carol Lawrence, widely known for her role as Maria in the original Broadway production of *West Side Story*, as Catherine. Miller's friend and University of Michigan classmate, Norman Rosten wrote the screenplay. Interior scenes were filmed in a Paris studio, and exterior scenes were filmed in Red Hook, the same neighborhood where the drama takes place and where Miller conducted his research (Marino 2010: lxv). Miller and Inge Morath visited Brooklyn during the filming of the location shots. Morath's photos of the actors and Miller on the Brooklyn Bridge (Figure 1.26), along with Miller signing autographs for the Red Hook longshoremen, are a vivid coda for this important work (Figure 1.27).

Broken Glass

Much of the action in *Broken Glass* occurs in 1938 in the same Brooklyn neighborhood where Miller grew up, presumably Midwood/Gravesend. As in *A View from the Bridge*, Miller uses the Brooklyn locations in *Broken Glass* with thorough accuracy and emphasizes their importance in the lives of the characters who regularly refer to streets, neighborhoods, department stores, shops, restaurants, and movie theaters.

Figure 1.27 United States. Brooklyn, New York. 1961. Arthur Miller signing autographs for longshoremen during the production of *A View from the Bridge*. © Inge Morath/Magnum Photos

Of note is Ocean Parkway, particularly in its association with the important character Dr. Harry Hyman. Miller's East 3rd Street boyhood home was a few blocks from the wide boulevard known as Ocean Parkway. This famous Brooklyn thoroughfare traverses directly through the borough with its terminus, as the name indicates, at the Atlantic Ocean. In *Broken Glass*, Dr. Harry Hyman rides his horse every afternoon on the bridle paths—now pedestrian walkways that formerly lined this boulevard—riding all the way down to Brighton Beach where Ocean Parkway ends (Figure 1.28). Riding is important for Hyman's character. Critical discussion has pointed out how "horse riding is clearly used as a metaphor in the play" (Marino 2002: 141) especially of Hyman's powerful sexuality. His unorthodox treatment of Sylvia's physical paralysis spills over into the sexual paralysis that exists between her and Philip.[8]

Hyman is a local Brooklyn doctor who practices medicine out of a neighborhood office, which apparently dissatisfies his wife, Margaret. To her, Manhattan has more stature which is quite evident from her remarks. In the very first scene, she explains to Phillip her husband's sterling reputation as a doctor, despite him practicing in Brooklyn, by name-dropping that they "met in Mt. Sinai when he was an intern." Of course, residency at this prestigious

Figure 1.28 Former bridle path on Ocean Parkway, c. 2023. Photo by Katie Murray.

Manhattan hospital gives a physician some real cachet. She reinforces his professional reputation by claiming that "They call him from everywhere Boston, Chicago. By rights he ought to be on Park Avenue if only he had ambition, but he always wanted a neighborhood practice. Why I don't know—we never invite anybody, we never go out, all our friends are in Manhattan" (Miller 1994: 6). Margaret reinforces the prestige, perhaps still existing today, for a doctor to have a mid-Manhattan office, to be a "Park Avenue" doctor, Brooklyn obviously being a backwater compared to Manhattan.

Despite this, Brooklyn remains at the core of the events in *Broken Glass*. Phillip too is associated with very defined Brooklyn locations that are intimately connected to his character. He is the proud head of the Mortgage Department of Brooklyn Guarantee and Trust, which he explains is the largest lender east of the Mississippi River. He proclaims that he is the only Jew in its employ, a crucial fact because *Broken Glass* focuses on Sylvia and Phillip's identification as Jews. It seems that Miller named this company for buildings located in what Brooklynites call "Downtown Brooklyn,"[9] actually the Brooklyn Civic Center, adjacent to Brooklyn Heights, where Miller lived from 1940 to 1956. Miller seems to have based the name of Phillip's company on the Brooklyn Trust Company whose former headquarters is a historic bank building located at the

The Brooklyn Plays 93

Figure 1.29 Landmarked buildings that housed the National Title Guarantee Building and the Brooklyn Trust Company, c. 2023. Photo by Katie Murray.

corner of 177 Montague and Clinton Streets, one block from Miller's former address on Pierrepont Street (Figure 1.29) (see Chapter 1). Miller also seems to have based the Title Guarantee Company that is mentioned in the play on The National Title Guarantee Building at 185 Montague Street, where the building is still located in Brooklyn Heights.

Phillip's role as a mortgage lender takes him to many locations throughout the New York metropolitan area that create a geographic sweep to the play similar to *Death of a Salesman*. Phillip says he "got caught in traffic in Crown

Heights" (Miller 1994: 54), a neighborhood in mid-Brooklyn. He travels to New Jersey for a zoning meeting or checks out property across from the A&S department store on Fulton Street. His boss Stanton Case speaks of sailing his boat "out through the Narrows," (Miller 1994: 57) which is the strait between Brooklyn and Staten Island that the Verrazzano Bridge now spans.

Many notable places to Brooklynites—department stores, shops, restaurants—named in the play are located in Downtown Brooklyn including: Greenberg's on Flatbush Avenue; the A&S department store on Fulton Street where Philip and Sylvia bought their bed; Schraffts, the famous restaurant on Fulton Street where Sylvia and Philip went for a soda during their courtship (Figure 1.30).[10] The characters also evoke other places that are part of the routine of life in Brooklyn in 1938. Hyman says he found Sylvia to be an unusually well-informed woman, especially for their neighborhood. In fact, Sylvia tells Hyman that she is reading the novel *Anthony Adverse*, which she explains: "I rent it from Womrath's" (Miller 1994: 65) as did Miller's mother, Augusta, a biographical fact that he incorporated into the play. The importance of Womrath's in the reading habits of mid-twentieth century New Yorkers cannot be understated as the most widespread chain in New York that targeted a broad demographic,[11] especially middle-aged women as Sylvia.

In 1938, movie going was a regular pastime and Brooklyn neighborhoods were filled with theaters. Two theaters are mentioned in the play when Philip and Sylvia consider going to a show. Sylvia says, "At the Beverly they got Ginger Rogers and Fred Astaire" (Miller 1994: 30). The Beverly Theatre was located at 111 Church Avenue in Flatbush, not far from the neighborhood where *Broken Glass* is set.[12] Amazingly, Miller gets the film exactly correct because in the fall of 1938, the time of the play's events, the movie *Carefree* starring the famous dance couple Fred Astaire and Ginger Rogers had been released on September 1, 1938. Kristallnacht was November 9–10, 1938. Similarly, Sylvia says that "Jimmy Cagney's at the Rialto, but it's another gangster story" (Miller 1994: 30). The Rialto Theatre in Brooklyn (there was also one in Manhattan) was located at 1085 Flatbush Avenue, again a short distance from the presumed location of the Gellburgs' home (Figure 1.31).[13] He also accurately names the movies that were current at the time: *Boy Meets Girl* starring James Cagney, which was released on August 27, 1938, but *Angels with Dirty Faces* was released on November 26, 1938, a few weeks after Kristallnacht.

There is one important Queens location, in Long Island City, that is mentioned in the play. Sylvia is characterized as keen and intelligent by many

Figure 1.30 The famous Schrafft's restaurant in Downtown Brooklyn, c. 1940. Courtesy Municipal Archives City of New York.

characters. Before her son Jerome was born, she had an important position as Head Bookkeeper at Empire Steel, a company that Miller did not entirely fabricate. There is a company named Empire City Iron Works that operated in that neighborhood at the time of the play and still exists. Of course, Miller knew the neighborhood quite well, having been a delivery boy in 1932 for

Figure 1.31 The Rialto Theatre in Flatbush, c. 1940. Courtesy Municipal Archives City of New York.

Milton Shapse's father, who owned a company there. Miller's rather extensive familiarity with the neighborhood he put to greater use in *Focus* (see Chapter 3), and it is amazing how he would reach back to that memory and use it in a play in 1994 when he completed *Broken Glass*.

Although *Broken Glass* is filled with references to places in Brooklyn, there is one notable Manhattan location that has considerable importance in the play. Phillip's boss Stanton Case is interested in purchasing a building for which he only gives an address as # 611, a location that he believes will

Figure 1.32 Cable Bldg 611 Broadway, c. 1940. Courtesy of the Municipal Archives City of New York.

make a fine annex for the Harvard Club (located on 44th Street) of which the waspish Mr. Case is obviously a member. Because Phillip describes the building as being two blocks from Wanamaker's, the famous department store that was located on 8th Street and 770 Broadway, we can assume the #611 address is for Broadway. Miller's accuracy in this is remarkable; for the building located at 611 Broadway, then and now, is a beautiful landmarked building in the Soho section of Manhattan called the Cable Building (Figure

Figure 1.33 The famous Wanamaker's Bldg at Broadway and 8th Street, c. 1999. Courtesy of the New York City Landmarks Preservation Commission.

1.32), actually located a few blocks from the Wanamaker's building. The Cable Building in the late 1930s and 1940s became the location for many garment manufacturing businesses, and it is located not far from Orchard Street, where Sylvia reminisces about shopping for bargains in the Lower East Side Jewish neighborhood, where the Millers and Barnetts originally settled. In addition, in its retail history, Wanamaker's department store was created from the A. T.

Stewarts store which Willy mentions in *Death of a Salesman*. The establishment originally opened at 280 Broadway and moved to the Wanamaker location at 8th and Broadway, a building that in recent years has been occupied by Meta (Facebook), Yahoo, and a Wegman's supermarket (Figure 1.33). Phillip disappoints Stanton over the evaluation of the property, a significant event in the play that is a catalyst to Philip's downfall.

Finally, there is a scene in *Broken Glass* where Miller dips again into the well of autobiography. He uses another version of his aunts and uncles, the Balsams and Newmans, who had moved to Brooklyn after the First World War, a story that he relates in various forms in "A Boy Grew in Brooklyn," *The American Clock,* and *Timebends.*

> Sylvia: As a child, when we first moved from upstate there were so many birds and rabbits even foxes here—Of course that was real country up there –
> In Coney Island, we used to kill rabbits with slingshots. (Miller 1994: 107)
> Brooklyn was beautiful. Mother used to stand on our porch and watch us all the way to school, right across the open fields for—must have been a mile. (Miller 1994: 108)

For Miller, Brooklyn remained a beautiful source of artistic inspiration for the length of his career. Gregory Mosher, who directed the 2010 Broadway revival of *A View from the Bridge*, observes that "Brooklyn is Miller's waterfront, or the Loman House being dwarfed by new buildings, and that little garden he's planting. He made us see a place differently, and that's a trick not may artists can pull off" (Stapinski 2016: 6).

2

The Manhattan Works

A Memory of Two Mondays, After the Fall, The Price, The Ride Down Mt. Morgan, Mr. Peter's Connections, Homely Girl, A Life

Miller set much of the action of five plays and his novella in Manhattan. *A Memory of Two Mondays, After the Fall, The Price, The Ride Down Mt. Morgan, Mr. Peter's Connections* and *Homely Girl* depict the economic, social, and cultural forces of the borough on the lives of the characters in the twentieth-century decades in which each work takes place. The characters' casual mention of New York locations illustrates how much the city is an integral part of their regular lives and how accurately Miller depicted the vibrancy of life in the city that he knew so well.

In form and style, the plays all can be classified as "memory" plays. The one-act *A Memory of Two Mondays* is a dramatized recollection of the period Miller worked at an auto parts warehouse in Manhattan. Because, as the title states, it is a memory play, the form is not strictly realistic; rather, Miller employed a style that combines romanticism, expressionism, realism, and naturalism. Miller's 1968 play *The Price* takes place in the attic of a brownstone on Manhattan's West Side, a building that is slated to be torn down, and the play gives insight to the changing physical and social fabric of the neighborhood. It is the only stylistically realistic play of the five, yet because the characters recall how crucial past events of their lives affect the present, memory plays an important role. *After the Fall, The Ride Down Mt. Morgan,* and *Mr. Peter's Connections* are strict "memory" plays in that their action takes place in the internal thoughts of the main characters; as such, Miller employs many of the same expressionistic techniques he used in *Death of a Salesman*. However, much of the imagined action is rooted in vital physical locations in Manhattan that provide a measure of reality for the reveries of the characters.

In *Timebends,* Miller proclaimed that, "I loved the city, was feverishly curious about all our lives lived in it" (145) and he clearly dipped into the well of autobiography for the plots, characterizations, and themes of these plays. *A Memory of Two Mondays* is based on the two years from 1932 to 1934 when Miller worked as a stock clerk at the Chadick-Delamater auto parts warehouse in Manhattan before he attended the University of Michigan. In *Timebends,* Miller relates the circumstances in which he was hired for the job, his duties, and the many places where auto parts were delivered throughout New York City. The characters in the play are thinly disguised versions of the actual workers at the plant, including the character Bert, who is Miller's literary doppelganger.

After the Fall is the most controversial of these plays, if not the most debated of Miller's career. Written for New York's newly formed Lincoln Center Repertory Theatre that debuted in 1964, Miller directly used autobiographical incidents from his life. He dramatized many scenes about his formative years and his parents' family conflicts (some of which overlap with similar scenes in *The American Clock* and *The Price*), such as his mother Gussie's resentment about her forced marriage, his father Isidore's illiteracy, and the impact of Miller's father losing his fortune. He changes the names of the real-life figures, but he keeps the name of the actual principal from his grammar school, Miss Fisher (Miller 1987: 17), whom he writes about in *Timebends.* He also depicted his three marriages to Mary Slattery, Marilyn Monroe, and Inge Morath, and his personal and professional relationship with the director Elia Kazan who "named names" before HUAC. His testimony in 1952 caused a breach with Miller that lasted until Kazan directed *After the Fall*'s premiere in 1964. Critics found the most scandalous autobiographical incidents to be the scenes about Miller's marriages, especially to Monroe. Miller's depiction of the character Maggie was seen as too closely resembling Monroe, who died in August 1962, a year and a half before the play's debut. Many judged that Miller had taken unfair advantage of Monroe's apparent suicide at the relatively young age of thirty-six, which elevated her to legendary status. They also saw as hypocritical Miller's fictionalizing of Kazan's testimony before HUAC in the characterization of Mickey.

The Price contains several autobiographical strains. In it, Miller returned to illustrating conflict between two brothers, as he had done in *The Man Who Had*

All the Luck, All My Sons, and *Death of a Salesman.* The play revolves around two estranged brothers meeting in the attic of a Manhattan brownstone where their father's possessions have been stored for fifteen years since his death. The building is being torn down and the brothers are meeting an appraiser to sell the items. Miller's father Isidore died in 1966 and Miller explained in *Timebends* that the "characters were not based on Kermit and me, we were far different from these two, but the magnetic underlying situation was deep in my bones" (Miller 1987: 13). Miller actually based the character of Victor on his boyhood chum, Sid Franks, who had lived in the adjoining apartment at 45 W 110th Street. Like Miller's father, Mr. Franks had lost his business during the Great Depression and in the late 1930s he and Sid were living in a second-floor apartment on W. 47th Street and Sixth Avenue in Manhattan. Miller used their address to convince the authorities that he was living there independently from his family and had limited income so he could qualify to work for the government-sponsored Federal Theatre Project which employed promising young playwrights a living wage of twenty-three dollars a week. To prove this to a Welfare Dept inspector, he "allegedly" lived with Mr. Franks, Sid's father, in the apartment over a tobacconist shop where he set up a cot and stored some clothes. This is also the neighborhood location for Frank's Chop House in *Salesman.* In *Timebends,* he provides a description of the Franks' piled-up furniture (245) and a daughter who committed suicide, details he would use in *The Price.* Sid had become a New York City police officer and Miller projected him onto the characterization of Victor; he used Frank's daughter's suicide as the basis for Solomon's daughter's suicide.

Despite Miller's assertion that the characters were not based on him and Kermit, there are blatant autobiographical incidents about Miller's parents that he used in the plot, particularly their extravagant upper middle-class lifestyle and his father losing his business. The original set of the play also included a poignant autobiographical touch. The attic is filled with the old furniture of the Franz family, and when set director Boris Aronson was accumulating pieces for the production, Miller's sister Joan Copeland (who was the understudy for Kate Reid as Esther) reminded him that their parents' dining room table had been given to their Aunt Blanche, his father's "baby" sister, when the Millers moved out of their East 3rd Street home to a small apartment. Miller trekked out to Brooklyn to see the table, which aroused in him memories of his mother dancing on it one New Year's Eve (Miller 1987: 13–14). With Aronson's

Figure 2.1 Cast on the set of *The Price* with Augusta Miller's dining room table on stage, c. 1968. Credit Line: Photo by Friedman-Abeles © Billy Rose Theatre Division, The New York Public Library for the Performing Arts

approval, the dining table was centered on the stage at the Morosco Theatre when *The Price* opened on February 7, 1968 (Figure 2.1).

The plots of *The Ride Down Mt. Morgan* and *Mr. Peter's Connections* are certainly not autobiographical, but critics have noted how the situations of both plays have connections to Miller's life and themes that he had explored in other plays. *Mt. Morgan* revolves around the bigamist Lyman Felt who has juggled two lives with two wives. He has crashed his car in a snowstorm in upstate New York, and both wives are inadvertently summoned to the hospital where they meet and discover his decades-long duplicity. In this late-career play, Miller returned to the issue of adultery and sexual desire between an older man and a younger woman, as he had done in *The Crucible*, *A View from the Bridge*, and *After the Fall*—plays seen by many critics as Miller artistically working through his feelings over his failed first marriage to Mary Slattery and his relationship with Monroe—although Miller's biographer Christopher Bigsby suggests that Lyman Felt's libidinous desires more closely resemble those of Elia Kazan (Bigsby 2005b: 378).

In *Mr. Peter's Connections*, Miller again dramatized the complicated relationship between brothers as he did in his Michigan plays and Broadway dramas. The central action revolves around Mr. Peter's trying to find "the subject" of his life, especially through "conversations" with his dead brother Calvin, who is an actual character on the stage. However, Harry does not appear to recognize him until late in the play. Miller also created a character named Cathie Mae, Mr. Peter's dead lover, who is clearly a Monroe-esque figure and also appears on the stage. Miller used this same technique with the on-stage appearance of his dead brother, Ben, in *Death of a Salesman*. There are other characters: Mr. Peter's wife Charlotte, his daughter Rose, and her paramour, Leonard, who are apparently alive, but since the action occurs in the synapses of Mr. Peter's mind, whether any of these events are real is the difficulty with understanding this complicated play. However, Miller included a blatantly autobiographically based recollection by Mr. Peters about his childhood. He recalls his mother and the maid—before the advent of washing machines—boiling sheets, washing laundry, and banging rugs on the roof of their New York apartment building. In *Timebends,* Miller detailed these exact same routines of his family when they were living on West 110th Street in Manhattan (Miller 1987: 64).

Although Miller wrote these plays over more than a forty-year period, all are centered in Manhattan locations not far from each other. *A Memory of Two Mondays* takes place at the Chadick-Delamater auto parts warehouse which was located at Broadway and 63rd Street, the current site of Lincoln Center for the Performing Arts on the borderline of Midtown and the Upper West Side. *The Price* is set a few blocks south in a brownstone building on the West Side, off Seventh Avenue. Although the real-time action of *The Ride Down Mt. Morgan* transpires as Lyman lies in a hospital bed in upstate New York near the city of Elmira, he has reveries that occur in Manhattan locations on the Upper East Side. Similarly, in *After the Fall* the events in Quentin's "mind, thought, and memory" include various Manhattan places. *Mr. Peter's Connections* takes place in an old abandoned night club in an undetermined neighborhood in Manhattan.

Even though *After the Fall, The Ride Down Mt. Morgan,* and *Mr. Peter's Connections* are not realistic plays, in that their action is dictated by the internal thoughts of the main characters, much of the imagined action is rooted in vital physical locations in Manhattan that provide a measure of reality for the reveries of the characters and for the theatrical experience of the audience. The locations also indicate how Miller used his familiarity with Manhattan

New York References in *After the Fall*

After the Fall is intriguing for the way Miller meshed locations associated with his own life into the fictional events. Most notable is the hotel that Quentin mentions where he is living, which is likely the famous Chelsea Hotel (Miller 1964: 2) where Miller lived after his divorce from Monroe and that he used as a Manhattan base during the early years of his marriage to Inge Morath. In 2002, Miller published an essay, "The Chelsea Effect," in which he detailed the colorful characters, famous and notorious artists, actors, writers, and musicians who inhabited that famous New York residence. In recent years, the Chelsea has received notoriety for its renovation as a first-class hotel (Figure 2.2).[1]

Miller used his familiarity with the geography and streetscape of Manhattan in the scene where Quentin first meets Maggie at a park bench (Miller 1964: 42). She is looking for the bus stop and asks, "What bus is this?" Quentin responds, "Fifth Avenue. This is the downtown side" (Miller 1964: 42). This indicates that the bench is one of the Central Park benches that line the park side of Fifth Avenue (Figure 2.3), probably around a street in the East 80s because Quentin also refers to a Museum of Art, likely the Metropolitan Museum of Art (Miller 1964: 43), along what is now known as Museum Mile. Quentin's direction that, "This is the downtown side," needs to be explained. Currently in New York, Fifth Avenue is one way running south. However, at the time that *After the Fall* occurs, it was a two-way avenue (It became one way in 1966). Park benches are located on the downtown side of Fifth Avenue along the stone border wall of the park. This indicates just how much detail Miller reveals about New York and how much we learn about Manhattan at the time.

During her conversation with Quentin, Maggie tells a male passerby that she is looking for a discount record store, and he responds that there is one located on Twenty-Seventh and Sixth Avenue (Miller 1964: 45). Of course, Miller would know this because this location is a few blocks from the Chelsea Hotel. However, Quentin also conveys that, "There's one around the corner, you know," which indicates that there also was a record store on Madison Avenue in the East 80s. During this conversation, Maggie reenforces the

Figure 2.2 Miller lived at the famous Chelsea Hotel after his divorce from Marilyn Monroe and during the early years of his marriage to Inge Morath, photo c. 1973. Courtesy of the New York City Landmarks Preservation Commission.

location when she explains to Quentin that she had a friend whose family lived "right over there on Park Avenue" (Miller 1964: 47) which is two avenues east of Fifth Avenue.

Miller also conveys the accuracy of New York Manhattan telephone numbers in 1963: (Miller 1964: 53, 54) by using the geographic area format

Figure 2.3 Central Park benches line the west side of Fifth Avenue, c. 2024. Photo by Jane K. Dominik.

for the phone number location that was used before the companies switched to numbers. Thus, Max's phone number "Murray Hill 3-4598" indicates the Manhattan neighborhood where he lived. The play also gives insight into the price of a taxi at the time: Quentin is outraged at giving fifty dollars to a cab driver (Miller 1964: 100). When Lou is killed by a subway train (Miller 1964: 58), although the play gives no indication of the line or station, the fact that there "there was no crowd at 8 o'clock" indicates that his death occurred after "rush hours," which most New Yorkers would know (Miller 1964: 100). The play also refers to Columbia University (Miller 1964: 3) where Holga is attending a conference, and Hunter College, formerly a women's college (Miller 1964: 17) where Augusta had an academic scholarship.

The play mentions two significant locations outside of Manhattan. New York's Idlewild (Miller 1964: 61) Airport was renamed John F. Kennedy International Airport after the president's assassination in 1963. The set of *After the Fall*'s 2004 Broadway revival set the play in an airline terminal that resembled the iconic and now landmarked TWA terminal, designed by architect Eero Saarinen, at JFK. The building has now has been integrated into the TWA Hotel complex at the airport.

Figure 2.4 First Lady Jacqueline Kennedy christening a ship at the Groton Shipyard, c. 1962. Courtesy of US Navy.

However, the more intriguing location that the play references is the Groton Shipyard that is located in Connecticut, and has played a vital role as a building location for American naval vessels. Maggie tells Quentin that she christened a submarine at the shipyard because she was voted the "favorite of all the workers" (Miller 1964: 72). There is no evidence that Monroe—on whom Maggie is modeled—christened a submarine there. However, it is quite fascinating that First Lady Jacqueline Kennedy christened the *USS Lafayette* at Groton on May 8, 1962, (Farrington, M.C. 2019), and Miller likely used this as the source for Maggie's visit (Figure 2.4). The irony of this cannot be lost because of the rumors of President John F. Kennedy's relationship with

Monroe. Her singing "Happy Birthday, Mr. President" to him at Madison Square Garden on May 19, 1962, is legendary. Fun fact: Miller's father Isidore was her "date" at the event (Miller 1987: 593).

New York References in *The Ride Down Mt. Morgan*

The Ride Down Mr. Morgan mentions Manhattan locations that are almost exclusively on the Upper East Side, a fitting neighborhood for an upper socioeconomic class family such as the Felts to reside. Lyman's daughter Bessie says she lives on East 74th Street (Miller 1992: 14); Leah explains that she and Lyman often stay at the exclusive Carlyle Hotel (Figure 2.5) (35 East 76th Street) four blocks from Theo's house (Miller 1992: 114); Lyman strolls with Leah, looking at the expensive shops on Madison Avenue (Miller 1992: 115). In one of the flashbacks, Theo gives insight into the upper-class lifestyle that she and Lyman led at one time, attending the New York City Ballet and eating at high-priced establishments. She describes "getting tickets for the Balanchine. And a table at Luigi's afterwards" (89). Lyman also describes to Tom, his lawyer, "the red river of taillights gliding down Park Avenue on a winter's night" (30).

The only location mentioned not on the Upper East Side is an appetizer store on Ninth Avenue and 40th Street (Figure 2.6), that Lyman recalls his father owned, which fits into his description as the proprietor of a Jewish delicatessen. Lyman describes to his lawyer how his father "connected to life; couldn't wait to open the store every morning and happily count the pickles, rearranging the olive barrels" (26). Lyman refers a few times to his father's store: "I was dreaming of my father's store" while in a deep troubled sleep (33) and recalls his grandfather "losing three fingers under the Ninth Avenue trolley" (77). One can also speculate that this is the very neighborhood where *The Price* brownstone is located.

Other Manhattan locations that the characters reference are: Leah attending the NYU School of Business (12), and Lyman selling poems to the *New Yorker* and a story to *Harper's* (44). An intriguing reference to a character who "got a woman stashed in Trump Tower and two in L.A." (69) likely refers to the famous Trump Tower on Fifth Avenue.

Figure 2.5 The exclusive Carlyle Hotel, c. 2024. Photo by Jane K. Dominik.

An interesting dichotomy exists in the play between life in the city (Downstate in New York City) and life in the country (Upstate in Elmira). Leah hopes to get a place in Manhattan because of the vibrancy of life in the city (13). However, there are many places in upstate that are evoked: the city of Elmira, Lyman staying at a Howard Johnson's hotel (35), Lyman suggesting to Theo that she fly upstate, rent a car, and fly through Cherry Valley (47). Cornell

Figure 2.6 Fruit and vegetable market on Ninth Avenue, c. 1940. Courtesy Municipal Archives City of New York.

University in Ithaca figures prominently in the play (and reflects Miller's many references to the Ivy League school in *Timebends*). Lyman recalls hitchhiking back from Cornell (68) where he met Theodora and getting advice about sex from an English instructor at Cornell (71). Theodora recalls skinny dipping at the river past the campus's Chemistry building. This, of course, is the famous gorge and its falls at Cornell. There is one reference to Long Island: Lyman and Theo go on a two-day sail off Montauk Point (55).

New York References in *Mr. Peter's Connections*

Mr. Peter's Connections is a difficult and confusing play. The disjointed action in the synapses of Peter's mind challenges the reader/audience to ground the events in reality. However, the references to places in Manhattan help give us an understanding of Mr. Peter's memories of his actual past life in various decades in the city.

The play takes place in an old abandoned night club in an undetermined part of New York City during the late 1990s when Miller completed the play, and it premiered at Manhattan's Signature Theatre in 1998. The evidence indicates the club may be located on the Lower East Side: the multiethnic neighborhood has Jews, Koreans, and "Chinks" (100). The characters mention that the structure formerly housed a bank (a bank owned by the Morris Family (96), the Frick Museum, the Astor 42nd Street Library, Morgan Library, and the Rockefellers (96) and was a cafeteria in the 1930s called the "Eagle Cafeteria" (97). The entire action of the play takes place in front of this structure, and characters, dead and alive, pop in and out of Mr. Peter's memories and real time.

The New York locations that Mr. Peter and his brother mention include Sheepshead Bay, Brooklyn (86, 123), and Floyd Bennett Field in Brooklyn (91), and their familiarity with these adjoining areas indicates they may have lived there. Other places include Lenox Hill Hospital (102), the Radio City Rockettes (118), Bear Stearns on Wall Street (120), and Weehawken, New Jersey (123).

New York References in *The Price*

The dialogue of *The Price* implies that the play is set in a brownstone building on the West Side of Manhattan, probably Midtown, on the cusp of what is called Hell's Kitchen. Esther tells Victor that she will pick up his suit from the dry cleaner right off Seventh Avenue (Miller 1968: 24), and late in the play (Miller 1968: 105) Victor recalls that he walked to Bryant Park from their attic apartment and witnessed unemployed men camped out behind the 42nd Street Library. With this, Miller depicted the reality of the economic conditions of life in Manhattan during the Depression years of the 1930s, as he did in *The*

American Clock. "What you saw behind the library was not that there was no mercy in the world, kid" (Miller 1968: 107). The play depicts the effects of the Depression not only on the Franz father but others like him, such as the men in the park. Solomon explains that his ex-wife is "still living by Eighth Avenue over there," which perhaps indicates that the brownstone is between Seventh and Eighth Avenues. (It is also possible that the brownstone is located further uptown, near Lincoln Center, and where the Chadwick-Delamater was located because the entire area was demolished for the construction of Lincoln Center (Figure 2.7). However, Victor would have had to make a rather long walk to Bryant Park from there.)

The Price takes place in 1968, a time when that area in Manhattan was being reconstructed: As Victor says, "They tear down old buildings every day in the week, kid." (Miller 1968: 10). This was especially true in the Theatre District/Hell's Kitchen during that time. Solomon gives insight into the decrepitude of the area when he says about the exquisite furniture, "In this neighborhood, I never expected such a load" . . . "You're lucky they're tearing the building down" (Miller 1968: 30). Solomon, as a furniture dealer, also claims that he was vice president (62) of the Appraisers Association, an accurate depiction of an organization that actually existed in Manhattan. When the association first organized in 1949, they met at the Belmont Plaza Hotel located at Lexington and 49th Street in the Grand Central Station area of Manhattan.[2]

The Manhattan-centric attitude that we see in *Death of a Salesman* and *A View from the Bridge* is evident in *The Price* when Victor explains to Solomon where his "beat" as a cop is located: "I'm out in Rockaway most of the time, the airports," and Solomon jokes: "That's Siberia, no?" (Miller 1968: 33).

New York References in *A Memory of Two Mondays*

Perhaps the most important of these Manhattan plays is the lesser-known *A Memory of Two Mondays*. Even though *After the Fall* and *The Price* include fictionalized versions of events in Miller's life, Miller had a special fondness for the autobiographical aspects of *A Memory of Two Mondays*.[3] Among the other plays included in his 1958 *Collected Plays—All My Sons, Death of a Salesman, The Crucible,* and *A View from the Bridge*—he felt about *A Memory of Two Mondays* that "Nothing in this book was written with greater love, and

Figure 2.7 Many buildings in the San Juan Hill neighborhood of Manhattan were razed to construct Lincoln Center. Among those was the Chadick-Delameter Auto Parts Warehouse. United States. New York City, 1963. © Inge Morath/Magnum Photos

for myself, I love nothing printed here better than this play" (Miller 1968: 164). After all, the two years that Miller spent at Chadick-Delamater were an important time in his personal, intellectual, and artistic growth. Stymied by his poor grades in high school and his family's economic circumstances, the seventeen-year-old Miller was unable to attend college and fulfill his desire to become a writer. He was forced to work a series of odd jobs including at his

Figure 2.8 Contemporary view of the Lincoln Center complex, c. 2024. Photo by Jane K. Dominlk.

father's business, as a truck driver and delivery man for the father of his friend Milton Shapse, and as an on-air tenor for a Brooklyn radio station. Then he answered a newspaper ad for a stock boy at the auto parts warehouse in Manhattan. The warehouse was located on the site that is now Lincoln Center for the Performing Arts (Figure 2.8).

Miller spent two of his formative late teenage years from seventeen to nineteen toiling at the warehouse, but he clearly learned much about the human condition from the lively, lonely, and troubled co-workers, all struggling under personal, economic, and moral duress during the depths of the Great Depression. Miller said that "The play speaks . . . of rent and hunger" (Miller 1957: 164)—and years later he would transform his and their experiences into art. Miller described *A Memory of Two Mondays* as a

> pathetic comedy; a boy works among people for a couple of years, shares their troubles, their victories, their hopes, and when it is time for him to be on his way he expects some memorable moment, some sign from them that he has been among them, that he has touched them and been touched by them. In the sea of routine that swells around them they barely notice his departure. (Miller 1968: 164–5)

In *Timebends*, Miller relates how ten years after he left the warehouse, he found himself in the neighborhood of Chadick-Delamater and popped in to say hello. He ran into a worker, Huey, who did not recall the young man beside whom he had worked a decade before. But the young man who left the warehouse to go to college and become a writer remembered him and all the other workers whose lives he dramatized for posterity (Miller 2002d).

Miller explains that he wrote the play "in part out of desire to relive a sort of reality where necessity was open and bare; I hoped to define for myself the value of hope, why it must arise, as well as the heroism of those who know, at least, how to endure its absence" (Miller 1968: 164). In *Memory*, Miller clearly applied his prescription, as he laid out in "Tragedy and the Common Man," of seeing tragedy as ending not in despair, but in hope. Miller, in the guise of Bert, spent his two years there in hopes of eventually leaving for college, and he was troubled by, and yet marveled at, how the workers in the warehouse had little hope of leaving the dire conditions, but nevertheless carried on despite this.

In the previous chapter, I detailed how Miller exhibits his extensive knowledge of the New York subway system with extraordinary accuracy. It is fascinating how he explicitly details exact trips from one location to another in the city. Why would he do this? Perhaps he wanted to re-create the experience of the often-long rides to and from the city, that is, Brooklyn to Manhattan/Manhattan to Brooklyn, trips he took literally hundreds of times over the years so that the routes imprinted themselves on him—an experience that certainly can be shared by many New Yorkers. This experience must have been terribly impressionable on the young Arthur, as for two years he made the trek from his Brooklyn home to the Chadick-Delamater warehouse. In *Timebends*, Miller details getting the job (Miller 1987: 216) and explicitly describes his step-by-step trip from his Brooklyn home on East 3rd Street: "I was on the trolley rocketing down Gravesend Avenue to the subway stop at Church and then up to Times Square and a change to the local train to Sixty-sixth Street, then a short trot over the Sixty-Third and up the steel stairs into that quiet, cool, establishment" (Miller 1987: 216).

Moreover, the opening scene of *A Memory of Two Mondays* begins with that exact subway ride. The character Bert—the fictionalized Miller—arrives for work carrying a thick book, a lunch bag, and the *New York Times*, as the young Miller likely looked after taking his long subway ride:

Raymond the manager enters:
Raymond: What are you doing in so early?
Bert: I wanted to get a seat on the subway for once. But, it's nice to walk around in the streets before the crowds get out . . .
Raymond (*he has never paid much attention to Bert, is now curious, has time for it*) How do you get time to read that paper?
Bert: Well, I've got an hour and ten minutes on the subway . . . .(Miller 2022: 4)

This conversation reveals much about Bert's (and Miller's) life as a New Yorker, particularly as a young Brooklynite learning about the experience of traveling to and working in the city. The characters' casual mention of New York places shows how the city is an integral part of their regular lives. Bert has arrived at work early because he has learned that riding the subway during rush hour dramatically reduces one's chance of getting a seat in the crowded cars. Bert, the aspiring college student, reads the *New York Times* every day, and most New Yorkers know the difficulty of reading the *Times* while standing in a subway car—for which, of course, the "subway fold" was invented for reading the large broadsheet. In addition, young Bert is amazed at how the Manhattan streets are much less crowded in the early hours. Moreover, he accurately describes the approximate time it takes to get to the warehouse from his home in Brooklyn. As a sensitive observer of human life, Bert delivers a plaintive speech about subway riders that likely echoes how Miller felt: "Why does it make me so sad to see them every morning? It's like the subway. Every day I see the same people getting on and the same people getting off and all that happens is that they get older" (Miller 2022: 36).

In addition to absorbing much about the hopes and dreams of the workers, Miller also learned about the prejudice endemic in the Manhattan workplace, especially against Jews. In fact, Miller experienced anti-Semitism for the first time when he answered the newspaper ad for the stock boy position at Chadwick-Delamater. When he initially applied for the job, he was rebuffed because he was a Jew. However, the father of his friend Milton Shapse, for whom Miller once worked as a delivery man in Long Island City, intervened to get him the position. In *Timebends,* Miller also related an incident when he was working at the warehouse about one of the workers slurring him as a Jew (Miller 1987: 214–15). In 2002, Miller contributed a short essay in *New York* magazine recalling how the prejudice was not only reserved for him. He wrote, "I was the only Jew. The guy who worked there after me was Italian. They hated him, too" (Miller 2002a: 122). However, he does not dramatize anti-Semitism in the play, likely because he wanted the overall tone to be sentimental rather than stark realism. Nevertheless, he imbues the play with a high dose of ribald ethnic comments about the Irish, Poles, and American Indians that display the stereotypes that the workers have about each other. Miller presents this, and the attitude toward the female employees, as a regular part of the work environment. As the only Jew at the plant, there would be no one for the young Bert/Arthur to share a repartee with, and as a teenager, he certainly would not have vocalized any bias or comments to his fellow workers.

Other autobiographical references that Miller applies to Bert include: receiving bad marks in high school (4), saving money for college (5) (the five hundred dollars Miller needed for the University of Michigan), reading *War and Peace* on the subway (5) (Miller was turned on to the Russians in the library of Abraham Lincoln High School), reading the *New York Times* in the office (4), and his poignant feeling at leaving the job (53).

The play's location in New York is crucial. Miller's dialogue accounts for the various New York ethnic dialects, accents, and colloquialisms. Of particular note is the Slavic accent of Gus and the lilting Irish accent of Kenneth. Moreover, native New Yorkers do not all share the same speaking style, and there are various dialects within the city's boroughs. For example, Bert, as the stand-in for Arthur Miller, approximates a "Brooklyn" accent that Miller himself retained his entire life. Mr. Eagle, a Dartmouth-educated college graduate who is wealthy and upper class, speaks a sophisticated vernacular. In addition, there is a working-class dialect of incorrect grammar and idiomatic language, such as when the mechanic says, "It like sticks out, except it don't stick out" or "I brung over a couple a friend of mines . . . "(Miller 2002a: 26).

A Memory of Two Mondays is chock-full of geographic references. In fact, because the warehouse delivers auto parts throughout the city and the workers travel throughout the metropolis, there is a geographic sweep to locations and specific neighborhoods that are mentioned throughout New York's five boroughs: the Staten Island Ferry, Bryant Park, the West Bronx, Williamsburg, Brooklyn, the Hudson Tubes, Long Island City, Staten Island. On his drunken cavort on the final night of his life, Gus travels much of Manhattan: "Got right up Third Avenue and hit the bars on both sides. And got up to about Fourteenth Street, in around there, and we kind lost track of the car someplace" (Miller 2022: 54).

Miller himself acquired a sense of geography when he worked as a delivery man for Shapse's warehouse that was located in Long Island City. In *Timebends*, Miller relates how he got lost many times traveling to many places in that Queens neighborhood as he delivered auto parts. He explains how he "moved the truck through the streets, back and forth across the bridges, up into the Bronx and out to Brooklyn" (Miller 1987: 214) and got to know "working class neighborhoods like Long Island City" (Miller 1987: 214). He obviously retained a powerful memory of the area, its adjacent communities, and the city's outer boroughs, which he used to full effect in *A Memory of Two Mondays* and in his novel *Focus* (see Chapter 3).

Chadwick-Delamater also delivered parts to businesses upstate and on Long Island, so the locations there are referenced as well: Atlantic City, New Jersey; Skaneateles, an upstate town; Riverhead on Long Island in Suffolk County; Jersey City; Scranton, Pennsylvania; and Peekskill, an upstate town.

The introduction detailed Miller's fascination with cars from a young age, and Miller admittedly took this youthful attraction to automobiles into his adulthood. In fact, throughout *Timebends*, he consistently describes cars in some extraordinarily specific detail, with references to the many cars that Miller owned, rented, and drove throughout his life. The use of cars in his plays and fiction is extraordinary.[4]

By the time he was nineteen, Miller had extensive experience working in two businesses that were centered on automobiles. As a driver for Milton Shapse's father, Miller picked up auto parts from Chadwick. From the young Miller's vantage point as a driver, Chadwick had a "certain panache, handling the best brands that serviced parts for similar luxury cars he was attracted to as a youth: Bear ignitions, Timken roller bearings, Detroit axles, Brown and Lippe transmissions, Packard-Lackard ignition wires, Prestone anti-freeze, Gates gaskets and radiator hoses, Perfect Circle piston rings and wrist pins—these were heavy names that bespoke grave and established firms sold as rock" (215). Miller proudly admitted that he "had come to understand something about the business" (Miller 1987: 214).

Miller's judgment that he had come to understand "something" about the auto parts business is an understatement because he clearly used in his plays what he learned about cars at Shapse's place and Chadwick-Delamater. *A Memory of Two Mondays* is filled with references to specific cars, makes, models, and parts. Miller clearly offers a primer on cars in 1934. The dialogue and stage are literally strewn with auto parts: manifolds, Model T Ford mufflers, Marmon valves, ignition stuff, Maxwell differentials, Locomobile head nuts, rear-end gears, fenders for an old wrecked Ford. Larry purchases an expensive Auburn because, "They got the most beautifully laid out valves in the country on that car" (Miller 2022: 15); an old coal truck is identified as a Mack, but the engine is American-La France. Toward the play's end, Gus's long speech overflows with references to cars:

> When there was a Winton Six I was here. When was Minera car I was here. When was Stanley Steamer I was here, and Stearns Knight, and Marmon was good car; I was here all them times ... When was Locomobile, and Model K Ford and Model N Ford—all them different Fords, and Franklin was good car, Jordan car, Reo car, Pierce Arrow, Cleveland car—all them was good cars. All them times I was here. (Miller 2022: 51–2)

It is quite impressive to see what the young Miller absorbed and later used in his work.

Homely Girl, A Life

Perhaps none of Miller's work depicts the geographical sweep of Manhattan more than *Homely Girl, A Life*. The 1992 novella relates the story of Janice Sessions, the homely girl of the title, as she traces through memory and time her life as a "plain girl" (the title of the work in England) living in New York from the 1930s to the late 1970s. The plot details how Janice, cast as unattractive by her own mother, searches for an identity in the political and social milieu that constituted Manhattan through the Depression, the war years, and the postwar decades. Raised in the middle-class materialism of her Jewish parents, she marries a radical Communist sympathizer, Sam Fink, alternately embracing then rejecting both him and his politics. When she meets a blind classical musician, Charles, a man who cannot see her homeliness, she ultimately "lives into beauty."

The commentary that exists on the story mostly focuses on its sociopolitical implications and not the significance of the New York locations. Thomas Adler has examined the work as a reading of the text of the Jewish body, marked and stigmatized as the other. Malcolm Bradbury sees it as an allegory that spreads across the years of Miller's own writing using the political, cultural, and social events that influenced it. Christopher Bigsby sees a direct connection between Janice and Miller's own idealistic devotion to political and social causes and their ultimate awareness that these do not ultimately constitute the essence of their lives (2005b: 460–2).

The settings in Manhattan are central to the text. In the fifty-year time span of the narrative, Janice traverses the borough's streets from the East Side to the West Side, from riverside to riverside, from upper Broadway to the Village. She occupies residences in its distinctive neighborhoods and visits its bars, restaurants, schools, theaters, and retail stores. The story blatantly points out scores of locations in Manhattan: Greenwich Village, picket lines at Columbia University, the 90 Church Street Army recruitment office, the piers on the Hudson, dusty Irish bars, movies on Irving Place. Janice attends school at Hunter College; she and Sam live on East 32nd Street in the 1930s. She frequently strolls the city streets: from the dead East Side to the tenements on slummy Sixth Avenue; she shops on Madison Avenue. Her experiences in these Manhattan haunts become central to her character—the identifying mark of her existence. Miller uses the streets and buildings of Manhattan to create a literary landscape as significant as Gustave Aschenbach's Venice or Leopold Bloom's Dublin. Janice's story is the story of death and the city, sex and the city, ugliness and the city, all intimately connected to her identity—which she herself realizes when she declares, "I love this city!" In Janice's New York, sex becomes love, homeliness becomes beauty, and death becomes life.

One of the strongest effects of the story is how Miller realistically conveys the ethnicity, social classes, and politics of Manhattan neighborhoods, an aspect that pervades much of his work, as other chapters in this text show. For example, Janice's father is a middle-class Jew who lives in the gloom of a West End apartment, and Janice is repulsed by the objects which to her typify her parents' class: the heavy European silverware, the overstuffed chairs, the Oriental rugs, and the doomed weight of the tea service—items that resemble much of Miller's family's furniture that he describes as stored in the attic in *The Price*. Similarly, Janice's first husband, Sam Fink, was a Jewish Communist radical with whom she attended rallies and meetings in downtown Manhattan lofts and West End Avenue living rooms in the 1930s. They fear walking through Yorkville on the Upper East Side because its predominantly German residents are holding rallies in favor of Hitler and threatening Jews as they walk on 86th Street, the enclave's central thoroughfare.

Particularly striking examples of how Miller strongly connects politics to places in Manhattan occur on three significant historical dates associated with the Second World War and further exhibit how Miller weaves history into his fiction. On August 23, 1939, Hitler and Stalin formed their non-aggression pact in the dark days preceding the war—an event which is described as "a permanent stinging memory" for Janice. She had been shopping for shoes on 34th Street; in fact the text specifically describes her shopping foray along the shopping strip that stretches from Macy's department store on the West Side to B. Altman's on the East Side (Figure 2.9). Along the way, she passes a typical New York corner candy store newsstand and reads the awful headline of the news in the *New York Times*. She walks to Madison and 31st Street, reading the paper, simultaneously wondering what the reaction to the news will be in another Manhattan neighborhood tied to politics: West End Avenue. That same evening, she goes to dinner with Sam at a Barclay's restaurant on 8th Street in the Village, whose residents are stunned by the news. Miller then fast-forwards to the next date: June 22, 1940, and places Janice in Times Square with an immense crowd on the day France was vanquished by the Nazis (Figure 2.10). Then he shifts again to the summer of 1941, the day when Hitler attacked Russia, breaking the pact, and the politically left-leaning residents of the "Village relaxed" (Miller 1992: 21).

Miller structured *Homely Girl* as a series of non-chronological flashbacks, and Janice's first memories in the text are directly connected to the setting. In fact, the very first lines present the importance of Manhattan in its connection to Janice. The story begins with death: Janice awakens to find her second husband, Charles, dead in the bed next to her. But even before she becomes conscious of him lying beside her, she surfaces from her sleep thinking of the previous warm June day in that famous bucolic place directly in the center of Manhattan— Central Park. Ironically, it is the only pastoral scene in the entire story.[5]

Death, both literal and figurative, pervades *Homely Girl*. In fact, there is an inversion—of death to life—rather than life to death. The story clearly frontloads the literal deaths: the death of Charles is followed by a flashback to the death of Janice's father years earlier. That entire episode is not only rooted in Manhattan settings but also emphasizes the physical condition of the city. After her father's funeral service in a synagogue on the Upper West Side, Janice, her brother, Herman, and his wife stroll down Broadway toward downtown.

Figure 2.9 B. Altman's flagship store on Fifth Avenue at 34th Street signified the best in luxury shopping, c. 1940. Courtesy Municipal Archives City of New York.

During this walk, Herman, whom Janice describes as the "last Republican Jew in New York," also enforces the sociopolitical importance of the Manhattan settings. Herman is a sort of dabbling real estate broker, and on their walk down Broadway, he is entranced by the numerous stores out of business and the many vacant apartments, all clearly a result of the Depression, a situation that Miller accurately depicts. He complains that refugees, obviously escapees from the impending war in Europe, are buying up properties on Amsterdam Avenue and proposes that he and Janice pool together their share of their

Figure 2.10 Crowd gathers in Times Square to get the news about the invasion of France, c. 1939. Photo12/Ann Ronan Picture Library/Alamy Stock Photo.

father's inheritance so they "could pick up buildings for next to nothing" (Miller 1992: 9). Of course, this emphasizes physical structure, vacancy, and the value of real estate during the Depression years, but also foreshadows the destruction of the important Crosby Hotel at the end of the story some forty years later.

They end up in an Irish bar on 84th Street and Broadway modeled after a bar that stood there at the time (Figure 2.11). The action in this bar strengthens the importance of death in the story. Janice and Herman carry with them the box containing their father's ashes. On her way home in a taxi, Janice realizes she has left the ashes at the bar and she returns to find them, but they are gone. The Irish bartender consoles her with a martini, and Janice spends the night talking with him about different kinds of death: "sudden and drawn out, the death of the very young and the old." (10). The conversation about death is crucial because Janice encounters many literal deaths, all ultimately leading to the most important death in the story: the death of her plainness. Her conversation with the bartender results in Janice's first realization in the story. She releases herself from "waiting to become someone else" and declares that she is Janice forever (Miller 1992: 11), accepting the homeliness to which her mother consigned her. It is significant that as she walks down Broadway after her realization, she is described as smiling perversely at her new liberation, the freedom now to be herself. Moreover, as she continues her walk down the

Figure 2.11 Janice and Herman wind up in an Irish bar on 84th Street and Broadway, c. 1940. Courtesy Municipal Archives City of New York.

avenue, she is amused by the thought of her father left on a bar in the box, trapped, outraged, banging to get out (Miller 1992: 11), a notion which leads to another realization: "that the body was more of an abstraction than the soul, which never disappeared." Janice has realized that she is a person whose soul, whose anima, whose spirit counts more than her appearance.

This emphasis on the body is a crucial aspect of Janice's identity, for many of the revelations Janice has about herself are connected to her body. Janice's awareness of her body began in childhood when her mother put an Ivory soap advertisement in Cosmopolitan magazine up to her face and pointed it out as an example of beauty. Janice herself had witnessed the reactions of men who first had seen her from behind and then subsequently saw her plain face. Consequently, Janice used her innate sense of style to emphasize her obviously "very good compact body" (Miller 1992: 4). And Janice's awareness of her body leads to extramarital relationships with Lionel Mayer and Professor Kalkofsky, ultimately liberating her from the marriage with Sam.

The affair with Professor Kalkofsky, Janice's graduate school art teacher at Hunter College, occurs when Sam has been shipped off to Europe. It is notable that the spark for Janice's affair with Oscar occurs during one of her walks on the streets of the city. She decides to stop in an Argosy store on lower Fifth Avenue to get off her feet and find something to read. When the professor ambles into the store, she is drawn into his "self-mocking smile and wry fatalism" (Miller 1992: 28). A few months later, walking in Manhattan one day and pained by the impending return of her husband from the war and her desire to divorce him, she decides to go see the professor to talk, not about art, but about life. Janice's own sense of her body is tuned into Kalkofsky's attraction to her. Their subsequent affair provokes another crucial revelation in her: that she is a woman of value who chooses to grant her body to the professor, and being able to choose liberates her. Janice's relationship with the professor illustrates how important the acts of strolling and walking "endlessly" (Miller 1992: 27) through Manhattan to significant locations are in the novella during other turning points in Janice's life, such as walking with her brother down Broadway, patronizing the old movie house on 72 Street and Broadway to see a Garbo film, and walking with Charles for the first time from the Crosby Hotel to the subway. As Miller does in other works, their walk to the subway exactly maps the correct streetscape as they turn right from the hotel to walk to Broadway to the subway line that takes them to the 59th Street station where the Athletic Club, Charles's destination, is located.

The most significant Manhattan location in the story is the Crosby Hotel where the final action occurs. After leaving Sam, Janice moves to the seedy hotel with a Parisian ornateness on 71st Street off Broadway; it serves as a crucial catalyst to Janice's ultimate revelation about herself, for there she meets her second husband Charles, who is literally blind, but comes to see the real beauty within her. Miller's model for the hotel is likely one of many of the beautiful hotels in that area (Figure 2.12).

Figure 2.12 The fictional Crosby Hotel is modeled after the many resident hotels on Manhattan's Upper West Side, c. 2024. Photo by Jane K. Dominik.

Before Janice meets Charles in the elevator of the hotel, Janice receives a visit from her brother Herman, and he again highlights the importance of Manhattan real estate, as he did on the day of their father's funeral. Now working and buying real estate in Chicago, Herman disapproves of her apartment at the Crosby, saying: "You picked a real good dump to waste your life in" (Miller 1992: 34). He again wants her to invest with him in Manhattan buildings that are undervalued, an irony because eight years before he proposed the same deal and has done nothing about it. He asks her: "How can you live in this dump, everything falling apart?" In Janice's reply: "I like everything falling apart; it's less competition for when I start falling apart," (Miller 1992: 35). She herself makes the crucial connection to the figurative importance of the Crosby Hotel. After Herman asks whether she ever found their father's ashes, a not-so-subtle reminder of the importance of death in this story, he asks if she has any friends, Janice replies: "Maybe I'm not ready to have friends. Maybe I'm not fully born yet. Hindus believe that you know—they think we go on being born and reborn right through life, or something like that." Then Janice declares, "I love this city. . . . I know there are ways to be happy in it, but I haven't found any. But I know they're there" (Miller 1992: 36).

Janice sees hope for her future not in the monetary value of individual Manhattan real estate, but in the pulsing life of the metropolis. And in the next scene, Janice indeed finds her happiness in the city; she is reborn when she meets Charles in the elevator of the Crosby Hotel. The moment they meet, she feels "a freedom close by, a liberation swept her up as for one instant he stared sightless into her face" (Miller 1992: 39). And all the elements of the story come together: they stroll down Broadway; they make love in his hotel room. "His hand discovered her good happy body" (Miller 1992: 42). Charles loves her body, not her face. He declares her beautiful. The Hindu allusion is crucial because Janice connects herself to the cycle of creation and re-creation. Thus, the Crosby Hotel becomes no less than the place of reincarnation for Janice: the place of death, rebirth, destruction, and life.

The story ends with Janice, now living in the Village in the 1970s, on a visit to the Crosby, which is being demolished for a new apartment house in an ever-changing Manhattan. She stands in front as men, having already demolished the top floor, are working their way toward her apartment. She notes that "Each generation takes part of the city away, like ants tugging twigs" (Miller 1992: 45). She walks up to the front doors and stands trying to catch the haunted earth-cold smell of a dying building, trying to recapture the feeling when she first walked out of the hotel's front doors and walked with Charles down Broadway toward the subway on the last day of her homeliness. Janice turns away and she is surrounded by the dirt and squalor of New York in the late 1970s. Janice says almost aloud, "Oh, Death, of Death" (Miller 1992: 46). But *Homely Girl* does not end in the despair of death and destruction. Ironically, Janice finds happiness in the most unlikely place—in the destruction of the Crosby Hotel. This is a story which inverts the process, leading not from life to death, but death to life. The tale ends with Janice crossing the street at a green light, an affirmation of life, not death, and with apologies to F. Scott Fitzgerald, her orgiastic future both behind and before her as she is filled—in the last words of the text—"with wonder at her fortune of having lived into beauty."

3

Focus

A Novel about Queens

Focus is a novel that Arthur Miller may not have ever written if not for the stunning failure in 1944 of his first Broadway play, *The Man Who Had All the Luck*. Disappointed by the critical reception of the production that closed after only four performances, Miller was convinced that he would never write another play; in fact, he would not write another drama until *All My Sons*, which premiered in 1947. However, as he explained in a 2004 interview with Christopher Bigsby (Miller 2006: 68), knowing that he had a natural talent for writing prose, in 1945 Miller published his only novel, *Focus*, which is one of the first important works about American anti-Semitism. The novel was quite successful, selling 90,000 copies. Miller's sister, the actress Joan Copeland, related in an interview in 2007 their mother's pride at her son's accomplishment:

> But when he wrote *Focus*, my mother used to carry the book around with her. She was very loquacious and she could talk to anybody. She could talk the birds off the trees! She was a very charming lady. She carried the book around with her. And when we'd go to a restaurant, she'd sit next to somebody and get into a conversation with them. She'd say, "What do you do?" And she would then know the whole history of the person. Women liked to talk to her , but the men would be a little bit—you know men don't like to talk to strangers—you know, women converse with each other in that kind of situation. She would then, sooner or later, right before dessert came, say: "Have you read this book?" [*Laughter*]

> SM: It's ironic that he had that success with that novel before the success with *All My Sons*. The novel was 1945. No wonder your mother carried it around.

JC: Yes, she would try to sell it! Nobody in those days read. We would go to Juniors and I suppose she was responsible for selling a few of those copies. (Copeland 2008: 49)

The plot of *Focus* centers on Lawrence Newman, who at the outset of the novel, lives with his mother in a one-family house in the New York City borough of Queens. The gentile Newman is the personnel manager of a large Manhattan company that refuses to hire Jews, a policy that he enforces. Newman is forced to wear glasses because of failing eyesight. Thus, the title of the novel possesses literal and figurative meanings. Although the glasses help him see clearly, they make him look like a Jew. He is suddenly viewed differently and becomes the object of discrimination and persecution. His bosses want to remove his desk to a corner office so that visitors do not see him. He refuses, quits, and cannot find another job because of his appearance. Moreover, he becomes an outcast to his neighbors on his street because they too suspect that he is Jewish, especially when he shows sympathy for the corner candy store owner, Finkelstein, is reluctant to participate in removing undesirables from their Queens neighborhood, and is unwilling to attend hate rallies. Newman suspects that his next-door neighbor, Fred, is allied with the Christian Front, who is responsible for harassing Newman and Finkelstein with actions such as overturning their garbage pails. Newman's wife Gertrude plays a complicated role in the novel. They first meet at a job interview at which Newman refused to hire her because he suspected that she was Jewish; conversely, she thought he looked Jewish. Ironically, Gertrude once worked for an anti-semitic organization, exhibits intrinsic anti-Semitism, but she, too, is taken for a Jew when she and Newman marry. Newman suspects that the Christian Front plans an assault against Finkelstein. One night, walking home with Gertrude, Newman himself is attacked on his street by the Christian Front, who also target Finkelstein in his store. However, Finkelstein escapes the store and comes to Newman's defense, the two fending off the attack. Emboldened by identification with a man he now sees as a fellow Jew, Newman reports the attack to the police.

Focus powerfully tackles a subject that Miller would make a major part of his later dramatic canon: all humanity shares a responsibility for the suffering of the Jews. This is evident in his so-called Holocaust plays: *After the Fall, Incident at Vichy, Playing for Time,* and *Broken Glass.* Responsibility for all humanity is a major theme in *All My Sons*, and the idea of a person's growing awareness of taking a stand on an issue is illustrated by Thomas Stockmann in *Enemy of the People*, John Proctor in *The Crucible*, and Prince Von Berg in *Incident at Vichy*. Similar themes run like threads in Miller's dramatic canon—guilt, betrayal, the complexity of accepting full responsibility for one's actions, to whom the individual is responsible: oneself, one's family, or society—and are also evident in *Focus* as well.

Although the action centers on anti-Semitism, the work is not only about prejudice against Jews in New York City during the Second World War. The novel also portrays biases pervasive in every aspect of New York City society at the time: in the workplace, in neighborhoods, in the subway, in families, corporations, retail establishments—and for many ethnic and racial groups: the Puerto Rican, the Black, the Irish, the Catholic, the Wasp, the rich, the poor, the working class. *Focus* is particularly notable in how the New York settings enforce the prejudices at the heart of the novel. The tale emphasizes how the rampant anti-Semitism in the borough of Queens in 1944 mirrors the same anti-Semitism operating in the workplace in Manhattan, and by extension in the world at war outside the novel. For it is notable that Miller wrote *Focus* while the Second World War was still raging in Europe and the atrocities of the Holocaust were about to be fully revealed. Miller possessed a boldness in writing a tale about American anti-Semitism when the Holocaust was in its final chapter.

The same way that some critics view *Titus Andronicus* as the ur-text for many of Shakespeare's tragedies, *Focus* also operates as an ur-text in its use of New York City in many Miller works that followed—both drama and fiction. *Focus* not only provides a sweeping panorama of the city as other Miller plays and stories do, but also depicts the city's inherent ethnic, racial, religious, and class divisions. New York was at odds with the melting pot image of American society; in reality, the fire of racial and ethnic hatred was bringing that pot to a boil.

Previous chapters in this book discussed Miller's plays set in Brooklyn and Manhattan, but *Focus* is unique in that much of the significant action occurs in the outer borough of Queens—the only major prose work to do so, except for the short story "I Don't Need You Any More" which takes place in Far Rockaway (see Chapter 4). It is worth noting that the novel has been mistakenly identified as taking place in Brooklyn. For example, Hillary Daninhirsch writes that Newman "lives in Brooklyn with his wheelchair-bound mother" (Daninhirsch 2011: n.p.). The IMDb opening page proclaims: "In late WWII, Brooklyn neighbors wrongly think a couple is Jewish" (*Focus* IMDb: n.p.), and the back cover of the novel's Penguin reissue for the film version states that, "As World War II draws to a close, anti-Semitism is alive and well in Brooklyn" (Miller 2001c.). This is likely due to Miller's strong identification with the borough. In addition, the novel indicates that Newman and his mother once lived in Brooklyn and that she is a frequent reader of *The Brooklyn* Eagle. However, Miller's boldness in confronting for the first time in American literature the issue of anti-Semitism is integral to the Queens neighborhood—Woodside— where he placed Lawrence Newman's home.

Focus had a long germination period. Like many of Miller's plays, the novel came out of his personal experience as a boy and young man, particularly his exposure to anti-Semitism in New York detailed in earlier chapters. Miller's extensive commentary on his upbringing traces his gradual awareness of the complications of being Jewish in New York. In many essays and interviews, he conveyed his alarm at a brewing anti-Semitism in the city in the 1930s and early 1940s during the Second World War—an awareness that instigated his writing of the novel. His exposure to the stereotypical nascent fear of Catholics by many Jews, a fear first instilled in him by his great-grandfather (see "Introduction") became justified by the railings of radical "Radio Priests" such as Father Charles Coughlin and Father Edward Curran—whom Miller characterized in the novel.

In an introduction that Miller wrote in 1984 for the reissue of *Focus*, he recounts how the immediate catalyst to pen the novel occurred during his time working as a shipfitter in the Brooklyn Navy Yard from 1941 to 1943, a place where Miller describes sixty thousand men and a few women from every ethnic group in New York working. (Miller's story, "Shipfitter's Night," based on his experience in the Navy Yard, is discussed in Chapter 4.) He relates how he witnessed a certain level of hostility toward Jews. A not uncommon remark was that the United States had been "maneuvered into this war by powerful Jews who secretly controlled the federal government" (Miller 1984: v). Seeing the volatile mixture of those ethnic groups in the Navy Yard made him wonder that "when peace came, we were to be launched into a raw politics of race and religion and not in the South but in New York"

(Miller 1984: v). His intention in writing the groundbreaking novel was clear: "As far as I knew at the time, anti-Semitism in America was a closed if not forbidden topic for fiction—certainly no novel had taken it as a main theme" (Miller 1984: vi).

In 2001, Miller wrote a piece for the *New York Times*, "Shattering The Silence, Illuminating The Hatred," in which he detailed further the social conditions and personal experiences that caused him to write the novel.

> *Focus* sprang off the streets of New York in the 30s and 40s. With no money for college, I had spent three years driving trucks, pushing carts in the garment district and working as a parts clerk in a warehouse. I knew what I knew, what I had seen and heard, and too often it didn't match what I was reading in the papers and hearing on the radio. Especially the Big Secret—the city was pulsing with hatred. (Miller 2001b: E1)

As with other works, Miller folded his personal experience into real events, for the novel is also rooted in New York's history—many situations occurred or existed in the city during the novel's time span in the summer and fall of 1944 and early winter of 1945: ethnic and religious hatred bubbling in the boroughs, Fascist rallies, political hysteria, a brutal heat wave.

Miller's knowledge of the section of Queens where he sets the novel no doubt came from his time working as a delivery boy in Long Island City for his friend Milton Shapse's father a few months before starting work at the Chadwick-Delamater Auto Warehouse in 1932. He admits that he managed to get lost in Long Island City several times a day (Miller 1987: 213–14). Despite getting lost, Miller gained very specific knowledge about the adjacent Woodside neighborhood where he locates Newman's home. In fact, in the novel, Miller illustrates his familiarity with how both neighborhoods looked in the early 1940s: for example, in one scene, Newman and Gertrude drive through the streets passing old factories, boarded-up homes, and the slate-colored windows of Long Island City, and as they near their Woodside neighborhood, two-family houses appear among open lots and trees.

In *Focus*, Miller accurately maps the geography of Lawrence Newman's Woodside neighborhood: his home address, the locations of subway and elevated train lines, meeting halls, and the area's shops, movie houses, and residences. His clear purpose is to convey the characters' thorough identification with the locale. The residents are trying to create a homogeneous, ethnically pure neighborhood devoid of racial or ethnic types. Ironically, many residents belong to ethnic and religious groups that were formerly at the bottom of the social ladder when they immigrated to New York in the mid-nineteenth century, such as the Irish who were now a power group in New York City and composed a large population of Woodside, or even the Italians, proud of their Mayor La Guardia, groups whose rise came because, Miller points out, as Christians they worshipped the same as the white Anglo-Saxon Protestants who were the earliest power group in America. In the 1930s and 1940s, Jews in New York City were easy targets and Blacks were completely marginalized. As he recalls searching want ads in the *New York Times*—ads that specified "white," "Gentile," "Protestant," or "Cath, firm," Miller intuited those as a warning for Jews to stay away (Miller 1987: 214–15). As Erika Doss explains:

> Anti-Semitism was rampant in the United States both before and during the Second World War . . . Jews were denied full access to higher education, barred from certain jobs, discriminated against in housing and widely disliked. A 1938 Gallup poll found that 50% of Americans held a "low-opinion" of Jews; a 1939 Roper poll reported that 53% believed that "Jews are different and should be restricted"; and a 1946 survey showed that 64% of respondents reported hearing recent "criticism or talk against the Jews". In New York—home to about two million Jews (one third of all Jews in the US)—anti-Semitic violence was "part of everyday life", writes historian Eva-Maria Ziege. Jewish cemeteries and synagogues were regularly defiled with graffiti and swastikas and Jewish school children frequently assaulted by youth gangs. (Doss 2016: 11–12)

Stephen Norwood describes the anti-Semitism that prevailed in New York City during the same period "as Irish Catholic youths terrorized Jews in the streets, beat, stabbed, and even physically mutilated them, and tore the clothes off Jewish girls" (Norwood 2003: 233). Alson J. Smith explained that entire neighborhoods were terrorized by anti-Semitic gangs inspired by the almost entirely Irish and Catholic Christian Front who harassed Jewish storekeepers and stole and damaged their merchandise. They desecrated nearly every synagogue in Washington Heights, inscribing "pornographically hateful descriptions" of Jews on synagogue walls, and hurled Jewish prayer books into toilets. Vandals had desecrated Jewish cemeteries throughout Brooklyn, Queens, and other areas of Long Island, overturning gravestones and painting swastikas on them (Doss 2016: 10).[1]

In *Focus*, Miller portrayed life in an outer borough of New York City as he did in the Brooklyn plays. Whereas the Brooklyn dramas often represent the borough as rural and pastoral or as identifiably ethnic communities, he depicts Woodside, Queens, in the early 1940s as suburban, where residents have moved from the city, that is, Manhattan, to the developing neighborhood where tract housing was being built. Most importantly, people moved to Newman's block, as the neighbor Fred proclaims, to "get away from the element" (Miller 1945: 11), the element clearly meaning "others": Jews, Blacks, and Puerto Ricans.

The Woodside section of Queens had undergone the same rapid development as many other New York City outer borough communities at the beginning of the twentieth century and between the wars. The neighborhood had been created out of farmland that formerly dotted that area of Queens. All types of housing were sprouting in that part of the borough: mostly two-story single-family homes were being built on block after block, as well as multiple-dwelling apartment houses of all sizes, such as the Boulevard Gardens. Architecturally, homes were attached and semi-attached, with garages accessible by slim driveways behind the homes or built under the living area of the homes, level with the street entrance or slightly below grade ("Woodside Queens" 2005). The narrator of *Focus* describes the type of homes on the block:

> A stranger on the block could never have noticed any difference between Mr. Newman's house and the others. They stood in flat-topped line, attached two-story brick, with garages built in beneath the high front porches. Before each house grew a slender elm which was neither thicker no much thinner than its neighbor, all of them planted in the same week seven years ago when the development was finished. (Miller 1945: 4, 5)

No other work in Miller's canon, except *Focus*, places a character's residence on an actual street and address in New York City. For example, although Miller has specifically stated how the Willy Loman house in *Death of a Salesman* was modeled after his own Brooklyn home at 1350 East 3rd Street, the Loman house is given no specific address or neighborhood. *A View from the Bridge* takes place in the Italian American neighborhood of Red Hook, but a correct street for the Carbone House is not conveyed (see Chapter 1); the Gellburgs in *Broken Glass* live in a Jewish neighborhood in Brooklyn, but the street is not identified. Even "The 1928 Buick," a blatantly autobiographical short story set on Miller's East 3rd Street block, does not clearly identify the home address.

There are two sections of the novel from which the reader can deduce the exact location of Newman's home. The novel clearly places Newman's home on 68th Street, a block that a police officer describes as "bad" (Miller 1945: 216) because of the ethnic strife. However, that street number is not apparent until the next-to-last page of the narrative when Newman is in the police station reporting the attack on him and Finkelstein by the Christian Front gang. Newman does not give the cops the actual address of his home, only the 68th street name, but the exact house number is implied from an earlier incident in the novel (Miller 1945: 124) when Newman suspects that Fred is conducting a meeting of the Christian Front at his home. Two men, looking for Fred's house, ask Newman, "Beg your pardon, Which one is 41–39?" "Right next door," Newman said, pointing to Fred's house (Miller 1945: 124), which means that Newman's house is located at 41–35 68th Street according to the layout of streets and addresses in Queens.[2]

A search of the houses that currently exist at the addresses Miller uses in the novel shows homes that match the fictional residences on Newman's block as described in the novel (Figure 3.1). The garage underneath, the porch, the attached homes were typical of the type built in that neighborhood. Although the novel indicates that all the houses on the block were identical, the current houses on that block of 68th Street show mixed construction (Figure 3.2). The narrator's description states that development was completed seven years earlier, which would have been sometime in the mid-1930s. Newman's fictionalized block more likely resembles other streets in the Woodside neighborhood (Figure 3.3), such as 62nd Street in 1940 and today, or as depicted in the film version of the novel (Figure 3.4). Miller's intention is to use the location as a fictional representative, but he obviously was quite familiar with the kind of housing construction in the neighborhood because the similarity to the novel's description is uncanny.

Many descriptions of the block show how the residents of 68th Street attempt to enforce a homogeneous atmosphere on their "little suburban street." In the chapter when Newman exits the subway after quitting his job, he walks up the block, and there are neighbors out on the street engaged in various activities typical of a summer evening: Mrs. Depauw spraying her lawn, Mrs. Bligh sitting on her porch, and the Kennedy boy saying hello. The blend of ethnic names produces a sort of "acceptable" melting pot—except for the excluded groups. Newman has been targeted as an "other" because he looks like a Jew.

Figure 3.1 Home at Newman's address in Woodside, c. 2025. Photo by S. Marino.

He desires to fit in, so he paints his window shutters to look the same as all the others on the block, a very common characteristic of Queens neighborhoods. Newman senses a "presence of animosity" as people view him—judged for his looks in public, in the workplace, on his block, so he desires his house and himself to blend in with the homogeneity and not be one of the "elements."

There is an extensive amount of travel in the novel that emphasizes a geographic sweep that typifies much of Miller's New York work: characters journey by foot, by automobile, and by public transportation such as the subway, trolley, and bus. The travel bolsters the network of prejudice in the novel.

For example, Newman takes long walks through his Woodside neighborhood to and from his 68th Street block in three crucial scenes as he confronts the extreme anti-Semitism that is consuming society: when he attends the Christian Front Rally; when he and Gertrude walk home from the movies; and when he

Figure 3.2 Attached homes in Woodside in 1940 as described in the novel, c. 1940. Courtesy Municipal Archives City of New York.

walks to the police station after he and Finkelstein fend off the attack from the Christian Front. Miller integrated the exact streetscape of the neighborhood into these literary walks, including fictionalized versions of actual structures that existed at the time. In the growth of the neighborhood, Woodside did not develop an exactly neat geometric numerical street grid; rather, roads that had originated during colonial times and during the nineteenth and early twentieth centuries remained, some retaining their original names. Moreover, the city's construction of highways and boulevards, elevated train/subway

Figure 3.3 Same attached homes in Woodside today, c. 2025. Courtesy Municipal Archives City of New York. Photo by S. Marino

Figure 3.4 Still from the film version of *Focus*. Directed by Neil Slavin. Produced by Neal Slavin, Robert A. Miller, Mike Bloomberg; Production Companies: Enfoque Producciones, Carros Pictures, 2001. Filmed in Toronto, photos shows attached houses as depicted in the movie © Paramount Pictures, 2001. All rights reserved.

Figure 3.5 Miller may have modeled the Woodside National Bank as the location for the hate rally, c. 2025. Photo by S. Marino.

lines, and railroads created an irregular and confusing street pattern to many except for non-residents.

If we map out Newman's three walks as described in the novel, you can see just how accurately Miller portrayed the cityscape. Newman travels to the Christian Front Rally on foot from his 68th Street home across vacant lots not yet built on. The rally takes place in a hall with a "heavily columned facade" which had once been a bank (Miller 1944: 153–4) located at the end of a block, perhaps Broadway, a main neighborhood commercial thoroughfare. We can deduce this because on his journey home he crosses under the Roosevelt Avenue El, a few blocks from his residence on 68th Street, and he notes that he had walked halfway home. If Newman is halfway home at Roosevelt Avenue, this implies that the rally occurred on Broadway where a large building such as a bank may have been located (Figure 3.5). In fact, a similar structure still exists two blocks from Newman's address and could be the model. As Newman staggers home after being assaulted at the rally, he walks alone through a vacant lot, then two blocks with Finkelstein, who has followed him from the rally, before getting to their block where he notes "the location of the El in relation to his corner" (Miller 1945: 170).

The penultimate scene in the novel is the attack on Newman and Finklestein after Gertrude and Newman walk home from seeing a movie at a neighborhood

Figure 3.6 The Fisk Theatre, c. 1940. Courtesy Municipal Archives City of New York.

theater. This exciting scene builds great suspense as they quicken their pace through the Woodside streets while being followed by men of the Christian Front. Exactly what route they took from the movie theater is unclear because the text is ambiguous about the exact movie theater they attended. Newman plans to go to The Beverley, but that movie theater did not exist in Woodside; it was actually located on Church Avenue in Brooklyn, something Miller knew from his youth and which he referenced in the late-career play *Broken Glass* in 1994 (see Chapter 2).

In the 1940s, three movie houses were located several blocks apart from Newman's home on 68th Street: the Fisk at 68–02 Woodside Avenue at 69th Street (Formerly Fisk Avenue), the Deluxe at 62–02 Roosevelt Avenue, and the Woodside at 58–02 Roosevelt Avenue which was later transformed into St. Sebastian's Roman Catholic Church (Figures 3.6, 3.7, 3.8, and 3.9). The novel indicates that two of the movie houses were located several blocks apart on a business street that certainly matches the locations of the Deluxe and the Woodside that were only four blocks from each other on Roosevelt Avenue, then as now a major commercial street. Considering the location of these theaters in relation to Newman's home on 68th Street, one can conjecture about the various routes he and Gertrude may have walked home which the novel details as having taken six blocks. This section of the novel is slim on

Figure 3.7 Part of the Fisk Theatre structure survives as a tire shop, c. 2025. Photo by S. Marino.

noting specific landmarks on their rushed walk home, except that they pass a "tree-lined parkway," (Miller 1945: 197) but it is unclear what roadway Miller refers to as a parkway. Queens Blvd seems possible because of the number of blocks that the novel enumerates, but none of the movie houses would require a walk on Queens Blvd. The parkway could be Fisk Avenue, now 69th Street, which is a relatively wider street and a main thoroughfare that did contain a fair number of trees in those days.

The previous discussion of *Broken Glass* (Chapter 1) speculated about the movies that Sylvia and Phillip discuss seeing; they specifically name actors and theaters, so it is relatively easy to see Miller's accuracy about the film that Sylvia and Phillip saw in 1938. *Focus* provides fewer clues about the movie that Gertrude and Newman see. Gertrude merely describes an actor as the "new boy," but it is not at all clear that the movie they actually see features this actor. However, the narrative provides a scene-by-scene harrowing description of a half-finished movie that Newman and Gertrude walk in on. The film depicts atrocities occurring in Europe in the Second World War: a poor Russian or Polish town, people hiding in an apartment with a priest, an old bearded rabbi leading the group in prayer. The film climaxes with the people brought to the

Figure 3.8 The Loew's Woodside Theatre, c. 1940. Courtesy Municipal Archives City of New York.

town square to be executed on the gallows by the Germans. The rabbi and the priest exhort the soldiers not to murder the Jews.

The movie is so intimately tied to the novel's subject matter that it is intriguing to consider if Miller was referring to an actual contemporary film. In 1944, scores of war movies were released, many being action films. A few films did focus on the Holocaust, the most notable being *The Seventh Cross* about seven inmates, one Jewish, who escape from a concentration camp and

Figure 3.9 Today, the Woodside Theatre functions as St. Sebastian Roman Catholic Church, c. 2025. Photo by S. Marino

Majdanek: Cemetery of Europe, one of the first films to use actual footage of concentration camps (Reimer and Reimer 2012: n.p.). Surprisingly, in 1944 a few films addressed war trials, anticipating what would occur when the conflict ended. *None Shall Escape* portrays a Nuremberg-like trial in which a Nazi is brought to account for his crimes. The movie contains situations that are remarkably similar to the film that shocks Gertrude and Newman. Of note are a priest and a rabbi as characters, their resistance to the Nazis, and the brutality of the Germans. The movie also concludes with a scene in the town square where Jews are rounded up not on the gallows, but in railroad cars. In the movie that Newman and Gertrude view, the rabbi starts to make a speech, but is killed, after which the priest jumps on the gallows and delivers an impassioned speech against the Nazis. In *None Shall Escape*, the rabbi delivers a fervent diatribe and is killed, after which the Nazis slaughter the Jews. It is interesting to speculate if Miller saw this film and used elements of it in *Focus*. Newspaper listings for May 1944 indicate the film was indeed playing at theaters close to Miller's Brooklyn Heights apartment on Joralemon Street near Borough Hall and Downtown, including the Century's Tivoli on Fulton Street, the Duffield at Duffield/Fulton Streets, and the St. George Playhouse on Pineapple Street ("Feature Films . . . " 1944: 17).

The longest walk that Newman takes is the final scene in the novel. After the attack on him and Finkelstein, Newman walks to a police station to report the assault. The narrative describes him as walking along a "parkway" the distance of two subway stops. At the time of the novel, there was a police station located within reasonable distance from Newman's home: the 110th Precinct at 94–41 43 Avenue. It is likely that Newman walked to that precinct, which is approximately two stations along the Roosevelt Avenue El.

In *Focus*, Miller exhibits extreme familiarity with the entire transportation system that the lifelong New Yorker gained from his experiences in the city; characters ride the subways, the elevated lines, and trolleys (which at that time had not been replaced by the bus system). For example, in Chapter 2, Newman waits on the "front end" of the station platform which reveals Miller's keen knowledge of riding the subway because, as Newman, and any New Yorker knows, "the first car was always the emptiest" (Miller 1945: 6). In a striking chapter devoted exclusively to him, Finklestein takes the subway to Sheepshead Bay in Brooklyn (Miller 1945: 139) then travels on the subway and a trolley line to visit his father's burial place located in "populous graveyards at the northern edge of Brooklyn" (Miller 1945: 140). Many of Miller's family relatives are buried in the Jewish cemeteries in those areas, and by the time Miller was writing *Focus*, his great-grandfather and grandfather had passed and were buried in Union Field Cemetery and Mount Judah Cemetery. Thus, Finklestein rides on a trolley through Bushwick, transferring to where the trolley line converges with a subway or elevated train, likely the Jamaica el. The narrator mentions Finklestein shopping at a toy firm in Bushwick, which may very well be the Bargain Town store with its distinct red and white stripes, formerly located on what is now Malcolm X Blvd and Broadway near the Kosciusko Avenue station on the elevated Jamaica line. These are routes that Miller likely took. In fact, *Death of a Salesman* reveals Miller's familiarity with that exact neighborhood when Hap recalls Biff taking him to have sex for the first time with that "big Betsy thing on Bushwick Avenue" (Miller 1949: 11).

The novel details Newman's extensive travel on New York's subway system, which foreshadowed Miller's consistent use in his later dramatic canon, as previous chapters discussed. Newman's home on 68th Street is within walking distance of two train lines, the elevated Roosevelt Avenue line and the IND Queens Blvd line. Newman refers to both in many events in the novel. For his usual trip to work in Manhattan, Newman walks down his street to the corner where Finkelstein's candy store is located and where the entrance "down" to the subway is apparently located. Miller has taken some liberty with the exact locations of the subway and El, but the convergence of the two lines is close to Newman's block. The Roosevelt Avenue El is two blocks away from the actual street address, but Newman thinks about the "location of the el in relation to his corner" (170).

Miller vividly illustrates how the subway system operates like a network of prejudice. As Newman waits for the train, he reads the graffiti written on the steel pillars, the columns holding up the subway stations. It is telling that Miller writes, "With an acute squint he screwed the pupils of his eyes into focus" (Miller 1945: 6). Note how this word—"focus"—the novel's title, foreshadows the literal and figurative use of vision in the novel. Newman notices graffiti scrawled on the pillar with an anti-Semitic remark: "*Kikes started WAR.*" Below it, "*Kill kikes killki*," and "*Fascists!*" (Miller 1945: 7). Newman is terribly affected by the sight:

> Nothing he ever read gripped him so powerfully as did these scrawled threats. To him they were a kind of mute record that the city automatically inscribed in her sleep; a secret newspaper publishing what the people really thought, undiluted by fears of propriety and selfish interest. It was like finding the elusive eyes of the city and staring into her true mind. (Miller 1945: 7)

This implies that beneath the facade of the city—in the very transportation network that unites it—exists a seething hatred that Miller referred to in his *Vanity Fair* essay, a seething hatred which can travel throughout the city. Miller's biographer, Christopher Bigsby, explains that the "city itself is the source of paranoia as people have to endure the forced propinquity of the subway, pressing flesh against alien flesh, and crowds are charged with the potential to transform into mobs" (2005b: 67). Bigsby describes how Newman "shuttles to and fro through the flying underbelly of New York reading there subterranean truths which belie the apparent moral stability of the world above his head" (2005b: 67).

Miller here accurately portrays the type of graffiti that dotted the subway system during these times. James Agee observed in a 1939 essay, "All over the city on streets and walks and walls the children, and the other true primitives of the race, have established ancient, essential, and ephemeral forms of art,

Figure 3.10 Bernard Perlin's *Orthodox Boys*, 1948 © Bernard Perlin. Courtesy of the Estate of Bernard Perlin and Tate Images.

have set forth in chalk and crayon the names and images of their pride, love, preying, scorn, desire." (Agee 1972: 189) But Erika Doss clarifies that graffiti actually "was mainly made by street kids and youth gangs to mark their turf, or to markup sacred Jewish spaces" (Doss 2016). The artist Bernard Perlin depicted such action in the subways in his 1948 painting *Orthodox Boys* 1948 (Tate N05956; Figure 3.10), As Erika Doss explains: "Perlin personally experienced anti-Semitism, noting in his diaries a particularly disturbing encounter on a New York subway in 1936 in which two older women called him a 'dirty Jew kike' and insulted him with homophobic slurs" (Doss 2016: 10). Newman himself is subject to an anti-Semitic remark—"You people"—on the subway (Miller 1945: 72).

There is great irony in Newman's revulsion at the anti-Semitic sayings because he himself possesses an inherent anti-Semitism. When the train for Manhattan approaches the station, Newman notices two women smelling of cherry soap, which to him washes away the dirtiness of the graffiti. Newman brushes against one of the women and the cherry smell gets stronger, and he is comforted because, "He likes to travel with people who were well kept"

(Miller 1945: 8). However, the subway is not a place of pristine homogeneity. Rather, the subway is a heterogeneous place where all classes of society mix, and Newman observes his fellow passengers, observations that reveal his own prejudices: a Ukrainian-Polish worker whom Newman judges as "soiled and stupid," a Negro upon whom he ruminates on exploring the various types of "niggers," and a man who Newman guesses by the "Hindenburg bags" (Miller 1945: 8) under his eyes must be a Jew. Newman plays a mind game of recognizing a Jew, a recognition that is unwittingly turned on him on his street and in his workplace.

On the subway, Newman also encounters his next-door neighbor, Fred, the man who is the locus of racial and ethnic hatred in the novel. Fred discusses moving the "element" out of the neighborhood: His fear is that "They'll be moving niggers in on us next" (Miller 1945: 11). Fred desires to preserve the neighborhood: "Only reason most of the block moved way out here to get away from that element, and now they're trailin' us out here" (Miller 1945: 11). When Fred addresses his concern that Finklestein is moving his relative into a house on a corner, Newman conveys his fascination with Fred for saying "things you felt and dared not say." Yet, Newman feels a sense of foreboding around Fred: "It was the same feeling he got around the pillars—something was building up inside the city, something thunderous and exhilarating" (Miller 1945: 11). Fred invites Newman to a meeting to help clean out the neighborhood, especially the Jews on the block, and "then we'll help the boys across the avenue with the Spics" (Miller 1945: 12). This important scene reveals all the seething prejudices in the city as typified by Fred. The fact that this takes place in the subway car moving throughout the city shows how the bias is spreading, still underground, not yet surfacing. As Newman exits onto the sunny sidewalk, he tries to think of his block and the identical houses all in a row like pickets on a fence. "The memory of their sameness soothed his yearning for order" (Miller 1945: 13). But he longs for a sameness which does not exist; for on that block lives Fred, whose hatred actively surfaces later in the novel.

In chapter 8, Miller again uses the subway to indicate the seething network of prejudice in New York, including Newman's. He is riding to Manhattan on the Eighth Avenue subway line and focuses on the pillars of the subway, the same ones with the scrawled anti-Semitic phrases. In this scene, Newman has little fear and anxiety because at this point in the novel he believes he is no longer a target of the anti-Semitic attacks on his block, so he feels a "new comradeship" (Miller 1945: 57) with his neighbors. This newfound feeling is reinforced when Newman sees more graffiti, "Jew," scrawled on an ad in the subway car. Significantly, "The tinge of embarrassment that would have disturbed him once did not occur this morning" (Miller 1945: 58). He sees a few "brethren" standing beneath the advertisement, and Newman feels a sense of power. Moreover, he plays the game of trying to recognize a Jew, and as he does, he "raised his eyebrows with the pleasing awareness of the man's stupidity—a man who could sit so leisurely and calm while his very doom was written on the wall above his head" (Miller 1945: 59).

Even though the main setting of the novel is in Queens, crucial events occur in locations in Manhattan. Miller certainly depicts the borough as the economic center of the city where the characters are employed in corporations that Miller modeled after actual businesses. Most importantly, the workplaces enforce the anti-Semitism that is at the heart of the action.

At the beginning of the novel, Newman works for a corporation for which he carries out its policy not to hire Jews, a practice which existed widely in New York, as Miller himself experienced in his job search. The corporation for which Newman works is likely a midtown Manhattan location. Based on the evidence in the novel, Newman had a one-train subway ride to the city on either of the subway lines close to his home. From the subway exit, he walks one block to the building, which he enters "passing through the Gothic entrance of the Corporation's skyscraper" (Miller 1945: 13). Many buildings in 1940s New York fit such a description, such as the New York Life Insurance Building on Park Avenue or the Metropolitan Life Building on Park Avenue. The novel describes it as a large multinational corporation, emphasizing the "mammoth size of the company" (Miller 1945: 13.). By implication, the company's ethnic and racial policies would be enforced around the globe. Moreover, Newman's boss, who looks out at the river (whether it is the East or Hudson is unclear) from his office, is appropriately named Gargan, that suggests "gargantuan." His massiveness is enforced when he orders Newman to switch jobs on the order of a superior VP because he is too Jewish-looking. The boss is standing "at his full height, which is much higher than Mr. Newman's" (Miller 1945: 38). Mr. Gargan, indeed, is "gargantuan" in this scene because of the power of the anti-Semitic corporation overshadowing Newman.

After he quits his job, Newman interviews for a position at the office of the Akron Corporation which is located downtown near Wall Street. He has taken the Eighth Avenue subway line all the way down to lower Manhattan, an appropriate location for this crucial scene. The interviewer judges that Newman is a Jew when he hears his last name and denies him employment. After his job rejection, Miller constructs for Newman an exact walk through the Manhattan financial center (Miller 1945: 65). Newman travels west toward the "Bay," that is, New York Bay or harbor, to catch the Eighth Avenue subway back to Queens. The narrator emphasizes the desertion of the Wall Street area at that time of day, indicating that business hours have passed. (At the time of the novel, the financial district did not contain many residences as it does today and very much resembled a ghost town, compared to the hubbub during business hours.) On his way to the subway, the despondent Newman stops at New York's famous Trinity Church (Figure 3.11), located on the intersection of Wall Street and Broadway. He sits on the high stone curb around an iron lawn railing with a lamp post, pondering his predicament. Newman's reflection on being taken for a Jew takes place as he looks toward the adjacent ancient graveyard (Figure 3.12), which is one of the most important surviving colonial burial places in Manhattan, distinguished as the resting place of Alexander Hamilton: "The tombstones now swept him with their cold meaning" (Miller 1945: 67), the significance, of course, being the symbolic death of Newman's former self. His new awareness of anti-Semitism is born, and he walks toward the subway two blocks away.

Despite the pervasive discrimination against Jews in the workplace, there were establishments that maintained open hiring practices. Miller illustrates one such business in the novel when he interviews for a job at Meyers-Peterson, whose headquarters he specifically locates on the tenth floor of a building on 29th Street in Manhattan, which is quite close to the factory where Isidore Miller's Miltex Corporation was located in the 1920s. The main plant was in Paterson, New Jersey, and likely modeled on one of the many plants that Miller knew made fans and electrical equipment in peacetime in that city. At his arrival, Newman perceives that the receptionist is a "Jewess," which comforts him. Coincidentally, he is interviewed by Gertrude Hart, his future wife, whom he recognizes as the woman he rejected for employment at his previous firm because he suspected that she was Jewish. She too recognizes

Figure 3.11 Trinity Church, c. 1940. Courtesy Municipal Archives City of New York.

him, and she says "You thought I was a Jew." "You don't need your experience for this place. They hire anybody in this place. All they do is ask if you're a citizen. Jews, niggers, wops, anybody" (Miller 1945: 82).

New York's famous Central Park is a significant location at a crucial point in the novel, and the scene illustrates the exactness with which Miller constructs the streetscape of Manhattan and mentions famous New York locations. Gertrude and Lawrence walk from the Meyers-Peterson office on 29th Street. up Fifth Avenue to Central Park on 59th Street, to the Plaza Hotel, and face the hotels on Central Park South. The narrator notes how the couple went to a show at Radio City Music Hall two nights before (Figure 3.13). When Newman

Figure 3.12 Trinity Church graveyard. Maciej Bledowski/Alamy Stock Photo.

asks Gertrude if she wants to go to a nightclub, she asks if he has ever been to a nightclub, and he conveys that he has been to one in Queens, and she asks in surprise, "a Queens night club?" (Miller 1945: 90) showing the inferiority of nightlife in an outer borough, a similar attitude that Miller illustrated in *A View from the Bridge*, *Broken Glass*, and *The Price* (see Chapters 1 and 2). The couple takes a stroll into the park (an action he would use again in *Homely Girl* in 1992), entering exactly at Fifth Avenue and 60th Street across from the Plaza Hotel, and ambling towards the lake near the famous Wollman skating rink (Figure 3.14). The highlight of this chapter is Newman and Gertrude helping a distraught woman whose friend had gone off with a sailor. The park is filled with couples having random sex, which contrasts with the romanticism of Gertrude and Lawrence falling in love. This important scene takes place in the natural setting of the park that contrasts with the city: "Staring up through the leaves of the tree he could see the faint glow of light that the city surrounding the park threw up against the sky" (Miller 1945: 98).

Miller's canon is distinguished by taking actual events and situations that he experienced and transposing them with fictional precision in his work, as he did in *A View from the Bridge*, *Broken Glass*, and *After the Fall* (see previous chapters). One striking example in *Focus* shows how anti-Semitism was enforced in a location outside New York City.

Figure 3.13 Radio City Music Hall, c. 1985. Courtesy of the New York City Landmarks Preservation Commission.

In Chapter 13, Newman and his new bride Gertrude are driving outside the city for a weekend getaway. During their conversation in the car, she reveals that she was born in Staten Island; she had concocted the story of being from Rochester in order not to be mistaken for a New York Jewess, a common

Figure 3.14 Entrance to Central Park facing the Plaza Hotel, c. 1969. Courtesy of the New York City Landmarks Preservation Commission.

practice. They intend to stay at the Riverview Hotel somewhere up the Hudson Valley. Miller based this scene on an actual incident he had which he reported in *Vanity Fair* in 2001. Miller went for a drive in the country on a Sunday afternoon with a friend and his girlfriend. In New Jersey, they saw a small sign at the driveway entrance to a country hotel that read: "Restricted clientele, Christian." Miller recalls that the notion of "being forbidden to so much as enter the place somehow exploded something in my brain. It was like being shot at. The hatred in that little sign was indigestible" (Miller 2001a).

This is exactly what Miller re-created in *Focus*. Gertrude and Lawrence are denied a room at the Riverview Hotel, an inn where Newman had stayed five years earlier, but which now is "Full up," something which Lawrence and Gertrude know is untrue. They are denied entrance for looking Jewish. When they leave the premises, Newman notices a sign "Restricted Clientele" which he had not previously noticed. Jonathan D. Sarna has revealed how some hotels even explicitly advertised policies of "No Hebrews" (Sarna 2004: 219). As they search for another hotel in the car, Gertrude confronts him with a huge question: "Why do always let them make a Jew out of you?"(Miller 1945: 117) another needling on Newman's journey to identification with Finklestein at the novel's conclusion.

Despite the importance of these settings, Woodside, Queens remains the locus of prejudice where the most harrowing scene in the novel occurs: Newman's attendance at the hate rally. Gertrude's judgment about the anti-Semitism that consumes New York is a preamble to this crucial scene. She proclaims: "I never saw such Jew hate as there is here. New York is crawling with it. It's everyplace you go. You know that. I don't have to tell you that" (Miller 1945: 131). The hate rally scene is particularly important as it concludes with Finklestein's provocative questioning of Newman about his anti-Semitism, which becomes a catalyst for his identification as a Jew and his subsequent defense of Finklestein.

The hate rally chapter vividly illustrates how Miller wove historical events into the narrative. The novel frequently emphasizes summer heat over its two-year time span and accurately recreates a heat wave that engulfed New York City in 1944. Newman's mother asks if it was hot in the city, remarking: "Somebody said people were dropping dead on the streets" (Miller 1945:, 41). After supper, his neighbor asks: "Hot enough for you today?" (Miller 1945: 41). As the neighbors are out after dinner watering their lawns, Newman is warned: "You better water the grass. . . . It's burn up sure" (Miller 1945: 42)

As a native New Yorker, Miller experienced the unique ways that citizens coped with brutal summer heat waves. His 1998 New Yorker essay, "Before Air Conditioning," offers vivid recollections of the hot summers of 1927 and 1928—the last years Miller lived in Harlem—of people sleeping on mattresses on their fire escapes, hordes sleeping on the grass in Central Park. During the heat waves of the Depression, people cooled off by riding the open trolleys on Broadway or on the elevated trains on Second, Third, Sixth, and Ninth

Avenues. He describes the sweat and smell of the workers in his father's suit and coat factory. He is amused at how the heat "moved otherwise sensible people to repeat endlessly the brainless greeting, 'Hot enough for ya? Ha-ha!'" (Miller 1998: n.p.).

Miller lived through New York's historic 1944 heat wave which garnered significant media coverage. News reports detailed record high temperatures and their impact on the metropolitan area. In the long opening paragraph of chapter 16, Miller vividly details how New Yorkers coped as the heat spread throughout specific geographic places of the city where it had not rained for almost forty days: the sweltering days and choking humidity; people spilling out onto the streets and stoops of the city; crowded ice cream parlors, saloons, and beaches; citizens sleeping in Central Park, on tar roofs, and in the fire escapes of tenements. He catalogues terrible accidents caused by the heat: overworked refrigerators exploding; boys trying to get a cool breeze sticking their heads out of the windows of the Culver Line, decapitated by a stanchion; pregnant women delivering their babies early in buses; in the cafeterias the smell of souring milk. People and animals were reduced to heat hysteria: a man on Sixth Avenue was so aggravated by the heat that he took a shotgun and fired twice into the crowd; in the Bronx, dogs running loose, infected with rabies. In Brooklyn, there was an invasion of stinging flies; Queens was inundated with swarms of more mosquitoes (151–2). Amazingly, many events that Miller describes can be documented by actual newspaper reports, as the 1988 retrospective in the *New York Times* headline proclaimed: "August '44: A Month too Hot for Satan."

Miller purposely uses the literal heat wave to parallel the hot waves of hatred that consume the Christian Front Rally depicted in the novel. The hate rally that Miller vividly creates has a historical basis in the anti-Semitism that gripped New York in the 1930s and 1940s, for he was exposed to similar rallies that occurred in the boroughs.

The Catholic "Radio Priest" Father Charles E. Coughlin, in addition to his famous national broadcasts, also spoke at hate rallies throughout the country where he railed against the democracy of the US government, the policies of Franklin Delano Roosevelt, capitalism, communism, and Jews. He organized the National Union for Social Justice that in 1938 became the famous Christian Front. New York was the locus of the Christian Front's anti-Semitic attacks

Figure 3.15 Nazi rally at Madison Square Garden, c. 1939. Everett Collection/Alamy Stock Photo.

on Jews led largely by the city's Irish Americans. Coughlin spoke at rallies in New York, most notably at Madison Square Garden in 1935 and in Brooklyn in 1936 (Figure 3.15). The Christian Front received widespread publicity for participating in the Nazi rally sponsored by the German American Bund held in Madison Square Garden on February 20, 1939 that was a high point of their activity. The artist Bernard Perlin lived in Brooklyn in the late 1930s and was so affected by Coughlin's huge appeal that he created a 1938 lithograph, *Father Coughlin Speaking*, depicting the "demagogic 'Radio Priest' gesticulating in front of an admiring and sinister crowd" (Doss 2016: 5).

The Roman Catholic Diocese of Brooklyn led by Archbishop Thomas Molloy and its official publication *The Tablet* were seen as tacit supporters of this anti-Semitism. Miller obviously was aware of *The Tablet*'s editorial slant because when he and Gertrude leave the movie theater, a man is on the street corner hawking the paper. Notably, a priest of the diocese, Rev. Edward Curran, editor of *The Tablet*, delivered his own radio broadcasts and spoke at rallies, becoming known as the "Father Coughlin of the East." In Boston, infamous as the center of Christian Front violence against Jews, Curran spoke at South

Boston's Evacuation Day exercises in 1942, at South Boston High School in 1943, and in 1944 at Hibernian Hall, located in the Irish American section of Roxbury (Norwood 2003: 236). Curran (who later became the pastor of St. Sebastian in Woodside, a church within walking distance of Newman's fictional house, and the site of the former Woodside movie theater) may be the model for the "Boston priest" who speaks at the rally in the hall in *Focus*. As Miller portrayed his diatribe, he is likely an amalgam of Father Coughlin, Father Curran, and Joe McWilliams,[3] head of the Christian Mobilizers, who "often worked himself into a frenzy during his harangues, tearing off his collar and tie as he shouted anti-Semitic and anti-Roosevelt epithets" (Norwood 2003: 236).

At the rally, Miller parallels the extreme heat of the summer night with the crowd's fever pitch. Newman is overcome physically and emotionally as "the terrible heat of the people was beginning to fold upon him like wool" (Miller 1945: 155). The priest whips the crowd into a frenzy with his Jew hatred. The intensity of the rally turns on Newman when he is accused of being a Jew because he does not join in the hand clapping and the rabid screaming and yelling of the mob, and he consequently is pummeled by the crowd. In a crucial image, Newman realizes his glasses—the very item that makes his literal and figurative vision clear—were bent and broken.

Finkelstein observes the rally from outside and witnesses Newman's expulsion from the hall, following him home. This is an important scene for beginning the rapprochement between him and Newman, who "found he was more at ease with this Jew, for he was not imposing at all" (Miller 1945: 166). Finkelstein's telling remark to Newman, delivered out on their street that is the ground zero of hate, "In other words, when you look at me you don't see me" (168), forces Newman to reject his anti-Semitism and come to a new vision:

> A spasm of distress began to take hold of Mr. Newman's stomach. It was as though all the tokens of the known world had been switched, as though in a dream his own house numbers had been changed, the name of his street, the location of the El in relation to his corner, as though all the things that had been true were all catastrophically untrue. (Miller 1945: 170)

This crucial moment of revelation for Newman occurs in the geographic center of his existence: 68th Street. He has attempted to forge an identity with his place, and everything has been uprooted.

Miller concludes the novel with a powerful image of 1940s New York: the outside of a police station where Newman sees "the green lamps beside the doorway" (Miller 1945: 215) as he enters to report the attack on him and Finklestein. Emboldened by the "cleansing fury" (Miller 1945: 217) that the attack has given him, Newman is lifted of the weight he had been carrying: he starts to tell his story to the police officer.

4

Short Stories

The Presence of New York

One of the last short stories that Miller wrote and published is titled "Presence" (2003), a striking story whose plot involves an older man walking toward the beach in the early morning and happening upon a young couple copulating in the reedy brush. The man's observance of the couple and his encounter speaking to and swimming with the woman as the younger man lies asleep in the sand—spent after their sexual activity—leads to the older man's awareness of a "presence" the woman proclaims that he possesses. Miller also named his final collection of short stories, *Presence*, an apt title for the aging writer who perhaps wondered about the presence of his literary legacy after he passed.

Presence is also an appropriate way to consider the significance of New York settings when Miller's stories are taken as whole, for it is astonishing how the city's presence dominates most of the short fiction in his canon. Even in tales in which New York settings are not central, the city serves as a starting location in the narratives. For example, "The Performance" (2002) and "The Turpentine Still" (2004) have settings outside of the United States—in Nazi Germany and Haiti respectively—but the characters both begin their adventures in the city. Similarly, in "A Glimpse at a Jockey," a short narrative vignette, the aged rich jockey relates his past exploits in various geographic regions such as Argentina, Mexico, and Duluth, Michigan, where he reconnects with his long-lost father—all the while sitting in a saloon in New York.[1]

Much of Miller's short fiction is not only rooted in New York but also contains autobiographical aspects—to a lesser or greater degree. His stories can be divided into those tales in which he uses New York settings as part of (mostly) fictional events that are less autobiographical and others where the New York settings are a greater part of thinly disguised autobiographical events. Approached this way, stories such as "Bulldog" (2001), "The Bare Manuscript" (2002), "Fitter's Night" (1967), and "A Search for a Future" (1966) are the former; "Ditchy" (1944), "I Don't Need You Anymore" (1967), "The 1928 Buick" (1978), "In Memoriam" (1995), and "Fame" (1978) are the latter. Nevertheless, every story illustrates Miller's thorough familiarity with the cityscape, particularly its neighborhoods.

Miller was wary of biographical readings of his work. Christopher Bigsby comments that Miller resented "those who seek to decode his work purely in terms of autobiography, as if it were no more than elaborate subterfuge, a cover for confession. What matters, he insists, is the work. Some of his stories do find their inspiration in his own life. Their achievement, he insists, lies elsewhere, in characters raised to exemplary status, in stories that work by indirection" (Bigsby 2005a: 453). From this perspective, we can see how many autobiographical stories contain male protagonists who are of an age when a significant moment of crisis occurs: In "I Don't Need You Anymore," the five-year-old protagonist is in a psychological struggle in rejecting his pregnant mother, identifying with the strong figure of his father, and leaving childhood for the alluring world of men. "Bulldog" depicts a thirteen-year-old's emotional and physical confusion over his boyhood desire for a puppy and his adolescent lust awakened by his sexual initiation. "Presence" illustrates a man's recognition of how passion ebbs in middle age. "Fame" dramatizes a renowned artist's awareness of the limits of his reputation. "A Search for a Future" presents the two life crises of an actor who struggles with his artistic and political commitments while confronted with the imminent death of his institutionalized father.

"Bulldog" is a late-career piece (2001) published in the *New Yorker*, and the story is a striking illustration of how Miller blended autobiographical elements with an outright fictional event set in Brooklyn. The plot centers on a thirteen-year-old boy, seemingly modeled on Miller, who lives in Midwood, Brooklyn, with a family that strongly resembles Augusta, Isidore, and Kermit. The boy reads an ad in the paper about puppies, allegedly bulldogs, for sale, and he travels to an apartment in Brooklyn Heights to obtain one. At the apartment, the woman offers him much more than a puppy, and the boy has his first sexual encounter with her, an event that leaves him both confused and desirous of more. The second part of the tale relates the boy's—and the family's—failure at caring for the puppy that culminates in the animal eating an entire chocolate cake prepared by the mother, both left unattended by the boy who was distracted by his desire to go outside, tend his garden, and search the basement for a lost baseball. The puppy falls ill, and the family calls the ASPCA (American Society for the Prevention of Cruelty to Animals) for it to be taken away. The boy is both haunted and aroused by the memory of the sex, which he views as a precious secret he can keep from his family. The story concludes with him playing in unrestrained abandon on his admiring mother's piano.

The temptation to read this story of lost virginity as autobiographical is quite strong. However, this event may be pure fiction. In *Timebends*, Miller related that he had his first sexual experience at sixteen when his brother Kermit and friends took him to an apartment on the Upper West Side of Manhattan. Miller describes a "sensation of vacancy and remoteness" (Miller 1987: 161) about the encounter, feelings that are quite different from the boy's confusion about his awakened desire in "Bulldog." However, the family depicted in the tale—the mother, father, and older brother—is clearly Miller's, with the notable absence of the younger sister Joan; moreover, the family dynamics are remarkably like Miller's characterization of them in the Michigan plays, *After the Fall*, and *The American Clock*. For example, the story opens with the father taking a nap and his mother playing bridge. Gussie's piano playing and Miller's ineptness at it are central to the climax; the older brother is described as the sibling who "always knew what was right or wrong" (Miller 2001, 2016: 259), certainly an accurate depiction of Kermit in much of Miller's work.

Miller draws the Brooklyn settings out of his own experiences in an intriguing way. The family not only lives in his same Midwood neighborhood, but he clearly sets the story on the block of his East 3rd Street home, if not the same exact house—although he does not specifically identify it—and folds direct biographical experiences into the tale—all in one remarkable paragraph that describes the two-story house with its cellar, the back porch that Miller had built, and the pear tree and apple tree that he planted in the backyard.

He also describes the backyard of the house ending at a fence where Erasmus Field is located (Figure 4.1). The famous Erasmus Field has a storied history in Brooklyn as the site of the Erasmus High School football and baseball home games as well as professional games. The field, located on Gravesend Avenue and Avenue M, can be seen and heard from the backyard of the Miller home

Figure 4.1 Sid Luckman formerly Erasmus Field, c. 2023. Photo by Katie Murray.

on East 3rd Street, and the young Arthur undoubtedly watched many contests there, which the story details (Miller 2001, 2016: 263). The area looks much the same as when the story takes place, presumably in 1928 or 1929, when the Millers moved to the block; the field as it exists today is now known as Sid Luckman Field.[2] "The 1928 Buick" also takes place on this block with the final focus being on the cemetery that is located on the dead-end street next to Sid Luckman Field and Erasmus Field.

In a striking twist, Miller locates the apartment house where he obtains the puppy on the same Schermerhorn Street (Figure 4.2) in Brooklyn Heights where he lived from 1941–4 (See Introduction), although the story presumably takes place when Miller himself was thirteen. He also offers exact descriptions of the difference in housing from his Midwood haunts. The houses were made of brownstone, not like the clapboard ones on his block. The boy intuited that Jews did not live in the quiet neighborhood. No one sat outside in the sunshine, but many windows were open "with expressionless people leaning on their elbows and staring out . . . many of the women in their bras and the men in underwear trying to catch a breeze" (Miller 2001, 2016: 258–9).) This description accurately depicts how Brooklyn Heights looked in the late 1920s

Figure 4.2 18 Schermerhorn Street, c. 1940. Courtesy Municipal Archives City of New York.

and 1930s. In a 2004 interview with Christopher Bigsby, Miller describes the neighborhood in the 1930s and 1940s as being one of the cheapest in New York and having boarded-up windows, something quite different from the luxury of the historic district and million-dollar brownstones that typify the neighborhood today (Miller 2006: 65).

The boy travels on the subway to get from Midwood to Brooklyn Heights, and Miller details his exact trip, similar to how he describes traveling to the Chadick-Delamater Auto Warehouse in *Timebends* and how Catherine commutes to the plumbing shop in *A View from the Bridge*. The woman from whom he is buying the puppy explains the travel directions, and the precise route is detailed, including that the boy take the Culver Line, the elevated train directly behind Miller's East 3rd Street home, and that he must change subway lines at the Church Avenue station, a requirement even in today's system. In "A Boy Grew in Brooklyn," Miller describes the thrill of riding the Culver Line to Coney Island, but in "Bulldog" traveling north in the opposite direction on a Sunday, he offers a panoramic vision of the view from the almost empty elevated train. In empty lots, he sees old Italian women, their heads covered with red bandanas, bent over and loading their aprons with dandelions, and men standing in driveways watering their cars (Miller 2001, 2016: 257–8).

"Ditchy" is Miller's first published short story, appearing in October 1944 in *Mayfair Magazine*. Its existence was unknown to scholars until George Crandall discovered it in 1994 in a trove of Miller's papers at the Harry Ransom Center at the University of Texas, Austin. The story is Miller's fictional version of an incident from his childhood that he included in *Timebends* (Miller 1987: 22–3): He was roller skating in Central Park and was mugged and punched by a gang of Italian kids who also robbed him of his skates. However, the story does not simply retell the mugging (Figure 4.3); rather, Miller uses a twenty-something narrator who has returned to the same spot, and as the memory floods up, he

Figure 4.3 One of the north entrances to Central Park across from Miller's 110th Street home, c. 2024. Photo by Jane K. Dominik.

is accosted by three boys. He disarms them with his gentleness, particularly showing sympathy for one of the lads named Ditchy. The unnamed narrator judges that the boy's violence likely derives from the deprivation of his family's poverty, as evidenced by his rotten teeth. The narrator takes Ditchy to a dentist and has his teeth pulled. This story shows Miller's interest in the effects of nurturing on children, and how bleak naturalistic socioeconomic forces can ruin youth. Ten years later, Miller would research how similar forces resulted in the violent youth street gangs of Bay Ridge, Brooklyn (see Chapter 1).

"I Don't Need You Anymore" is one of Miller's better-known short stories, contained in his first collection in 1966. He considered this story important because he placed the tale first and also titled the nine-story collection, *I Don't Need You Anymore and Other Stories*. The story was published first in *Esquire* in 1959 and reprinted in the 1987 collection *The Misfits and Other Stories*. The story is clearly autobiographical. The events involve the emotional conflicts of five-year-old Martin, on the cusp of the age of reason, struggling to understand the different worlds that constitute his life: the community of men of his grandfather, father, and brother; the realm of women as personified by his pregnant mother; and the mysteries of religion and nature. Situations in the story exactly parallel Miller's life. The story presumably takes place in early October 1921 when Miller was five (He would turn six on October 17). The mother in the story is pregnant, and Gussie gave birth to his sister Joan on June 1, 1922. The story in many ways illustrates Miller's oft-quoted line: "How may a man make of the outside world a home?" (Miller 1956, 1978: 73) because the boy is looking to find his place among groups he does not understand.

"I Don't Need You Anymore" is set in a New York location that figured prominently in Miller's youth: the summer bungalow community in Far Rockaway where the family spent the bulk of every season until the loss of their fortune in 1928. This story, along with the novel *Focus*, are Miller's only works set in the outer borough of Queens (although Victor in *The Price* works in a precinct in Queens near Idlewild Airport, today known as JFK). For those unfamiliar with New York City's beaches, "I Don't Need You Anymore" provides insight into the summer seaside communities of the Rockaways that were overshadowed by Brooklyn's famous Coney Island but had a uniqueness that threatened Coney Island's reputation. Various bungalow communities stretched from Far Rockaway to Rockaway Beach from the early twentieth century until their heyday in the 1950s (Figure 4.4). The photos here depict

Figure 4.4 The Miller family spent their summers in a bungalow in Far Rockaway, c. 1940. Courtesy Municipal Archives City of New York.

the unique architectural construction of these tiny edifices squeezed onto small lots "using pattern book designs incorporating uniform facades, compact interiors, integrated porches and exposed rafters" (Figure 4.5) ("Far Rockaway Beach Bungalow Historic District" 2013). The bungalow communities were occupied by distinct ethnic groups, with largely Jewish

Figure 4.5 Rows of bungalows, c. 1940. Courtesy Municipal Archives City of New York.

population in the lower numbered streets of Far Rockaway and the Irish who rented or owned many of the bungalows in higher numbered streets up to Rockaway Playland Amusement Park on Beach 98th Street. Some of these bungalows have survived, and in 2013, the district of surviving bungalows was placed on the New York State Register of Historic Places, which automatically nominated the neighborhood to be on the National Register of Historic Places that became official in July 2013 ("Bungalows of the Rockaways") (Kensinger 2015). In 2010, a film documentary "The Bungalows of Rockaway" directed by Jennifer Callahan and narrated by Estelle Parsons told the unique story of the twentieth-century seaside community.

In an interview, Joan Copeland recalled life in the summers at the shore, particularly an incident when she was stung by an insect.

> Stephen Marino: So you don't remember those summers in Rockaway that Arthur talked about? Living in the bungalows?
>
> Joan Copeland: I have one memory of Rockaway and it's when I became ill, very seriously ill . . . suddenly. My mother, I suppose, called the doctor to come. And I had been bitten by a fly. My memory is that it was a horse fly. I don't know how I got to be so friendly with a horse fly?! And I didn't know at the time that horse flies resided [*Laughter*] in the leavings of the horses. Anyway, my leg swelled up to an enormous size. I was just a little girl at the time. I don't know maybe six or seven, something like that. Maybe even younger, because we went to Rockaway when we were still living in Manhattan.
>
> SM: Yes, that's the way Arthur tells it. You spent the summers in the bungalow. That stopped in '28 after the move to Brooklyn.
>
> JC: Yes, so I must have been 4 years old when this event occurred. I have a memory of lying on a wooden dining table, a round table, and people standing around me and the doctor being there. I didn't quite know what he was doing. But he cut open and drained the poison from the leg. And he [Arthur] said—of course, Arthur was so dramatic anyway—But he said to my mother that another ten minutes it would have been too late. My dad, when he came home from work and found out what happened—somebody told him that I had been bitten by a poison horse fly. So he said, "Well, I don't blame that horsefly," he said. "You are so sweet, and you can't fool a horsefly! [*Laughter*]. And to this day, when something happens that is a monumental event, I say, "Well, you can't fool a horsefly!" And all my life growing up, when I was correct about something, my dad would say "You can't fool a horse fly!" [*Laughter*] (Copeland 2008: 44).

In the tale, Miller connects his Jewish heritage with the important setting on the beach. The story takes place during the high holidays culminating in Yom Kippur. The men in the story—Martin's father, older brother, and grandfather—are fasting and have gone toward the ocean to cast their sins, rituals which the five-year-old is not permitted to do. He is left with his pregnant mother. In

Timebends, Miller recalls his youthful fascination with Jewish ritual when he was in the temple with his great-grandfather on the feast of Simchat Torah (see Introduction), and in this story, Martin expresses parallel sentiments. The boy's fascination with fasting is meant to parallel his spiritual hunger. Many of the incidents in the story are caused clearly by the boy wanting to satiate his desires. So there is food throughout the story: the bread the men cast into the water, the breakfast the mother wants Martin to eat, his reluctance to eat because he wants to fast like the grown-ups, all culminating in a blow-up at the meal breaking the fast. The boy's kicking of the pregnant mother and screaming the awful line, "I Don't Need You Anymore," indicates the boy's desire to separate from her. The boy's statement is particularly shocking to the older brother. There is also a sexual component to Martin's struggles, for he is confused by an encounter the mother has had with a former beau. The critic Alan Chavkin views this story as the dynamics of a patriarchal Jewish family operating in a family system theory "which assumes that to understand a particular individual one should look at this individual not in isolation but in the context of the individual's family" (Chavkin 2020: 142).

One interesting note about the time of year that this story occurs: In general, Labor Day marked the end of the summer season and the bungalow communities would empty, especially those with families because the school year began. In 1921, Labor Day was Monday, Sept. 5. Yom Kippur began on the evening of Tuesday, October 11 and ended on the evening of October 12. Thus, there are a few cultural questions that the story raises. If the school year has started, why is the family still at the bungalow? Did they come down to celebrate the holidays there? Did the brother not yet start school? Kermit was known to be a superior student and would missing school for the high holy days have been condoned for them? Also, in the year that the story likely occurs, 1921, New York City public schools did not have official days off for Jewish holidays; they did not become part of the school calendar until 1960 ("Dates").

"Fame" is another of Miller's biographical tales. Miller explained that the story is based on an actual incident when he ran into an old friend who did not recognize him as the famous playwright (Bigsby 2005a: 452). The fictionalized incident exists in three versions: an original short story published in *Esquire* in 1966 under the title "Recognitions" and re-titled "Fame" for the short story collection, *I Don't Need You Anymore and Other Stories,* in 1967; a short play version in 1970; and then a TV film that aired on NBC's *Hallmark Hall of Fame* in 1978, Miller's first TV script, that expanded on the original story. The plot of all three iterations centers on a famous New York Jewish playwright—Meyer Berkowitz in the story and play, Meyer Shine in the film—who is torn by the recognition that his success has brought him. On one hand, he is put off by the constant interruption of people greeting him in his public forays in Manhattan; on the other hand, he wants to be acknowledged. He has two plays currently on Broadway that keep his name in lights, but he worries about writing another successful comedy.

Miller structured the story as a series of Berkowitz's encounters with people who recognize him on the streets of Manhattan and in a restaurant, events that culminate in Berkowitz being approached by a man, Bernie Gelfand, who identifies him not as the famous playwright, but rather as a close high school buddy, whom Berkowitz does not at all remember, even though the man claims that they were best friends. Gelfand is proud of his business success, boasting about his position as a general manager in the shoulder pad industry. The internal narration informs the reader that Gelfand observes Berkowitz's unkempt appearance and frayed clothes (he cares little for the showy trappings of fame) and assumes that he has not done well in life. However, when Gelfand asks the usual New York question: What do you do?, Berkowitz reveals himself as the famous playwright. In shock, embarrassment, and recognition of his inconsequence, Gelfand shrinks away and exits the restaurant. Berkowitz is left sipping on an oxymoronic "hateful pleasure" of his renown.

"Fame" is another of Miller's tales that integrate Manhattan locales into the events. In fact, the story is structured so that Berkowitz walks through midtown, and the narrative points out specific places and thoroughfares. It is fascinating that the reader can map out the route that Berkowitz walks to eventually arrive at the Chinese restaurant where he encounters Gelfand. The story begins with Berkowitz leaving his agent's office located in a building on Madison Avenue. (Meyerwitz is deep in thought about having just collected a royalty for $750,000, and he is chafing at the $75,000, 10 percent commission he must pay his agent, whom he identifies as Billy. In these details, Miller mixes bio with fiction. The amount of the royalty is probably an accurate figure at the time the story was written, whereas Miller's longtime agent was not named Billy, but rather the famous agent Kay Brown.) As he steps onto the avenue, a woman recognizes him and smiles, and then a man stops him and asks, "You wouldn't be Meyer Berkowitz?" to which Berkowitz replies in denial, "No, I look like him, though" (Miller 1967, 2016: 149). Berkowitz then walks to the corner of Fiftieth Street and turns west to walk toward Fifth Avenue. A couple recognizes him. He notes a newsstand with copies of *Look* and *Life* with his face on the cover. After recollecting about his life before his fame—working at Burnside Memorial Chapel (perhaps this is Miller's nod to Manhattan's Riverside Memorial Chapel on W. 72nd Street)—he resolves to happily greet and acknowledge himself to the next person. When he gets to Fifth Avenue which he describes as "so clean, gray, and rich" (Miller 1967, 2016: 150), he walks downtown thinking, "Two blocks west, two blocks to the right of his shoulder, the housemen in two theaters were preparing to turn the lights on over his name; the casts of two plays were at home, checking their watches; in all, maybe thirty-five people, including the stage managers and assistants, have been joined together by him, their lives changed and in a sense commanded by his words" (Miller 1967, 2016: 150). From the description, we infer that Berkowitz likely has walked to at least 45th Street, because the major venues of the theater district are located on West 44 and 45 Streets, if we use Shubert Alley as a focal point of the district. Miller never had two plays playing simultaneously on Broadway at the time the story was written. However, it is likely that Miller may have been making an intended reference to Neil Simon, who had four shows running on Broadway in 1966 and certainly is a Jewish comedic writer closely resembling Berkowitz. In fact, Gelfand says that he and Berkowitz were students at De Witt Clinton High School, exactly the school that Neil Simon attended, and the story relates that Berkowitz is from the Bronx. Also, a review by Tom Shales of the story's TV production concluded that the character's plays "make him seem patterned more after Neil Simon than after Miller himself, although Hallmark publicity termed the work as 'somewhat autobiographical'" (Shales 1978: n.p.).

A significant New York location that is mentioned is the restaurant The Pavillon where Meyerwitz remembers he is to meet his director, producer, and their wives. This upscale New York restaurant was located in the famous Ritz Tower on Park Avenue and 57th Street which meant Berkowitz would have to walk back uptown thirteen blocks from his present location at the Chinese restaurant ("The King" 1966; Prial 1974, 9). As he walks down Fifth Avenue, a cab driver and his customers recognize him and call out, but Berkowitz seeks refuge and anonymity in the bar of a Chinese restaurant that Miller names Lee Fong, where he has his encounter with Gelfand.

In "A Search for a Future," Miller again melds his life story into fictional situations that involve characters walking through Manhattan neighborhoods. The autobiographical echoes are directly taken from Miller's life in 1966: his commitment to protesting the war in Vietnam, the playwright's father, Isidore, consigned to a nursing home, and a return to their haunts in Harlem.

The plot involves a veteran actor who is re-evaluating the two most important roles he has played in his life: as an actor and as a son. The first-person narration allows the reader a portrait of the actor's regret at playing many characters on the stage, but he "never got to play a part" in real life. He has never married, and he regrets the children he will never have. Moreover, he is waiting to play the part of a grieving son, for he awaits the news of his father's imminent death. He is visited by a young man, an actor, who reminds him of a commitment he has made to appear at an anti-war rally, an event that the actor is not fully engaged in, but he is moved by the young man's lively spirit and idealism, the excitement of doing everything for the first time and thinking he can "stop the world from ending" (Miller 1966, 2016: 203). The older man is aroused by the young man's enthusiasm, and he consequently gives an engaging performance that evening.

The next day he visits his father in the nursing home located on the Upper West Side of the borough, and he is overwhelmed by its "zoo smell" (Miller 1966, 2016: 203). He recalls his performance at the war rally the night before, and despite the enthusiastic reaction of the audience to his questioning the war, he is troubled by his actual insincerity. His father no longer fully recognizes him, and his stroke makes his language difficult to understand. However, the son perceives a spirit in him because despite his debilitation, "he had not given up on his future" (Miller 1966, 2016: 209). The actor—wallowing in his mid-life torpor—realizes the contrast between him and his father: "In fact, he was reaching toward his future even more energetically than I was toward mine. He really wanted something" (Miller 1966, 2016: 209). His father wanted to go home, where he insists, "I could live" (Miller 1966, 2016: 210).

At this point in the story, Miller again has a character, as he does in many other works, travel through the streetscape of Manhattan in an emotional crisis. Miller meticulously maps out the actor's journey. Leaving his father, the actor crosses

Figure 4.6 Dry cleaning store in Harlem, c. 2024. Photo by Jane Dominik.

Riverside Drive to its park and takes the bus to Harlem where he was born. In this section, Miller clearly melds his own biographical experience with the character's, particularly noting the contrast in how places look in the present as opposed to the past. A dry cleaning store (Figure 4.6) stands in place of one of the best restaurants in New York (Figure 4.7, 4.8). He recalls the smell of the freshly baked rolls and the manager who sat with him and his parents (Miller 1966, 2016: 212). A Black man looks out from the store and the actor has the desire to go in and tell him how he remembers what the neighborhood looked like in the past: when no garbage

Figure 4.7 Restaurant on Lenox Avenue, c. 1940. Courtesy Municipal Archives City of New York.

cans were on the street, the Daimlers, Minervas, and Locomobiles (again Miller's obsession with cars!) cruised by, and a cop on the corner would toss the ball back the ball when it escaped the outfield on 114th Street (Miller 1966, 2016: 212). But he does not enter the establishment, preferring to retreat to his dressing room to prepare for the evening's performance.

As he applies his makeup, he has a revelation—that his father may be "the only one who is not an actor . . . He just speaks from his heart" (Miller 1966, 2016: 212). That night he receives a call from the nursing home that his father has escaped and is wandering out in stormy weather without an overcoat.

Figure 4.8 Site of former restaurant on Lenox Avenue, c. 2024. Photo by Jane K. Dominik.

Harry is proud of his father's moxie: "his willfulness, his blind push toward what he has to have" (Miller 1966, 2016: 213). The actor tries to find him, hailing a taxi in the rain, but he is not successful. The next morning, he receives word that his father has been found in a luncheonette in Harlem. Harry visits him and he does not remember the past night's event. But when the actor asks, "You went to Harlem. Were you going home?" The father retorts that he is going home tomorrow. The actor is impressed by the father's indomitable will to have "a future that they will never be able to rip from him" (Miller 1966, 2016: 215), and the actor hopes this will instigate in him a "terrific desire to live differently" (216).

Miller devotes a substantial narrative in *Timebends* to the years that he worked in the Brooklyn Navy Yard from 1941–3. Miller was declared ineligible for the draft because of damage from a knee injury that he received while playing on the second squad of the Abraham Lincoln High School football team. Still struggling as a writer and newly married, Miller needed a steady income and worked the night shift thirteen out of fourteen nights from four in the afternoon to four in the morning as a shipfitter. He recounts the attitudes of the many Italian workers in the Yard, particularly their "Sicilian dramas, guys caught in the arms of somebody's wife and escaping over rooftops, or maneuvering a friend out of the way the better to get his girlfriend" (Miller 1987: 199). Miller offers insight into the sexual exploits of his boss, Ipana Mike who had a string of girlfriends and a wife whom he resented because he had been tricked into marrying her. Miller also tells about Mike's ability to make an art of avoiding work on the ships by finding "inaccessible corners" to sleep. Despite these moral failings, Miller explains that Mike could "turn into a phenomenally resourceful worker" (Miller 1987: 200).

Twenty years earlier, in 1967, Miller wrote a long story, "Fitter's Night," for the collection *I Don't Need You Anymore and Other Stories*, which he based on Mike's character, his miserable married life, his sexual imbroglios, and his work ethic. Miller structured the story so that fictional flashbacks of Mike's life— renamed Tony Calabrese—interweave with the realistic working conditions in the Navy Yard and his heroic repair in brutal winter weather of a British ship anchored in the Hudson River. He describes the raw winter winds biting into their faces, straightened steel and cracked struts as they relied on each other's help in avoiding falling into the icy waters. (Miller 1987: 200)

Figure 4.9 French battleship *Richelieu* passes Brooklyn Bridge, New York, with damaged turret for refitting at New York Navy Yard on January 30, 1943. Pictorial Press/Alamy Stock Photo.

There is unarguably no other story rooted in a New York setting that provides as vivid, detailed realistic description of the locale as does "Fitter's Night." Miller captures the frenetic atmosphere of the Navy Yard that operated during the war years on rotating shifts twenty-four hours straight. In fact, in "Fitter's Night," Miller offers a primer on the Navy Yard with accurate descriptions of its size, location, workers, and ships (Figure 4.9).

In the story, Miller refers to the famous Navy Yard by its formal name—the New York Naval Shipyard—but it is almost universally known as the Brooklyn Navy Yard (Figure 4.10). Operating since 1801, "The Yard was once the nation's most storied naval shipbuilding facility, which for over 150 years built and launched America's most famous fighting ships, including the USS

Figure 4.10 Aerial photo shows the vastness of the Brooklyn Navy Yard, c. 1940. Courtesy of US Navy Archives.

Maine, *USS Arizona*, and *USS Missouri* (Figure 4.11). The Yard also served as an important point of the passage, home, and workplace for countless veterans as they served our country" (Figure 4.12) ("Brooklyn Navy Yard" Mission). The Yard was closed in the 1960s and has now been transformed into an industrial and manufacturing park that includes Steiner Studios, the largest film facilities outside of Hollywood ("History of the Yard"). During the years Miller worked there, the shipyard spread over a wide area of eastern Brooklyn along the East River, encompassing over 350 acres. It can be reached by four subway stops. Miller was living on Schermerhorn Street when he worked there and could either walk to the yard's southern entrance or take the subway. In the story, Tony takes the subway (Miller 1967, 2016: 161).

Miller integrates Tony's internal thoughts into exact descriptions of the yard and its environs: "Coming out of the end of the street, he saw the cold stars over the harbor, a vast sky stretching out over the bay and beyond to the sea. Clusters of headlights coursed over Brooklyn Bridge (Figure 4.13), the

Figure 4.11 The *USS Missouri* under construction at the Navy Yard. The Japanese surrendered on the battleship at the end of the Second World War, c. 1942. Courtesy of US Navy Archives.

thickening traffic of the homebound who did not know they were passing over the Yard or the war-broken ships" (Miller 1967, 2016: 161).

In discussions of previous stories, I have noted how Miller's characters walk through the streets of New York City. In "Fitter's Night," the central event—Tony's repair of ship rails for the deployment of depth charges—occurs not in

Figure 4.12 The Five Sullivan brothers at the Navy Yard in 1942. The siblings served together on the *USS Juneau* and were killed together in action when their cruiser was torpedoed at the Battle of Guadalcanal. Courtesy of US Navy Archives.

the Navy Yard, but on a British ship docked in the North River, another name for the part of the Hudson River above mid-Manhattan (Figure 4.14). Tony and a crew that includes Hindu and Baldu (Miller does not seem to characterize himself for this incident, even though in *Timebends* he relates performing this job with Mike) are driven there by a sailor. Miller relates the exact route that the repair truck takes from Brooklyn to the West Side of Manhattan. The vehicle drives along the "donkey-engine tracks" and streets of the Navy Yard, exits the gate, and heads over the Brooklyn Bridge. This indicates that they exited the Navy Yard from a southern gate, likely the Sands Street gate, which is closer to the Brooklyn Bridge. Miller describes the drive into Manhattan with Baldu thinking how the "Brooklyn Bridge was unwinding from the tailgate of the truck, and how beautiful it was, how fine to be speeding along like this on a mission for the country, and everybody, even Tony, springing into action for the sake of the war effort" (Miller 1967, 2016: 179). He describes the trip across lower Manhattan: "As they crossed Chambers Street, the tall office and bank

Figure 4.13 United States. New York City, 1961. View of the Brooklyn Bridge. Shipfitters travel over the Brooklyn Bridge on their way to the ship repair. © Inge Morath/Magnum Photos.

buildings they saw were dark, the people who worked in them at home, warm, and smart and snug" (Miller 1967, 2016: 179). This route takes them to the West Side of Manhattan, and the pickup truck turns at the Hudson Riverfront under the West Side Highway, which at the time was an elevated structure, and continues until they arrive at the pier where the British ship is docked. Miller exactly describes the piers and the way ships docked: "The truck turned left and into the pier, past the long light bulb and the night watchman under it

Figure 4.14 New York's landmarked Municipal Building, c. 1966 which the shipfitters passed after crossing the Brooklyn Bridge on their way to the ship repair on the Hudson River. Courtesy of the New York City Landmarks Preservation Commission.

listlessly waving a hand and returning to his stove in the shack. Midway down the length of the pier shed, one big door was open, and the sailor coasted the truck up to it and braked to a halt, the springs squeaking in the cold as the nose dipped" (Miller 1967, 2016: 182). He describes how they approached the gangplank, "which extended into the pier from the destroyer's deck and walked up, glancing right and left at the full length of the ship" (Miller 1967, 2016: 183).

After Tony's heroic repair, Miller details the same exact route for returning to the Navy Yard: "Outside the pier the sailor braked for a moment, glancing right and left for traffic, and he turned downtown. Tony at the side window saw sailors coming down the gangplank of the destroyer. They were already casting off. The truck sped through the cold and empty streets toward Chambers and Brooklyn Bridge leaving it all behind" (Miller 1967, 2016: 199). When they return to the Yard, Tony makes the driver take them to the drydock where they had been working on repairing a cruiser.

"The Bare Manuscript" is another late Miller story, published in 2002, and is in many ways connected to "Bulldog," published the previous year, in its focus on sexual awakening. Although "Bulldog" centers on a thirteen-year-old boy's unexpected loss of virginity, "The Bare Manuscript" is a tale of a middle-aged man's reawakening of the physical and emotional love he has for his wife. Miller concocted an unusual circumstance for the story. The main character is a writer who had great success in his early career but has lost the mojo of creativity, which the story parallels with the loss of his love for his wife and the deterioration of their relationship. He has had numerous affairs during their marriage, which sometimes stimulate creativity. When he sees a woman walking on the beach, he gets the idea that becomes the central act of the story: actually writing on a naked woman may restore his creativity. His idea works because he composes an autobiographical story of the genesis of his relationship with his wife.

There are elements of this story that may be autobiographical. His wife Lena somewhat resembles Miller's first wife Mary Slattery. His description of the early years of Clement and Lena's marriage living in Brooklyn Heights, their parties, and delving into conversations about political and social causes echoes the Millers' lives.

The story contains flashbacks of Clement's wooing of Lena, the breakdown of their relationship, and their attempts at saving the marriage. Many of the recent events occur in New York, but the city is not central to the tale—although it is notable that the house where Clement is writing his story on the naked woman is located in the Chelsea section of Manhattan. Miller describes a dormer window from which one could see uptown as far as 23rd Street and the house as the "last remaining brownstone on a block of old converted warehouses and newish apartment houses" (Miller 2002c, 2016: 297). Later in the story, when he is seeking to place the ad for the naked woman, he picks up a copy of *The Village Voice* and stands on the corner of Prince and Broadway, an exact location.

Miller focused on another vehicle produced in 1928 when he published in 1978, "The 1928 Buick" in *The Atlantic*. This story is significant because not only did Miller return to focus on a vehicle manufactured in 1928 as in *Salesman*, but the story also is thinly disguised autobiography, arguably one of his most personal fictional pieces. And it illustrates how in tune he was to the significance of automobiles—even in circumstances of family tragedy. It is striking to see how Miller transforms his personal experience into art, for this story is one of the special times where you can parallel, as in *After the Fall* and *The American Clock*, the actual event with its fictional counterpart.

In *Timebends*, Miller relates the tragedy of his cousin Jean, one of the three daughters of his Aunt Esther (Miller's mother's sister) and Uncle Lee Balsam, the salesman, who, along with Manny Newman (the prototype of Willy), lived in the side-by-side houses in Brooklyn some ten years before the Millers in 1928. Jean, her husband Moe Fishler, and his mother lived across the street from the Millers on East 3rd Street. Moe was a "strikingly handsome man . . . who radiated an aura of competence and good fortune" (Figure 4.15) (Miller 1987: 88). During the Depression, when everybody else was financially gasping, Moe had steadily risen to become a prosperous textile executive. However, Miller perceived that something had come between Moe and his cousin Jean for they barely spoke to one another. He relates how his Aunt Esther and her three daughters were meticulous house cleaners; Millers says, "They were kept together by all the polishing they did" (Miller 1987: 88). This mania even transferred over to Moe, who would polish his red Buick's engine until it shone like the body paint.

Tragedy struck when Moe decided one hot summer afternoon to drive alone to Brighton Beach for a swim some two miles away. By sundown he had not returned. As darkness came, an unfamiliar car drove down the street out of which stepped a tiny hunchbacked man in a bathing suit—a doctor who had been lying on the beach when Moe collapsed and who had tried to revive him. He had Moe's body in the backseat of the car. Miller ends the recollection with the removal of Moe's body from the car, the wailing of Jean, and the mourning of Moe's mother who for months rocked on her front porch facing the cemetery beyond their dead-end street.

Miller places an odd interjection about a neighbor who helped carry Moe's body out of the car—a long digression about Mr. Clark and his obsession with his car (Miller's focus on people and their cars is extraordinary). That day Mr. Clark had just finished lubricating his Model A Ford, a car he rarely drove and kept shining in the garage where he had dug a grease pit for it. The vehicle had

Figure 4.15 The East 3rd Street home of Moe Fishler, his wife Jean, and her mother is located across the street from the Miller family home, c. 1940. Courtesy Municipal Archives City of New York.

less than three hundred miles on it and was eventually bought by Moe's sister, Mae. Miller judges that the "vehicle was less an auto than an icon—a symbol: the childless couple had nowhere to go; they merely needed something to care for and worry about and protect from the elements" (Miller 1987: 89).

In 1978, Miller transformed the tragedy of Moe and Jean into the short story and clearly uses the 1928 Buick as a symbol for Moe Fishler, changed to the character, Max Sions.[3] Miller leaves the basic true story intact but includes himself as a thinly disguised first-person narrator who is central in pointing out the significance of the vehicle for both Max and him. Miller immediately cements Max's connection with the 1928 Buick Coupe by beginning the tale with a detailed, sensual description: "He had been polishing her all morning in the driveway and I had watched as he rubbed her sides to a liquid shimmer. . . . She had a built-in radio, with antenna underneath the running boards, wooden steering wheel, leather seats, and a built in heater " (Miller 1978c: 49). The femininity of the car echoes the same "she-ness" that Miller uses in a *Timebends* recollection of driving with his father and uncle. In the story, the narrator is a fourteen-year-old boy (the summer of 1930, when Miller was fourteen), and Max is twenty-five. Although the narrator says he had every reason to respect Max (Miller 1978c: 49), this is, indeed, ironic understatement, for Miller devotes a long section describing Max physically: his teenage adulation of the man is obvious. At the start of the story, the narrator is driving with Max from the 3rd Street block to Virginia's house, the name of his cousin in the tale, for they are not yet married. Miller describes Max as beautiful to look at. Women and men, too, let their gazes linger on him (Miller 1978c: 50) (Later in the tale, even the doctor who tried to save Max describes him as resembling Michelangelo's statue of David, even in his shifted stance). Max's identification with the 1928 Buick is summed up in the narrator observing the happy couple just sitting and talking in in the vehicle that he finds "so powerfully promising" (Miller 1978c: 51). When Max and Virginia decide to take a drive to Sheepshead Bay, the narrator observes the car moving away from the curb, "its perfection of metal flashing back the sunlight all the way down the block" (Miller 1978c: 51). Thus, Miller clearly connects the power, promise, and perfection of the vehicle with the same in Max.

The second part of the story fast forwards seven years later; the narrator has been to college and is home for the weekend. This is the summer of 1936 or 1937 on a hot July day; in this, Miller alters the time frame because Moe actually died on June 21, 1942, according to his headstone and the records

Figure 4.16 Athletic field and the adjacent Washington Cemetery where Moe Fishler is buried, c. 2023. Photo by Katie Murray.

for Washington Cemetery ("Fishler": n.p.). The narrator foreshadows the impending tragedy through images: 3rd Street, a dead end stopping at a fenced-off school athletic field, and a cemetery beyond—the one where Max will be buried at tale's end (Figure 4.16). (The locales are the same in present-day Brooklyn.) But the narrator also highlights the 1928 Buick again—now parked "permanently" in the Sion's wide driveway for "the shine was gone and even at a glance one saw the deadly worms of rust along the cowling and the dull dying chrome of the radiator. Its wooden spokes had lost their yellow varnish and were as gray as clothespins. A purplish haze was spreading through the rear window where the glass laminations were quietly separating" (Miller 1978c: 51). The once beautiful machine is like the beautiful man and his fiancée, whose promise and power are now decayed. In this, Miller expands on the real-life saga: the unhappiness of Max and Virginia, the narrator's perception that Max and Virginia were breaking up, and Max's drive to the beach alone on a Sunday, leaving his wife and children at home. Miller has him drive away in a new green Caddy convertible, the potent and ironic symbol of Max's promising new life. This section ends with the narrator wondering if Max would sell him the '28 Buick cheap when he returned to college in the fall. He speculates that perhaps the time had come for Max to "dispose of such things" (Miller 1978c: 54), as he is disposing of his youth, his wife, and his family. Clearly, the narrator would like to recapture the power, promise, and perfection of that vehicle.

The next section details Max's death: the doctor—now driving not an "unfamiliar" car, but a Cadillac sedan—bringing the body. This narrative is an expanded version of Miller's autobiographical story: he adds a family doctor and Max's father. The story ends as does the *Timebends* account, with Max's mother, Eva in the tale, staring and rocking at the cemetery beyond the block, mourning her son. But the actual focus at the story's climax is on two haunting images of cars. In the final paragraph, the narrator notes that when he left for college in the fall, he was unable to ask Virginia to sell him the '28 Buick. Therefore, it will remain in the driveway, decaying with its worms of rust—not far from where Max's body lies too with worms—in the driveway of his grave. This signifies, too, the narrator's realization of his own lost youth. The final image of the story focuses on Eva's fear of unknown cars: "Whenever a large car turned into that street, especially one that was moving slowly, she would stare calmly at its approach and then turn her back on it and go into the house before it arrived" (56), her never-ending fear of the death and destruction any vehicle could deliver.

"Please Don't Kill Anything" and "Presence" are not set within the New York City limits; they are located in rural beach communities, likely out on Long Island. "Please Don't Kill Anything" has a strong autobiographical component, likely based on a fictionalized incident that occurred when Miller was married to Marilyn Monroe and they rented a beach house in the famous Hamptons, whose sale garnered much publicity in 2021. It may also be that Miller used elements of this in "Presence," which also takes place in a beach community on the south shore of the island. The story explains the unnamed main character's familiarity with the beach by describing "the sterling ocean, his hallowed homewater from so long in the past in childhood, when it loved him and scared him into sparkling and foamy white on top and dark below with live things in its holy depths. Once he has nearly drowned, at six, seven" (Miller 2003, 2016: 366). He may not be referring to the specific beach and rather the Atlantic Ocean itself, of which Far Rockaway is part of, although the story explains that "thirty years ago he had made love on this beach" (Miller 2003, 2016: 369) with a black-haired woman now long dead.

Figure 4.17 In his final recorded visit to Brooklyn on April 23, 2004, Arthur Miller crosses Remsen Street to attend the Arthur Miller Conference at St. Francis College. Pictured with him are Stephen Marino (l) and Christopher Gibbons (r). Courtesy of the Arthur Miller Society.

Arthur Miller was a boy from New York City who became a citizen of the world. He walked the sidewalks and crossed the streets of the metropolis and found the subjects of his great plays and fiction that give him a permanent presence in literary history (Figure 4.17).

Notes

Introduction

1. Some of the material in this section appeared in Marino, Stephen (2006), "Editor's Note," *The Arthur Miller Journal,* (Spring) Vol. 1, no. 1, 1-2; Marino, Stephen (2015), Marino, Stephen (2003), "Arthur Miller" (2003), *Twentieth-Century American Dramatists*: Fourth Series. Ed. Christopher J. Wheatley, *Dictionary of Literary Biography* Vol. 266. Detroit: Gale, 2003. Adapted with permission.
2. Part of the Austria/Hungary Empire at that time.
3. At that time, home births were the norm in New York City. Miller's birth certificate indicates how the birth was attended by the family physician Dr. Plotz (Bigsby 21), whose onomatopoetic name was the source of much joking in the family.
4. Amazingly, most residences, school buildings, and temples where Miller lived, learned, and worshipped in Manhattan and Brooklyn have survived the constant "build it, tear it down, re-build it" ethos that marks New York real estate.
5. West 110th Street is the northern border of the park, with its southern border being West 59th, also known as Central Park South. Thus, West 110th Street is also known as Central Park North, and further west as Cathedral Parkway for the famous Episcopal Cathedral of St. John the Divine, whose southern property line is located on 110th Street at Amsterdam Avenue. In today's burgeoning Harlem real estate market, large apartments such as the Millers' are broken up into co-op units, as is the case with 45 West 110th Street which underwent such renovation in 2009. In *Timebends*, Miller relates that his father was angered that fine apartments houses all around their 110th Street residence were being broken up by landlords renting single apartments. "When we moved to Brooklyn in 1928, our landlord was happily planning to lease our six room (Miller misremembered the number of rooms) apartment to two families, thus increasing his take and the eventual deterioration of the building" (49).
6. See Marino, Stephen. "The Greatest Cars Ever Built: Arthur Miller's Production Line of Chevrolets, Buicks, Studebakers, Marmons, Porsches and Other Vehicles

of Death and Destruction." *The Arthur Miller Journal,* Volume 2 No. 2, Fall 2007, 5-20.

7   Some of the material in this section appeared in Marino, Stephen. "Touring Arthur Miller's Brooklyn," Marino, Stephen. "It's Brooklyn, I know, but we hunt too:' The Image of the Borough in *Death of a Salesman*," and Marino, Stephen. "Mapping Arthur Miller's Brooklyn," adapted with permission.

8   The Miller's had a short stint renting "an ample half of a two-family house" (Miller 1987: 112) at 1277 Ocean Parkway before purchasing the East 3rd Street residence.

9   Miller first attended James Madison High School where his mother had convinced the administrators to admit him at 13 before he graduated grammar school so her "can be with his cousins" (Miller 1987: 22), the offspring of Manny Newman and Lee Balsam. Kermit had gone to Townsend Harris, a high school for intellectually gifted pupils located at City College, but he was pulled out when the family moved to Brooklyn. Miller's last two years were spent at the newly constructed Abraham Lincoln High School about two miles (to which Miller walked everyday) further down Ocean Parkway toward Brighton Beach and Coney Island.

10 As a delivery man for his father, as an on-air tenor for a Brooklyn radio station, (Miller 1987: 109). He was taken by his agent Harry Rosenthal to the Brill Building on Broadway near 50th Street for the radio audition and did two fifteen-minute radio shows for the Brooklyn station.

11 One of the first Brooklyn Heights single-family homes to be remodeled and converted into apartments.

12 In *Timebends* Miller relates that he and Mary spent summers in a rented bungalow near Port Jefferson, on Long Island and that he completed the play on "the porcelain-topped kitchen table" (Miller 1987: 268).

13 The home contained two duplex apartments and the Miller family occupied the upper floors while the lower floors were rented to the previous tenants, Mr. and Mrs. Henry Davenport, who was the president of the Brooklyn Savings Bank. In *Timebends*, Miller details the extravagant lifestyle of the Davenports, but rails at their complaints about problems with the apartment. Miller disliked being a landlord and wanted to sell the house (Miller 1987: 143), but he judged that he would need another hit play and more money to do this.

14 The home that Miller bought at 155 Willow Street in 1951 is considered a Brooklyn Heights architectural gem, one of three Federal-style brick row houses that are among the oldest in the neighborhood, having been built in the 1820s. The houses also played a distinct role in the American Civil War as havens on

the Underground Railroad. A plaque at 157 Willow Street explains that how the homes had underground storage space to hide runaway slaves as they escaped northward to Canada. In *Timebends*, Miller relates how he spruced up the house, installing a subfloor and cork floor in the entrance hallway and built conveniences in the kitchen (328). But he also details how he performed these acts as duty because, torn by attraction to Monroe, he felt his marriage to Mary was floundering.

Chapter 1

1. Sections of the previous discussion of *No Villain* appear in edited form in Marino, Stephen 2020, *No Villain,* Performance Review, *The Arthur Miller Journal* (Fall 2020), 169-173.
2. The form of *The American Clock* is one of the more spectacular in Miller's dramatic canon. The cast contains forty-six named characters, plus extras who in the revised version remain on the stage the entire time. Miller also penned a song, "You got me singing along" for the production. All of the action is punctuated by the music of the era performed by a live band onstage and sung variously by the characters.
3. When Miller was seventeen, he wrote a story, discovered by his mother during the original production of the play, called "In Memoriam" (See chapter 4) based on his own experiences with a Jewish salesman when he was working for his father a few months after graduating high school. In *Timebends*, he also relates that he had forgotten that in college he started a play about a salesman and his family and discovered the notebook for it when he was moving his papers out of his Willow Street home after his marriage to Mary Slattery ended. (He tells this a bit differently in a 1992 interview, claiming that he found the papers when he was moving from the 31 Grace Court house to 151 Willow Street.) Other influences on Miller included his own relationships with his father and brother that Miller had dramatized in his Michigan plays. Murphy points out Miller's observation that relationship with his father is similar to Bernard and Charley's (4).
4. The previous discussion appeared in edited form in Marino, Stephen 2000, "It's Brooklyn, I know, but we hunt too:' The Image of the Borough in *Death of a Salesman*" in *"The* Salesman *Has A Birthday"*: *Essays Celebrating the Fiftieth Anniversary of Arthur Miller's* Death of a Salesman, Lanham, MD: University Press of America. Reprinted with permission.

5   With the exception of the "G" between Brooklyn and Queens, the Franklin Avenue Shuttle in Brooklyn, and the Staten Island Transit, which is technically not part of the subway system.

6   The line runs from Coney Island into Manhattan and then into Queens, terminating at 179th Street in the Jamaica section of that borough. In the time of the play, it terminated in Queens at Parsons Blvd, then 169th Street.

7   The barge also functions as part of the Waterfront Museum that was founded to provide programs in education and culture aboard an historic vessel and to advocate for and expand public waterfront access in the New York Metropolitan area. The barge's arrival in Red Hook in 1994 transformed a former dumping area into what has been called "an ideal example of open space and waterfront access which provides an excellent complement to waterfront development." The Museum contains a permanent collection of sea artifacts, holds exhibits and events, and invites tour groups. Its jewel is the nearly century old wooden barge, listed on the National Register of Historic Places (http://waterfrontmuseum.org). See Review of the play in *The Arthur Miller Journal*, Fall 2018.

8   For further discussion of Hyman's treatment of Sylvia, horse riding metaphor and sex see: Marino, Stephen. 2007. "'Physician Heal Thyself': Arthur Miller's Portrayal of Doctors" in *Miller and Middle America*, ed, Paula Langteau, University Press of America,, 41-54.; Marino, Stephen. 20022, "Chapter Six, *The Ride Down Mt. Morgan* and *Broken Glass*." *A Language Study of Arthur Miller's Plays*: "*The Poetic in the Colloquial*," Lewiston: Edwin Mellen Press.

9   When the characters mention "downtown," that could be downtown Manhattan or Downtown Brooklyn, which is the borough's civic center, where Borough Hall is located that was the City Hall of Brooklyn when the borough was an independent city before the consolidation of the boroughs in 1898.

10 Schrafft's restaurants were known for "wholesome, all-American fare, served by fresh-faced Irish waitresses. Mothers and children ate there; so did movie stars. Schrafft's restaurants were located in high-end shopping districts, like Fulton Street in Downtown Brooklyn" ("All That Remains of Schrafft's in Downtown Brooklyn").

11 According to "NY Bookstores in 1946," Womraths had 31 branches in the city and eight in the Long Island, New Jersey and Westchester suburbs. Six of the city branches were in Brooklyn, one in the Bronx and two in Queens (Jackson Heights and Forest Hills). The remaining 22 were in Manhattan. Womrath's had 100,000 members who could rent a book for a three-day period or buy new books. Most of the books in the stores were recent releases. Periodically the stores advertised sales of older inventory or damaged copies at 50 to 80

percent off the list price. The typical Womrath member was a middle-aged female, although the store reported in 1946 that their male customer base had risen to 40 percent since the end of the war. It did particularly heavy business in light fiction, including bestsellers, romances and mysteries. Westerns were also popular. Most New Yorkers did not have space for an extensive personal library in their small apartments and, if they read books at all, depended on libraries and rentals. Unlike the public library, there was no long waiting list for the current bestsellers at Womrath's."

12 "The Beverly Theater was opened on January 17, 1920. It was another small house that was once run by United Artists and then the Golden Theater chain. It was a dollar theater before being twinned in January 1976, and going first-run. It closed in September 1981, with the lobby turned into retail use and the theater becoming a yeshiva. A few years back, the auditorium was completely demolished to become a Public School of the City of New York. The former front of the theatre and lobby are retained in retail use"("The Beverly Theatre, *Cinema Treasures*, cinema treasure.org).

13 "The Rialto Theatre first opened on March 19, 1916 with Harry Lonsdale in "The Ne're Do Well". It was one of the first "luxury" theatres built by A.H. Schwartz, many years before he started the Century Circuit. The Rialto Theatre never presented more than movies, but during the silent era it employed a small orchestra and organist to play during the programs and intermissions. The Rialto Theatre's success caused Schwartz to build a very similar Rialto Theatre in Jamaica, Queens, in 1918, with R. Thomas Short again as architect. In 1948 some remodeling was done to the plans of architect John J. McNamara. Century Theaters operated the Brooklyn Rialto Theatre until 1976, after which the theatre was converted into a church"("Rialto Theatre," *Cinema Treasure*, cinematreasures. org)

Chapter 2

1 For info on the renovations see, Werner , Laura. "Newly Restored But With Raffish Spirit Intact, New York's Hotel Chelsea Reopens." *Forbes*, "Travel" May 7, 2022. https://www.forbes.com/sites/lauriewerner/2022/05/07/newly-restored-but-with-raffish-spirit-intact-new-yorks-hotel-chelsea-reopens/; "New York's Literary Legendary Hangouts." *New York Times*. Aug. 26, 2021; "Dreaming Walls: Inside the Chelsea Hotel" – Asleep. Movie Review by Neely Swanson, |July 3, 2022. "Dreaming Walls: Inside the Chelsea Hotel" - Asleep [MOVIE REVIEW] - Easy Reader News

2   The building has undergone many changes since then, It used to be the Hotel Montclair, then the Hotel Belmont Plaza—Jerry Lewis and Dean Martin got their start in the Glass Hat club there – and finally the Doral Inn. and is now the W Hotel. Hotel Belmont Plaza | Ephemeral New York (wordpress.com); https://www.appraisersassociation.org/index The association is now housed at 212 West 35th Street, 11th Floor South in the garment district.

3   Some of the material in the discussion of *A Memory of Two Mondays* appeared in edited form in Marino, Stephen. "Commentary." Arthur Miller *A Memory of Two Mondays*. Methuen Drama, 2022, used with permission.

4   For example, on a trip to Hollywood studio in 1945 he sees a bulky old Minerva open touring car driven by a uniformed chauffeur, the "kind of glorious limousine that Sid Franks and I had loved to watch lining the curb on 110th St." out of which stepped W.C. Fields (Miller 1987: 286-87). He also observes Clark Gable's "silver Mercedes gull wing coupe" (Miller 1987: 472) and watching Gable for the last time getting into a "big Chrysler station wagon" (Miller 1987: 486) four days before he would die. Miller describes himself driving down Sunset Boulevard in "my clunky rented green American Motors mess" (Miller 1987: 486). He also remembers riding in a new green 1940 green Chevy van when traveling in North Carolina (Miller 1987: 498). After he and Marilyn Monroe separated, she went up to Miller's Roxbury, Connecticut home and noted his new Land Rover, which Miller details as specially outfitted for the planting of trees on the property. The photo section of *Timebends* includes a picture of him with his children with the curious caption, "With, Jane, Bob, and a new Ford." Miller's attraction for automobiles, particularly his penchant for the Mercedes-Benz, was well-known late into his life. As in much of his canon, Miller transformed this personal experience into art. The number of cars which appears in Miller's work is staggering. *The Man Who Had All the Luck* contains the Marmon and the death car of Hester's father; *Death of a Salesman*, the Chevrolet, and Studebaker, *A View From the Bridge* contains references to cars, taxis, and images of riding; in "The Misfits" a pickup truck is used in a crucial perversion of a cowboy roundup; the short story "The 1928 Buick" uses autos as symbols of sensual male power; in *The Ride Down Mt. Morgan* a Porsche both destroys and liberates Lyman Felt; an Austin and a Land Rover deliver the characters of Miller's 2004 novella, "The Turpentine Still" to their fate. In many works, the automobiles are particularly central to the action.

5   The only part of the novella not set in Manhattan is when Sam enlists in the service after Pearl Harbor and Janice accompanies him to Oklahoma for his officer training. It is during this boring time in Middle America that Janice

realizes: "Here in Oklahoma, deep in America, she understood that secretly she was part of nothing larger than herself, a ridiculous person" – the implication that in Manhattan she is part of something. Moreover, she declares that she "had never understood life, and now it was death bewilders her" (23); this evocation of death contradicts her previous revelation about death in the Irish bar. She comes to view the whole apple cheeked country as fraud. —and in this mood, she begins her affair with Lionel who awakes her sexually and she describes herself "free once more, as she had when her father died."

Chapter 3

1. An understanding of the street grid of Queens clarifies the address. Miller knew that the Queens street layout runs opposite of Manhattan, (where avenues run north to south and streets from outward from Fifth Avenue east and west). The Queens grid is laid out where the avenues run east to west and streets run north to south: the lower number avenues begin in the north; the lower number streets start in the west. Also, there are many neighborhoods that do not use street numbers, but names – Queens being a collection of "towns" i.e. neighborhoods that have retained their identity as postal code identification. For example, a Queens resident does not write "Queens, NY," but rather his town as in "Woodside, NY or Flushing, NY. In addition, house numbers are determined by the cross street or avenue or road and the lot number assigned by the city real estate division. Thus, the address of Fred's house, located at 41-39 68th Street., reveals that it is located south of 41 avenue in the 39th plot designation on the block, indicating that it is closer to 42 and 43nd avenues, the section of the neighborhood that straddles the neighborhoods of Jackson Heights and Sunnyside. We can also ascertain that he lives left of Fred because he turns left when he leaves Fred's house (Miller 1945: 177), to the right when you face the houses!) So Newman's address is 41-35 68th Street.
2. For further reading of American anti-Semitism, the Christian Front and the rallies, see: "Anti-Semitism in American History," *Anti-Defamation League*; Dinnerstein, Leonard. *Anti-Semitism in America*. Oxford University Press, 1994; Sarna, Jonathan D. *American Judaism*. Yale UP 2004.
3. Stephen Norwood writes: "Led by Joe McWilliams, the Christian Mobilizers, whose rhetoric was explicitly violent, were influential in many New York City neighborhoods. Although McWilliams was not Catholic, the advisory board of the Christian Mobilizers consisted almost entirely of Irish Americans. McWilliams

boasted that his twenty bodyguards were all former members of the Irish Republican Army (IRA). A former Christian Front activist, McWilliams was nicknamed "Joe McNazi" by liberals. He often worked himself into a frenzy during his harangues, tearing off his collar and tie as he shouted antisemitic and anti-Roosevelt epithets. McWilliams called Hitler "the greatest leader in the history of the world," and denounced President Roosevelt as "an amateur Englishman [and] a Jew. Alleging that Roosevelt was Jewish or had significant Jewish ancestry was a common theme of German propaganda broadcasts" (Norwood 2003:236).

Chapter 4

1 Miller used a similar technique in *All My Sons* which is set entirely in the Keller backyard in Ohio, but New York somewhat looms in the background. Ann and George Deever, the children of Joe Keller's partner, Steve, who is in prison for the crime of knowingly selling defective plan parts, for which Joe "pulled a fast one" and avoided jail time, have escaped the scandal by moving to New York. George is a New York lawyer and Joe and Kate fear his acumen in seeking the truth about Joe's part in the coverup; whereas Ann perhaps has lost her homespun Midwest innocence in New York by planning plan to use the letter that Larry wrote her.
2 For further history of Erasmus Field, see "Brooklyn Ball Parks and "Erasmus Field" at BrooklynBallParks.com – Erasmus Field (covehurst.net)
3 Sections of the discussion of "The 1928 Buick" appear in edited form in Marino, Stephen (2007), "The Greatest Cars Ever Built: Arthur Miller's Production Line of Chevrolets, Buicks, Studebakers, Marmons, Porsches and Other Vehicles of Death and Destruction," *The Arthur Miller Journal*, Volume 2 No. 2, Fall 2007, 5-20.

References

Abbotson, Susan C. W. (2007), *Arthur Miller, A Literary Reference to His Life and Work*, New York: Facts on File.

Adler, Thomas (2004), "To See Feelingly: Moral (In)sight in Arthur Miller's *Homely Girl, A Life* and *Broken Glass*," *Shofar: An Interdisciplinary Journal of Jewish Studies*, 22 (4): 14–21.

Agee, James (1972), "Southeast of the Island: Travel Notes," in Robert Fitzgerald (ed.), *Collected Short Prose of James Agee*, 189, London: Marion Boyars Publishers Ltd.

Antisemitism (n.d.), "Anti-Semitism in American History," *Anti-Defamation League*, Available online: https://antisemitism.adl.org/.

"All That Remains of Schrafft's in Downtown Brooklyn" (2007), *Mc Brooklyn*. http://mcbrooklyn.blogspot.com/2007/10/all-that-remains-of-schraffts-in.html.

Barron, James (1988), "August '44: A Month too Hot for Satan," *New York Times*, August 17, Section B, 2.

Barron, James (2023), "Honoring the Dockworker Killed for Defying the Mob," "Newsletter, New York Today," *New York Times*, September 15, 2023.

Bell, Bill (2017), "The Death and Lavish Funeral of Al Capone Associate Frankie Yale," *New York Daily News*, August 14, 2017. https://www.nydailynews.com/new-york/death-lavish-funeral-al-capone-associate-frankie-yale-article-1.803659.

"Ben Zinn Remembers Marilyn at Ebbets Field" (2022), *The Marilyn Report*, November 21, 2022. https://themarilynreport.com/2022/11/01/ben-zinn-remembers-marilyn-at-ebbets-field/

Ben-Zvi, Linda (1989), "'Home Sweet Home': Deconstructing the Masculine Myth of the Frontier in Modern Drama," in David Mogen, Mark Busby, and Paul Bryant (eds.), *The Frontier Experience and the American Drama*, 217–25, College Station: Texas A&M University Press.

Berger, Marilyn (2005), "Arthur Miller, Moral Voice Of American Stage, Dies at 89." *New York Times*, February 11, 2005, Section A, 1.

Bewley, Marius (1959), "Scott Fitzgerald and the Collapse of the American Dream," in *The Eccentric Design, Form in the Classic American Novel*, New York: Columbia University Press.

Bigsby, Christopher (2005a), *Arthur Miller: A Critical Study*, Cambridge: Cambridge University Press.

Bigsby, Christopher (2005b), "Fiction," in *Arthur Miller, A Critical Study*, Cambridge: Cambridge University Press, 460-462.

Bigsby, Christopher (2008), *Arthur Miller 1915–1962*, London: Weidenfeld & Nicolson.

Bigsby, Christopher (2011), *Arthur Miller 1962–2005*, London: Weidenfeld & Nicolson.

"Boulevard Gardens, Woodside Queens" (1994), Excerpt from Gregory, Catherine. *Woodside, Queens County, New York: A Historical Perspective, 1652–1994*. New York: Woodside on the Move.

Bradbury, Malcolm (1997), "Arthur Miller's Fiction," in Christopher Bigsby (ed.), *The Cambridge Companion to Arthur Miller*, 211–29, Cambridge: Cambridge University Press.

Brater, Enoch (1983), "Ethics and Ethnicity in the Plays of Arthur Miller," in Sarah Blacher Cohen (ed.), *From Hester Street to Hollywood: The Jewish-American Stage and Screen*, 123–36, Bloomington, IN: Indiana University Press.

"Break in Long Heat Wave Seen; Mercury 93°, a Record for the Date" (1944), *New York Times*, August 15, 1944. https://junkscience.com/wp-content/uploads/2019/08/87463472.pdf.

"Brooklyn Bowling Proprietor's Association" (1950), *Brooklyn Eagle*, April 21, 1950, 21. https://www.newspapers.com/article/brooklyn-eagle-brooklyn-bowling-alleys-1/18159136/

"Brooklyn Navy Yard" (n.d.), Brooklyn Navy Yard – History of New York City (shu.edu). https://blogs.shu.edu/nyc-history/2022/04/16/brooklyn-navy-yard/ (accessed September 29, 2024).

"Bungalows of The Rockaways" (n.d.), *Kehilla Links*, The Rockaways (jewishgen.org). https://kehilalinks.jewishgen.org/rockaways/index.html (accessed September 29, 2024).

Callahan, Jennifer, Dir. (2012), *The Bungalows of Rockaway Small Houses and Big Dreams on Gotham's Shore.* Harris, 2010. https://www.thebungalowsofrockaway.com/.

Chavkin, Allan (2020), "A Family in Crisis: A Family Systems Theory Approach to Arthur Miller's 'I Don't Need You Any More'," *The Arthur Miller Journal*, 15 (2): 141–62.

Cohen, Randy (2005a), " We'll Map Manhattan," *New York Times*, May 1, 2005, Section 7, 31. www.nytimes.com/2005/05/01/books/review/well-map-manhattan.html.

Cohen, Randy (2005b), "We Mapped Manhattan," *New York Times*. June 5, 2005, Section 7, 23. www.nytimes.com/2005/06/05/books/review/we-mapped-manhattan.html.

Copeland, Joan (2008), "A Conversation with Joan Copeland," Interviewed by Stephen Marino, *The Arthur Miller Journal*, 3 (1): 43–65.

"Coughlin Supports Christian Front" (1940), *New York Times*, January 22, 1940. https://timesmachine.nytimes.com/timesmachine/1940/01/22/94780913.pdf.

Daninhirsch, Hillary (2011), "Miller's *Focus* Holds Up as Timeless Condemnation of Anti-Semitism," *Pittsburgh Jewish Chronicle*, December 14. https://jewishchronicle.timesofisrael.com/millers-focus-holdsup-as-timeless-condemnation-of-anti-semitism/ (accessed May 13, 2025).

"Dates for the Jewish Holidays of Rosh Hashanah and Yom Kippur from 1900 to 2020," https://gist.github.com/jtoll/ce463b9e2727ac42389c (accessed March 28, 2023).

"Deluxe Theatre," *Cinema Treasures*. http://cinematreasures.org/theaters/4656.

Dinnerstein, Leonard (1994), *Anti-Semitism in America*, Oxford: Oxford University Press.

Doss, Erica (2016), "Anti-Semitism, Propaganda and Modernism," in *Orthodox Boys 1948 by Bernard Perlin*, London: Tate Research Publication. https://www.tate.org.uk/research/in-focus/orthodox-boys-bernard-perlin/anti-semitism-propaganda-modernism (accessed 6 October 2022).

"Dreaming Walls: Inside the Chelsea Hotel" Asleep. Movie Review by Neely Swanson, July 3, 2022. "Dreaming Walls: Inside the Chelsea Hotel" Asleep [MOVIE REVIEW] *Easy Reader News*.

"Edward Curran, Right Wing Priest " (1974), *New York Times*, February 16, 1974, 34.

"Erasmus Field" (n.d.), http://www.covehurst.net/ddyte/brooklyn/erasmus.html (accessed May 25, 2023).

"Far Rockaway Beach Bungalow Historic District" (2013), *National Register of Historic Places Program*, National Park Service, 2013.

Farrington, M. C. (2019), "When Caroline Kennedy Last Christened a Ship in the Name of Her Father," *Hampton Roads Naval Museum*, December 6. https://hamptonroadsnavalmuseum.blogspot.com/2019/12/when-caroline-kennedy-last-christened.html.

Faulkner, William (2007), *The Paris Review Interviews*, vol. II, 57, New York: Picador; also in *The Lion in the Garden: Interviews with William Faulkner 1926–1962*. New York: Random House, 1962.

"Feature Films Showing Today" (1944), *Brooklyn Eagle*, May 10, 17.

Ferguson, Alfred R. (1978), "The Tragedy of The American Dream in *Death of a Salesman*," *Thought: A Review of Culture and Idea*, 53: 83–98.

Fishler, Moe, *Find a Grave*, Memorial ID: 205850714, Washington Cemetery. https://www.findagrave.com/memorial/205850714/moe-fishler (accessed July 18, 2021).

"Fisk Theatre," *Cinema Treasures*. http://cinematreasures.org/theaters/7470.

Focus, IMDb. https://www.imdb.com/title/tt0246628/ (accessed May 13, 2025).

"Football Games at Ebbets Field," www.luckyshow.org (accessed October, 2023).
Gallagher, Charles R. (2021), *Nazis of Copley Square: The Forgotten Story of the Christian Front*, Cambridge: Harvard University Press.
Galvani, William (1992), "Presidents and Submarines," *The Submarine Review*, July 1992. https://archive.navalsubleague.org/1992/presidents-and-submarines-2
Gregory, Catherine (1994), *Woodside, A Historical Perspective 1652–1994*. New York: Woodside on the Move.
Gross, Barry Edward (1965), "Peddler and Pioneer in *Death of a Salesman*," *Modern Drama*, 7 (4): 405–10.
Hamm, Theodore (2020), *Bernie's Brooklyn: How Growing Up In The New Deal City Shaped Bernie Sanders' Politics*, New York: OR Books. https://d.docs.live.net/ (retrieved August 15, 2021).
"He Was No Misfit in Brooklyn" (2006), *On This Day in History: October 17*, Brooklyn Eagle, Published online October 17, 2006.
"Historical Vital Records," *The New York City Municipal Archives*. https://a860-historicalvitalrecords.nyc.gov/.
"History of the Yard," https://brooklynnavyyard.org/about/history (accessed October 1, 2024).
"Hotel Commodore: Past, Present, and Future" (2021), *The Harlem Line*, March 3, 2021. https://www.iridetheharlemline.com/2021/03/03/project-commodore-past-present-and-future-of-grand-centrals-railroad-hotel-part-1/ (accessed October 3, 2021).
Hylton, Hylton (2014), "Labor Noir: Murders and Funerals on the Brooklyn Waterfront," Transport Workers Union, 2014. https://www.transportworkers.org/node/1618.
Kensinger, Nathan (1915), "The Slow Resurgence of the Rockaway Bungalow," *Curbed New York*, The Slow Resurgence of the Rockaway Bungalow – Curbed NY, September 17, 2015. https://ny.curbed.com/2015/9/17/9920336/the-slow-resurgence-of-the-rockaway-bungalow (accessed April 9, 2021).
"The King" (1966), *Time*, February 4, 1966.
Laterman, Kaya (2013), "In Far Rockaway, Recognition for Bungalows," *Wall Street Journal*, January 28.
Laterman, Kaya (2016), "Superman's Building Goes Condo," *New York Times*, September 4, 2016, Section RE, 2. https://www.nytimes.com/2016/09/04/realestate/supermans-building-goes-condo.html.
Lebovic, Matt (2017), "When Boston was America's 'Capital' of Anti-Semitism." *The Times of Israel*. https://www.timesofisrael.com/when-boston-was-the-capital-of-anti-semitism-in-america/
"Loew's Woodside Theatre," *Cinema Treasures*. http://cinematreasures.org/theaters/6406

Mailer, Norman (1982), "Interview," *The Brooklyn Heights Press*, September 30.

"Marilyn Monroe and Arthur Miller's New York Apartment Hits the Market," *The Spaces*. https://thespaces.com/marilyn-monroe-arthur-millers-new-york-apartment-hits-market/ (accessed December 2, 2022).

Marino, Stephen (2000), "'It's Brooklyn, I Know, but We Hunt Too:' The Image of the Borough in *Death of a Salesman*," in *"The Salesman Has A Birthday": Essays Celebrating the Fiftieth Anniversary of Arthur Miller's Death of a Salesman*, Lanham, MD: University Press of America.

Marino, Stephen (2002), "Chapter Six, *The Ride Down Mt. Morgan* and *Broken Glass*" in *A Language Study of Arthur Miller's Plays: "The Poetic in the Colloquial*, Lewiston, NY: Edwin Mellen Press.

Marino, Stephen (2003), "Arthur Miller," Twentieth-Century American Dramatists: Fourth Series, in Christopher J. Wheatley (ed.), *Dictionary of Literary Biography*, vol. 266, Detroit: Thomson/Gale.

Marino, Stephen (2005), "Touring Arthur Miller's Brooklyn," *The Arthur Miller Society Newsletter* 11: 8–12.

Marino, Stephen (2006), "Editor's Note," *The Arthur Miller Journal*, 1 (no. 1): 1–2.

Marino, Stephen (2007a), "'Physician Heal Thyself': Arthur Miller's Portrayal of Doctors," in Paula Langteau (ed.), *Miller and Middle America*, 41–54, Lanham, MD: University Press of America.

Marino, Stephen (2007b), "The Greatest Cars Ever Built: Arthur Miller's Production Line of Chevrolets, Buicks, Studebakers, Marmons, Porsches and Other Vehicles of Death and Destruction," *Arthur Miller Journal*, 2 (2): 5–20.

Marino, Stephen (2010), "Commentary," in *Arthur Miller, A View From the Bridge* with Commentary and Notes by Stephen Marino. London: Methuen Drama.

Marino, Stephen (2015), "Introduction," in *Arthur Miller* Death of a Salesman/The Crucible*: A Reader's Guide to Essential Criticism*, New York: Palgrave/MacMillan.

Marino, Stephen (2018), "Arthur Miller In Brooklyn Heights," in Felicia Hardison Londré (ed.), *Modern American Drama: Playwriting in the 1940s, Voices, Documents, New Interpretations*, London: Bloomsbury Methuen Drama.

Marino, Stephen (2021), "*No Villain*, Performance Review," *Arthur Miller Journal*, 15 (2): 169–73.

Marino, Stephen (2022), "Commentary," in *Arthur Miller, A Memory of Two Mondays*, London: Methuen Drama.

Marino, Stephen (2024), "Arthur Miller as a Christian Writer," *Arthur Miller Journal*, 19 (1): 20–8.

Martin, Robert A. (1978), "Introduction," in Robert A. Martin (ed.), *The Theatre Essays of Arthur Miller*, xix-xlii. New York: Viking.

Martin, Robert A., and Steven R. Centola, eds. (1996), *The Theatre Essays of Arthur Miller*, Boston: DaCapo Press.

Miller, Arthur (1944), "Ditchy," *Mayfair Magazine*, October 1944: 37+.
Miller, Arthur (1945), *Focus*, New York: Penguin Books.
Miller, Arthur (1949), *Death of a Salesman*, New York: Penguin Plays.
Miller, Arthur (1955a), "A Boy Grew in Brooklyn," *Holiday* 17 (March 1955) 54+.
Miller, Arthur (1955b), *A Memory of Two Mondays*, New York: Dramatists Play Service.
Miller, Arthur (1955c), *A View from the Bridge* (one-act version) in *Arthur Miller, Collected Plays, 1944-1961*, New York: The Library of America, 2006.
Miller, Arthur (1956, 1978), "The Family in Modern Drama," in Robert A. Martin (ed.), *The Theatre Essays of Arthur Miller*, New York: Viking.
Miller, Arthur (1959), "I Don't Need You Anymore," *Esquire*, December 1959, 270+; *I Don't Need You Anymore*, New York: Viking, 1967, 3-52; *The Misfits and Other Stories*, New York: Scribners, 1987, 3-52, Rpt in *Presence*. New York: Penguin, 2016, 3-47.
Miller, Arthur (1960), "Please Don't Kill Anything," *Story* (1960), Rpt. in *I Don't Need You Anymore*, New York: Viking, 1967, 71-8, Rpt. in *The Misfits and Other Stories*, New York: Scribners, 1987, 71-8, Rpt in *Presence*, New York: Penguin, 2016, 64-9.
Miller, Arthur (1962), "Glimpse of a Jockey," *Story* 5 (1962). Rpt in *I Don't Need You Anymore*. Viking, 1967, 114-17. Rpt in *The Misfits and Other Stories*, New York: Scribners, 1987, 114-17, Rpt in *Presence*. New York: Penguin, 2016, 102-05.
Miller, Arthur (1964), *After the Fall*, New York: Penguin.
Miller, Arthur (1966), "A Search for a Future," *Saturday Evening Post* 13 August 1966: 64-8, 70. Rpt in *I Don't Need You Anymore*, New York: Viking, 1967, 224-40; Rpt in *The Misfits and Other Stories*, New York: Scribners, 1987, 224-40, Rpt in *Presence*, New York: Penguin, 2016, 201-18.
Miller, Arthur (1967), *Arthur Miller Death of a Salesman, Text and Criticism*, ed. Gerald Weales, New York: Penguin Books.
Miller, Arthur (1967a, 2016), "Fame," in *I Don't Need You Anymore*. Viking, 1967, 166-74. Rpt In *Homely Girl, A Life and Other Stories*. Viking: 1995, 49-58, Rpt. in *Presence*. New York: Penguin, 2016, 149-56.
Miller, Arthur (1967b, 2016), "Fitter's Night," *I Don't Need You Anymore*. Viking, 1967, 175-223. Rpt In *Homely Girl, A Life and Other Stories*. Viking: 1995, 61-115, Rpt in *Presence*. New York: Penguin, 2016, 157-200.
Miller, Arthur (1968), *The Price*, New York: Penguin Plays.
Miller, Arthur (1977), *A View from the Bridge* (Two Act Version), New York: Penguin
Miller, Arthur (1978a), "Introduction to the Collected Plays," in Robert A. Martin (ed.), *The Theatre Essays of Arthur Miller*, New York: Viking.
Miller, Arthur (1978b), "On Social Plays," in Robert A. Martin (ed.), *The Theatre Essays of Arthur Miller*, New York: Viking.

Miller, Arthur (1978c), "The 1928 Buick," *Atlantic*, 242: 49–51, 54–6.

Miller, Arthur (1978d), "The Family in Modern Drama," in Robert A. Martin (ed.), *The Theatre Essays of Arthur Miller*, New York: Viking.

Miller Arthur (1978e), "Tragedy and the Common Man," in Robert A. Martin (ed.), *The Theatre Essays of Arthur Miller*, New York: Viking, 1978.

Miller, Arthur (1978f), "Introduction to the Collected Plays," in Robert A. Martin (ed.), *The Theatre Essays of Arthur Miller*, New York: Viking.

Miller, Arthur (1978g), "The Family in Modern Drama," in Robert A. Martin (ed.), *The Theatre Essays of Arthur Miller*, New York: Viking.

Miller, Arthur (1981), *Arthur Miller's Collected Plays*, vol. 2, New York: Viking.

Miller, Arthur (1984), "Introduction," in *Focus*, New York: Penguin, v–x.

Miller, Arthur (1987), *Timebends, A Life*, New York: Grove Press.

Miller, Arthur (1989), *The Archbishop's Ceiling/ The American Clock*, New York: Grove Press.

Miller, Arthur (1992), *Homely Girl, A Life,* New York: Penguin.

Miller, Arthur (1994), *Broken Glass*, New York: Penguin, 1994.

Miller, Arthur (1995), "In Memoriam," *The New Yorker*, December 25, 1995 and January 1, 1996, 56–7.

Miller, Arthur (1996), *The Ride Down Mt. Morgan*, New York: Penguin Plays.

Miller, Arthur (1997) *Arthur Miller: An Interview*, A BBC Production, Films for the Humanities and Sciences, FFH 7295, 1997.

Miller, Arthur (1998), "Before Air Conditioning," *The New Yorker,* June 22 and 29, 1998, 144–7

Miller, Arthur (1999), "Walking with Arthur Miller," *The New Yorker,* January 25, 1999.

Miller, Arthur (2000), "A City of Stories," *New York Magazine*, December 18–23, 2000, 122.

Miller, Arthur (2001, 2016), "Bulldog," *The New Yorker*, August 13, 2001, Rpt in *Presence,* New York: Penguin, 2016, 257–67.

Miller, Arthur (2001a), "His Jewish Question." *Vanity Fair,* October 2001. https://www.vanityfair.com/culture/2001/10/arthur-miller-200110.

Miller, Arthur (2001b), "Shattering The Silence, Illuminating The Hatred," *NY Times*, October 22, 2001, E 1–2.

Miller, Arthur (2001c), *Focus*, New York: Penguin Books.

Miller, Arthur (2002a), "The Chelsea Effect," *Granta Online Edition,* June 28, 2002. https://granta.com/The-Chelsea-Effect/.

Miller, Arthur (2002b), "The Performance," *The New Yorker,* April 22/29, 2002, 176–88; Rpt in *Presence,* New York: Penguin, 2016, 269–87.

Miller, Arthur (2002c, 2016), "The Bare Manuscript," *The New Yorker*, December 16, 2002, Rpt in *Presence,* New York: Penguin, 2016, 297–319.

Miller, Arthur (2002d), "My New York Places That Changed Us," *New York*, December 10–25.

Miller, Arthur (2002e), "The Chelsea Effect," *Granta Online Edition*, June 28, 2002. https://granta.com/The-Chelsea-Effect/

Miller, Arthur (2003, 2016), "Presence," *Esquire,* July 2003, 106–9, Rpt in *Presence*, New York: Penguin, 2016, 366–71.

Miller, Arthur (2004, 2016), "The Turpentine Still," *Southwest Review*, 89.4 (2004): 479–520, Rpt. in *Presence* New York: Penguin, 2016, 320–65.

Miller, Arthur (2006), "A Final Conversation with Arthur Miller," Interviewed by Christopher Bigsby, *The Arthur Miller Journal*, 1 (no. 1): 61–77.

Miller, Arthur (2009), *Mr. Peter's Connections. Plays: Six*, London: Methuen Drama.

Miller, Arthur (2022), *A Memory of Two Mondays*, London: Methuen Drama.

Murphy, Brenda (1995), *Miller Death of a Salesman*, Cambridge: Cambridge University Press.

"New York's Literary Legendary Hangouts," *New York Times*, August 26, 2021.

Norwood, Stephen (2003), "Marauding Youth and the Christian Front: Antisemitic Violence in Boston and New York During World War II," *American Jewish History*, 91 (2): 233–67.https://doi.org/ 10.1353/ajh.2004.0055.

O'Toole, Fintan (2019), "The Irish Priest Who Paved the Way for Donald Trump," *The Irish Times,* March 9, 2019.

Patell, Cyrus, R. K., and Bryan Waterman, eds. (2010), *The Cambridge Companion to the Literature of New York*, Cambridge: Cambridge University Press.

Pitt, Amy (2001), "The Standish: Brooklyn's Most Expensive and Celebrity-Studded Building," *New York Times, Street East Reads*, July 28, 2023. https://streeteasy.com/blog/the-standish-brooklyn-celebrity-filled-condos/.

Poore, Charles (1945), "Books of the Times," *NY Times*, November 24, 1945, 17.

"The Precincts of the Patrol Borough of Queens," *Police NY.* http://www.policeny.com/thehousequeens1.html

Prial, Frank J. (1974), "Pavillon Closes Doors As a Dining Era Fades," *New York Times*, September 26, 1974, 9.

Reimer, Robert C., and Carol J. Reimer (2012), *Historical Dictionary of Holocaust Cinema*, Lanham: Scarecrow Press.

Richards, David (1994), "A Paralysis Points to Spiritual and Social Ills," *New York Times,* 25 April 1994, C11–13.

Robinson, Brian (1987), "The Geography of a Crossroads: Modernism, Surrealism, and Geography," in William E. Mallory and Paul Simpson-Housely (eds.),

Geography and Literature: A Meeting of the Disciplines, Syracuse: Syracuse University Press.

Rosenthal, Daniel (2010), "Arthur Miller's *Broken Glass* Reveals His Private Sorrow," *Independent*, September 22, 2010. https://www.the-independent.com/arts-entertainment/theatre-dance/features/arthur-miller-s-broken-glass-reveals-his-private-sorrows-2086849.html#.

Ross, Andrew, and David Dyte (n.d.), "Brooklyn's Semipro Fields," http://www.covehurst.net/ddyte/brooklyn/semipro_parks.html (accessed May 25, 2023).

Sarna, Jonathan D. (2004), *American Judaism*, New Haven: Yale University Press.

"Schrafft's, Downtown Brooklyn" (2015), *Forgotten New York*. https://forgottenny.com/2015/04/schraffts-downtown-brooklyn/.

Schwartz, Stephen (2004), "Arthur Miller's Proletariat: The True Stories of 'On the Waterfront', Pietro Panto, and Vincenzo Longhi." *Film History*, 16 (4): 378–92. www.jstor.org/stable/3815607 (accessed August 23, 2021).

Schwartz, Stephen (2005), "The True Lives of Tales on the Waterfront," *Cisco Houston*, 2005. http://www.ciscohouston.com/books/longhi_2.shtml (February 11, 2005).

Sciorra, Joseph (2021), "Chi è Pete Panto?" *Turnstile Tours*. https://turnstiletours.com/where-is-pete-panto-corruption-and-crusaders-on-nycs-waterfront/ (March 22, 2021).

Shales, Tom (1978), "*Fame*: A Provocative Feather," *Washington Post*, November 30, 1978.

"Site of 1928 Gang Shooting" (2013), *Atlas Obsura*, August 22, 2013. https://www.atlasobscura.com/places/site-of-1928-gang-shooting.

Skee, Joey (2009), "Chi è Pete Panto?" 1–3, *Chi è Pete Panto?* (iitaly.org) (July 14, 2009).

Sokolovskyi, Andrii (2025), "How Monroe Put on a Show at a Football Match in the US – Hit A Photographer and Nearly Got Injured," *Tribuna.com*. https://tribuna.com/en/blogs/how-monroe-put-on-a-show-at-a-football-match-in-the-us-hit-a/, 10 February, 2025, (retrieved February 28, 2025).

Stanton, Kay (1989), "Women and the American Dream of *Death of a Salesman*," in June Schlueter (ed.), *Feminist Rereadings of Modern American Drama*, Rutherford, NJ: Fairleigh Dickinson University Press.

Stapinski, Helene (2016), "Arthur Miller's Brooklyn," *New York Times*, January 24, 2016, MB, 1, 6.

Stapinski, Helene (2018), "A View From the Barge," *New York Times,* May 16, 2018. https://www.nytimes.com/2018/05/16/nyregion/a-view-from-the-barge.html.

Stapinski, Helene (2022), "Where is Pete Panto," *New York Times*, July 9, 2022, 1+. https://www.nytimes.com/2022/07/09/nyregion/pete-panto-dockworkers-union-mafia.html.

Streeteasy Team (2023), "The Standish: Brooklyn's Most Expensive and Celebrity-Studded Building," *Celebrity Homes*, May 8. https://streeteasy.com/blog/the-standish-brooklyn-celebrity-filled-condos/amp/ (retrieved May 14, 2025).

Sultan, Tim (2016), *Sunny's Nights,* New York: Random House.

Viswamohan, Aysha (2014), "Arthur Miller and the New York State of Being," *Studies in Theatre and Performance*, 34 (1): 62–74. https://doi.org/10.1080/14682761.2013.875715.

Walsh, Kevin (2014), "Hiding in Woodside," *Brownstoner*, September 2014. https://www.brownstoner.com/architecture/hiding-in-woodside/.

Ward, Nathan (2011), "Chapter One: "DOV'È PANTO?" *Dark Harbor, The War for the New York Waterfront*, New York: Picador.

Ward, Nathan (2019), "The Tragic Violent History of the Brooklyn Waterfront," *Crime Reads*, July 17, 2019.

Werner, Laura. "Newly Restored But With Raffish Spirit Intact, New York's Hotel Chelsea Reopens." *Forbes*, "Travel" May 7, 2022. https://www.forbes.com/sites/lauriewerner/2022/05/07/newly-restored-but-with-raffish-spirit-intact-new-yorks-hotel-chelsea-reopens/.

"When Marilyn 'Kicked Off' at Ebbets Field" (2021), *The Marilyn Report,* February 21, 2021. https://themarilynreport.com/2021/02/21/when-marilyn-kicked-off-at-ebbets-field/.

Whitaker, Jan (2008), "When Ladies Lunched: Schrafft's," *Restaurant-ing Through History*, August 27, 2008. https://restaurant-ingthroughhistory.com/2008/08/27/when-ladies-lunched-schraffts/.

"Who Was Frankie Yale and How Did He Die?" (2014), *National Crimes Syndicate*. https://www.nationalcrimesyndicate.com/who-was-frankie-yale-how-did-he-die/

Williams, Keith (2017), "How Lincoln Center Was Built (It Wasn't Pretty)," *New York Times*, December 21.

Winchell, Louisa (2020), "Beyond the Village and Back: The 'Marble Palace' A.T. Stewart Store at 280 Broadway," "Off the Grid," *Village Preservation*, September 21. https://www.villagepreservation.org/2020/09/21/beyond-the-village-and-back-the-marble-palace-a-t-stewart-store-at-280-broadway/.

"Womraths," *NY Bookstores in 1946*, New York City April 1946 – NY BOOKSTORES IN 1946.

"Woodside, Queens (History)" https://urbanareas.net/info/resources/neighborhoods-queens/woodside-queens-history/.

"Woodside, Queens, Part 1" (2005a), *Forgotten New York*. https://forgotten-ny.com/2005/10/woodside-queens-part-1/ (October 22, 2005).

"Woodside, Queens, Part 2" (2005b), *Forgotten New York*. https://forgotten-ny.com/2005/10/woodside-queens-part-2/ (October 22, 2005).

Index

Note: Page numbers in italics indicate figures and tables and after "n" indicates notes.

Abbotson, Susan 30, 55, 56
Abraham Lincoln High School 25, 73, 119, 180, 207 n.9
Adler, Thomas 121
After the Fall 4, 9, 101–2, 105
   Broadway revival 108
   New York References in 106–10, *108*
Agee, James 148
Akron Corporation 152
Albee, Edward 1
Alfieri (*A View from the Bridge*) 58, 77, 80–1
All My Sons 1, 43, 45, 131
   pre-Broadway tryout 43
   royalties from 52
   success with 30, *32*
America's Century 2
American anti-Semitism 7, 131, 133
American Clock, The 4, 9, 11, 21–2, 37, 39, 208 n.2
American Dream 8, 57, 60, 77
   American Legion 56
American Society for the Prevention of Cruelty to Animals (ASPCA) 165
American South 2
Angels with Dirty Faces 94
Anthony Adverse 94
anti-Semitism 4, 118, 132, 136, 154
Appel, Benjamin 47
Arab-Israel conflicts 2
Aronson, Boris 103–4
Arthur Miller Conference 27, *192*
Astaire, Fred 94
AT Stewart Store *71*
Auden, W. H. 27

Balsam, Lee 22, 188
"Bare Manuscript, The" (2002) 164, 187
Barnett, Louis 8–9, 18, 38

Beatrice (*A View from the Bridge*) 78, 80, 85
Beckett, Samuel 1
"Before Air Conditioning" (*New Yorker* essay) 157
Bellow, Saul 2
Berkowitz, Meyer 174–5
Bernie's Brooklyn 51
Beverly Theatre 94, 210 n.12
Bewley, Marius 57
Bigsby, Christopher 9, 18, 20, 25, 104, 122, 131, 148, 164, 167
Blanche, Aunt 103
Bloomgarden, Kermit 54
Blunt, Emily 71
Boulevard Gardens 137
Bowling Association list *88*
"Boy Grew in Brooklyn, A" (*Holiday* magazine) 22, 99, 168
Boy Meets Girl 94
Brantley, Ben xv
Bradbury, Malcolm 121
"Bridge to the Savage World" (essay) 56
Broken Glass (1994) 1, 4, 6, 23, 37, 42, 56–7, 90, 99, 144
   Brooklyn locations in 90
   Cable Bldg. 611 Broadway *97*
   Ocean Parkway 91, *92*
   Schrafft's Restaurant *95*
   Wanamaker's Bldg. *98*
Brooklyn Bridge 40, 184, 187
Brooklyn docks and piers 83
Brooklyn Dodgers 72
Brooklyn Heights 166–7
   duplex apartment *31*
   French Flats *28*
   Miller in *33*
   residences 28, *34*

Brooklyn Navy Yard   30, 181, *182*
Brooklyn plays   37
   birth of   42–57
   Depression encampments   *41*
   Empire State Building   *42*
   fictionalizing Brooklyn   61–99
   Gargiulio's Funeral Home in
      Red Hook   *49*
   ILA Headquarters   *50*
   literal and figurative Brooklyn   57–60
   No Villain   37–8
   Union Square   *40*
Brooklyn Promenade   33–4
Brooklyn-Queens Expressway   34
"1928 Buick, The" (autobiographical short
      story)   25, 137, 164, 166, 188
"Bulldog"   164
bungalow communities   170–1
Bungalows of Rockaway, The (film
      documentary)   172
Burns, George   15

Cagney, James   94
Calabrese, Tony   180
Callahan, Jennifer   172
*Cambridge Companion to Literature of
   New York, The*   5
Cantor, Eddie   15
Capone, Al   79–81
Capote, Truman   27
Carbone, Eddie   53, 55, 57–8
Carefree (movie)   94
Carlyle Hotel   110, *111*
Case, Stanton   94
Catherine (*A View from the* Bridge)   53,
      55, 78, 80, 85
Catholic War Veterans   56
Cavalcade of America (DuPont)   30
Chadwick-Delamater   26, 114, 118, 120,
      135, 167–8
Charley (*Death of a Salesman*)   62,
      68, 73, 75
Chavkin, Alan   173
Chekhov, Anton   1, 26
Chelsea Effect, The   36, 106
Chicago (Bellow)   2
Christian Front   132, 140, 158
   anti-Semitic attacks   158–9
   violence against Jews   159–60
Christian Mobilizers   160

Cobb, Lee J.   52, 77
Cohen, Randy   5
Cold War   2
Communist ties   56
Communist Witch Hunts   2
Coney Island   40, *40*
Copeland, Joan   10–11, 103, 131, 172
Cotton Club   15
Coughlin, Fr. Charles E.   134, 158
Crandall, George   168
Crucible, The (1953)   1, 35, 53, 133
   European premiere   55
   trial transcripts   35
cultural revolution of   1960s and
      Vietnam   2
Curran, Fr. Edward   134, 159

Damon, Matt   71
Daninhirsch, Hillary   134
Death of a Salesman   1, 3–5, 22, 31, 37,
      39, 42–3, 61
   American Dream   77
   Brooklyn home of Willy
      Loman in   6, 24
   Ebbets Field   72–3
   expressionistic techniques in   101
   Jewish salesmen   75
   New York colloquial reference   69
   production of   54
   AT Stewart Store   *71*
   Wagner firm   70
"Declaration of Honesty"   69. See
      also "New York State Regents
      Examinations"
"Ditchy"   164, 168
Domink, Jane K.   xiii, xiv
Doss, Erika   136, 149
Downtown Brooklyn   92, 209 n.9
Downtown Brooklyn Civic Center   27
downtown Manhattan   209 n.9
Dublin (Joyce)   2
DuBois, W. E. B.   33
Dunnock, Mildred   52, 77

Eagle Cafeteria   113
Ebbets Field   72–4, *73*
Empire City Iron Works   95
Empire State Building   *42*
Enemy of the People, An (Ibsen)
      31–2, 53, 133

Erasmus Field   165, *166*
Esquire   173

"Fame"   164, 173–4
"Family in Modern Drama, The" (1956 essay)   39
Father Coughlin Speaking (1938 lithograph)   159
Faulkner, William   2
Federal Theatre Project   103
Felt, Lyman   104, 110–12
fictionalizing Brooklyn   61
  Broken Glass   90–9
  Death of a Salesman   61–77
  View from the Bridge, A   77–90
figurative Brooklyn   57–60
Filene's   70
Findley, Fergus   47
Fink, Sam   121
Finkelstein (*Focus*)   132, 138, 147, 150
Fisher, Miss   14, 102
Fishler, Moe   188
  East 3rd Street home of   *189*
  Washington Cemetery   *191*
Fisk Theatre   143, *143*, 144
"Fitter's Night" (1967)   164, 180–3
Fitzgerald, Scott F.   129
Five Sullivan Brothers   *184*
Flatbush Avenue   86–7
Focus (1945)   4–5, 74, 131, 161
  anti-Semitism   133, 154
  attached homes in Woodside   *140, 141*
  Christian Mobilizers   160
  film version   *141*
  Fisk Theatre   143, *143*, 144
  graffiti   148–9
  home at Newman's address in Woodside   *139*
  Jewish cemeteries   136
  Loew's Woodside Theatre   143, *145*
  Nazi rally at Madison Square Garden   *159*
  New York's historic 1944 heat wave   158
  New York's subway system   147
  Plaza Hotel   *156*
  plot of   132
  Radio City Music Hall   *155*
  Radio Priests   134

Trinity Church   *153, 154*
Woodside National Bank   *142*
Woodside Theatre   143, *146*
Fox, William   9
Franks, Sid   11–12, 103
Fred (*Focus*)   132, 137–8, 150
French battleship *Richelieu*   181

Gargiulio's Funeral Home in Red Hook   49
Gelfand, Bernie   174
Gellburg, Phillip   57–9
Gellburg, Sylvia   57–9
Ginsberg, Alan   5
Giuliano, Salvatore   51 *See also* "Sicilian Bandit"
"Glimpse at a Jockey, A"   163
graffiti   148–9
Gramercy Park   40
Grand Hyatt New York   66
Grass Still Grows, The (1939)   37
Great Depression   2, 23, 39, 41, 103, 116
Great Disobedience, The   37
Gross, Barry   4
Groton Shipyard   109
Guthrie, Woody   51

Hard Times (Terkel)   39
Hardy, Thomas   2
Hart, Gertrude   132, 152
Herman (*Focus*)   123–5, *126*, 128
Hoffman, Dustin   77
"Holocaust" plays   19, 132
Homely Girl, A Life   4, 7, 101, 121, 123, 129, 154
  fictional Crosby Hotel   128
  settings in Manhattan   122
Honors at Dawn   37
Hook, The   32, 52–3, 84
Hoovervilles   41
House Un-American Activities Committee (HUAC)   1, 35, 102
Hylton, Forest   82
Hyman, Harry   23, 91, 94

"I Don't Need You Anymore"   6, 20, 164, 169
Ibsen, Henrik   31–2, 53
"In Memoriam"   164, 208 n.3
Incident at Vichy (Von Berg)   133

Inside of His Head, The 60
Irish Republican Army
   (IRA) 212–13 n.3
Italian Tragedy, An 53

Janice Sessions 123–5, *126*, 128–9
Jessel, George 15
Jewish cemeteries 136
Jewish heritage 172
Jolson, Al 15
Joyce, James 2
Judaism 18

Kalkofsky (*Homely Girl*) 127
Kazan, Elia 32, 47, 52–3, 102
Kennedy, Jacqueline 109, *109*
Kennedy, John F. 108–10
Krasinski, John 71
Kristallnacht 56, 59, 94

Labor Day 173
Lahr, John 43
literal Brooklyn 57–60
Loew's Woodside Theatre 143, *145*
Loman, Willy 4, 6, 20, 24, 43, 52, 54, 57, 59, 61, 65–7, 75, 77, 99, 137
Longhi, Vinny 51, 55
Look and *Life* 175
Luckman Field, Sid 166

Mailer, Norman 27, 30
Majdanek: Cemetery of Europe 146
Man in Black, The 57
Man Who Had All the Luck, The 28, 30, 131
Manhattan works 101
  After the Fall, New York References in 106–10
  A Memory of Two Mondays, New York References in 114–29
  Mr. Peter's Connections, New York References in 113
  The Price, New York References in 113–14
  The Ride Down Mt. Morgan, New York References in 110–12
March, Frederic 77
Marco (*A View from the Bridge*) 77, 80, 82–3
Marino, Stephen 172

Mayer, Lionel 127
McCullers, Carson 27
McWilliams, Joe 160
Melville, Herman 5
Memory of Two Mondays, A (1955) 3–4, 26, 53, 101, 105
  anti-Semitism 118
  Lincoln Center complex *116*
  New York References in 114–29
  "memory" plays 101
Mielziner, Jo 52, 63
Mikush (janitor) 18
Miller, Arthur Asher 1, 37, 42–3, 53, 101, 131, *193*
  boyhood home at 45 West 110th Street *10*
  Brooklyn boyhood 62
  Brooklyn boyhood home, 1350 East Third Street 20–7, *25*
  Chelsea Hotel at 222 W 23rd S 36, *107*
  family home on East 3rd Street Brooklyn *21*
  in front of Brooklyn Bridge *54*
  31 Grace Court 30
  life in Manhattan 7–20
  marriages 102
  62 Montague Street 28, *28*
  102 Pierrepont Street 30
  Regun Theatre *17*
  18 Schermerhorn Street *29*
  Skaters on Central Park lake *15*
  summers in bungalow *170*
  Sutton Place apartment at 444 East 57th Street 36
  232 Tophet Road in Roxbury 36
  vaudeville *16*
  45 West 110th Street today 11, *13*
  151 Willow Street home 33–4
  writer in Brooklyn Heights 27–35
Miller, Augusta (Gussie) 8–12, 14–15, 19, 22, 38, 43, 94, 108, 164
Miller, Jane *31*
Miller, Henry 27
Miller, Isidore (Izzie) 3, 8–9, 12, 15, 38–9, 102–3, 110, 152, 164, 176
Miller, Kermit 9–11, 14, 38, 103, 165, 173
  Bar Mitzvah instruction 18
  union organizers 38

Miller, Rebecca   11
Miller, Samuel   8–9
Miltex Company   9
Miltex Corporation   152
Miltext Coat and Suit Company
    factory   11, *12*
Misfits and Other Stories, The   169
Molloy, Archbishop Thomas   159
Monroe, Marilyn   1, 3, 32, 35,
    36, 102, 104
  divorce from   3
  soccer ball at Ebbets Field   *75*
Moore-MacCormack line Pier   3, *84*
Morath, Inge   3, 102, 106
Mosher, Gregory   99
Mr. Peter's Connections (1998)   4,
    101, 104–5
  New York References in   113
  plots of   104
Municipal Building   *186*
Murphy, Brenda   43
Museum Mile   106

"named names"   102
National Register of Historic
    Places   171–2
National Union for Social Justice   158
New World Order   2
New York colloquial reference   69
1944 New York historic heat wave
    158
New York Mets   73
New York References
  in *A Memory of Two
    Mondays*   114–29
  in *After the Fall*   106–10
  in *Mr. Peter's Connections*   113
  in *The Price*   113–14
  in *The Ride Down Mt.
    Morgan*   110–12
"New York State Regents
    Examinations"   69. *See also*
    "Declaration of Honesty"
New York State Register of Historic
    Places   171–2
New York subway system   68–9, 85,
    117, 147–8
New York Times   5
New York's historic   1944
    heat wave   158

Newman, Lawrence   132, 138,
    142, 150, 161
Newman, Manny   22, 43–5, 77, 99,
    132, 134, 142–4, 146–55, 157,
    160–1, 188
  home on East   4th Street   44
No Villain   11, 37–8
None Shall Escape   146
Norwood, Stephen   136

O'Malley, Walter   73
O'Neill, Eugene   1, 5
Ocean Parkway   91, *92*
Olivier, Laurence   56
"On Social Plays"   54
On the Waterfront (Kazan)   47
Orthodox Boys (Perlin)   149, *149*

Palmer Method of handwriting   13
Panto, Pete   45–9, 51–2, 55, 81–3, 87
  lay in unmarked grave   46
  Mafia gangsters   53
  Red Hook   47
Parker House   71
Parsons, Estelle   172
"Performance, The"   163
Perlin, Bernard   149
Playing for Time   56
"Please Don't Kill Anything"   192
Poore, Charles   5
"Presence"   163, 192
Price, The   4, 12, 101–3, *104*, 105
  New York References in   113–14, *115*
Prince and the Showgirl, The   56
Proctor, John   133
Pyle, Ernie   30

Queens street grid   212 n.1
Quentin (*After the Fall*)   105–9

Radio Priests   134
Raw Edge, The (Appel)   47
Reaganism   2
Red Hook   5–6, 46, *47*, *48*, 50, 56–8,
    77–82, 84–86, *86*, *87*, 89–90, 137
Red Scare   2
Regun Theatre   *17*
Restricted Clientele   157
Rialto Theatre in Brooklyn   94,
    96, 210 n.13

Ride Down Mt. Morgan, The 1, 4, 101, 104–5
   Carlyle Hotel 110, *111*
   fruits and vegetable market on Ninth Avenue *112*
   New York References in 110–12
Ritt, Martin 53
Roaring Twenties 2
Robinson, Bill "Bojangles" 15
Robinson, Brian 58
Rockaway Playland Amusement Park 171
Rodolpho (*A View From the Bridge*) 78, 80, 82
Rogers, Ginger 94
Roman Catholic Diocese of Brooklyn 159
Roosevelt Avenue El 142, 148
Rosten, Norman 27, 29
Rowe, Kenneth T. 39
Roxbury 3, 31, 36, 52, 160, 211 n.4

S. Miller and Sons 9
Saarinen, Eero 108
Sackett Street 45, 81, 87, 89
Sandy, Superstorm xiv, xv, 62
Sarna, Jonathan D. 157
"Scarface" 80
Schwartz, Stephen 51
Scott, George C. 77
"Search for a Future, A" 164, 176
Second World War 2
Seventh Cross, The 145–6
Shales, Tom 175
"shape-up" hiring system 45
"Shattering The Silence, Illuminating The Hatred" 135
Shaw 1
Sheepshead Bay 190
Shine, Meyer 174
short stories 163
   "A Glimpse at a Jockey" 163
   autobiographical stories 164
   "Bare Manuscript, The" 187
   "Bulldog" 26, 69, 164, 165, 168, 187
   "Ditchy" 18, 164, 168, 169
   "Fitter's Night" 180–3
   "I Don't Need You Anymore" 6, 11, 20, 164, 169, 173, 174, 180
   "In Memoriam" 164

"Fame" 164, 173, 174
"Please Don't Kill Anything" 192
"Presence" 192
"The 1928 Buick" 25, 137, 164, 166, 188, 190, 191
"The Performance" 163
"The Turpentine Still" 163, 211 n.5
"Search for a Future, A" 176
"Sicilian Bandit" 51. *See also* Giuliano, Salvatore
Simmons, J. H. 70
Simon, Neil 175
Situation Normal 30
Skee, Joey 45
Slattery, Mary 27–8, 70, 102, 104, 187
Smith, Alson J. 136
Soviet Union, fall of 2
Stalin 123
Standish Arms, The 71–2, *72*
Stanton, Kay 4
Stewarts, A. T. 70, 98
Stewarts, F. H. 70
Stock Market crash of 1929 3
Stockmann, Thomas 133
Story of G. I. Joe, The 30
Streetcar Named Desire, A 52
Strindberg, August 1
"submarines" 82

Tablet, The 159
Terkel, Studs 39
Testament of Dr. Mabuse, The (Fritz Lang film) 52
Thacker, David 57
They Too Arise 37
Timebends 1–3, 5, 8–9, 11, 23, 27, 51–2, 63, 102, 165
Title Guarantee Company 93
Titus Andronicus 133
"Tragedy and the Common Man" 54, 117
"Tragic Violent History of the Mob, The" (Ward) 82
Trinity Church 152, *153*, *154*
"True Life Tales 'On the Waterfront'" (Schwartz) 51
Trump, Donald 66
"Turpentine Still, The" 163
Two Fingers of Pride (Ward) 51

University of Michigan 3, 11, 26, 27, 29,
    37–9, 53, 57, 90, 102, 119
USS Arizona 182
USS Lafayette 109
USS Maine 181
USS Missouri 182, *183*

View from the Bridge, A 1, 4–6, 35,
    37, 42–3, 77
  submarines 82
  union organizer 83
Viswamohan, Aysha 4–5
Von Berg, Prince 133

Wagner firm 70
Ward, Nathan 82

Waterfront Barge in Red Hook 86
Waterfront Museum 209 n.7
Wessex (Hardy) 2
Wharton, Edith 5
Whitman, Walt 5
Williams, Tennessee 1
Wolfe, Thomas 27
Woodside National Bank *142*
Woodside Theatre 143, *146*
Wright, Frank Lloyd 36
Wright, Richard 27

Yale, Frankie 81

Zinn, Ben 74
Zvi, Linda Ben 4